COVID-19 and European Banking Performance

Resilience, Recovery and Sustainability

Edited by
Paul Wachtel and Ewa Miklaszewska

Routledge
Taylor & Francis Group
LONDON AND NEW YORK

First published 2024
by Routledge
4 Park Square, Milton Park, Abingdon, Oxon OX14 4RN

and by Routledge
605 Third Avenue, New York, NY 10158

Routledge is an imprint of the Taylor & Francis Group, an informa business

British Library Cataloguing-in-Publication Data
A catalogue record for this book is available from the British Library

Library of Congress Cataloging-in-Publication Data
Names: Wachtel, Paul, 1945– editor. | Miklaszewska, Ewa, editor.
Title: COVID-19 and European banking performance : resilience, recovery and sustainability / edited by Paul Wachtel and Ewa Miklaszewska.
Description: Abingdon, Oxon ; New York, NY : Routledge, 2023. |
Includes bibliographical references and index. |
Identifiers: LCCN 2023004886 | ISBN 9781032316567 (hardback) |
ISBN 9781032316611 (paperback) | ISBN 9781003310754 (ebook)
Subjects: LCSH: Banks and banking—Europe—History—21st century. |
COVID-19 Pandemic, 2020—Influence.
Classification: LCC HG2974 .C68 2023 | DDC 332.1094—dc23/eng/20230203
LC record available at https://lccn.loc.gov/2023004886

ISBN: 978-1-032-31656-7 (hbk)
ISBN: 978-1-032-31661-1 (pbk)
ISBN: 978-1-003-31075-4 (ebk)

DOI: 10.4324/9781003310754

Typeset in Times New Roman
by codeMantra

Contents

Figures and tables

Figures

Tables

Contributors

Paola Bongini is Full Professor of Banking and Finance at the University of Milano-Bicocca, Italy, and Director of the PhD program in Business for Society. Her research interests are in empirical banking and financial regulation and most recently in financial literacy, also serving as a member of the Scientific Committee of the Italian Foundation for Financial Education.

Paola Brighi is Professor of Banking at the Department of Management at the University of Bologna. She obtained her PhD from the University of Ancona. She has published articles in journals on the following topics: ESG, bank efficiency, cooperative banks, relationship lending and SME finance.

Giuseppina Chesini is Associate Professor of Economics of Financial Intermediaries. Her main research interests include the evolution of financial markets and stock exchanges, the bank-firm relationship, international banking and financial markets regulation, bank management and performance evaluation.

Pedro J. Cuadros-Solas (PhD, University of Granada) is Associate (tenured) Professor at CUNEF Universidad. His research is focused in banking, financial digitalisation and corporate finance. He has published many papers in *Journal of Corporate Finance*; *Journal of Financial Stability*; *Journal of International Financial Markets, Institutions & Money*; *European Journal of Finance*; among others.

Marcin Czaplicki is Assistant Professor at the Warsaw School of Economics and an expert in Strategy Department at PKO Bank Polski. He is also a CFA Charterholder. His research interests are in macroprudential policy, monetary policy-and bank lending activity.

Małgorzata Iwanicz-Drozdowska is Full Professor of Finance at the Warsaw School of Economics and Chair of the Financial System Department. She has been involved in the business practice for about 30 years, including membership in supervisory boards of financial institutions and in 2019 he held the position of Deputy Chair of Polish Financial Supervision Authority.

Renata Karkowska is Associate Professor at the University of Warsaw. Her research activity includes areas of capital markets, banking, and portfolio management. She is the author of about 80 scientific publications, including papers, chapters and monographs. For many years, she has worked with practitioners and experts in the capital market and banking sector.

Stanisław Kasiewicz is Professor Emeritus of the Warsaw School of Economics and currently a scientific secretary of the Center for Research and Analysis of Financial System ALTERUM. He has been a member of supervisory boards of various financial institutions and an expert for Team Europe.

Krzysztof Kil is Assistant Professor at the Institute of Finance of Cracow University of Economics and a lecturer at the Jagiellonian University in Cracow. His research concentrates on the issues of bank stability and bank efficiency, as well as on the role and performance of the European cooperative banking sector.

Lech Kurkliński is Associate Professor at the Warsaw School of Economics, Head of the Digital Finance & FINTECH Department and Director of the Center for Research and Analysis of Financial System ALTERUM. He has been a member of management and supervisory boards of several Polish banks and an expert of Team Europe.

Caterina Liberati is Associate Professor in Statistics for Economics at the University of Milano-Bicocca, Italy. She is also a council member of the International Society of Business and Industrial Statistics (ISBIS). Her research interests are in business analytics, classification and credit risk modelling.

Ewa Miklaszewska chairs the Department of Banking and Global Financial System at the Institute of Finance of Cracow University of Economics. She is also a lecturer at the Jagiellonian University in Cracow and a member of the managing committee of the European Association of University Teachers in Banking and Finance – the Wolpertinger Group.

Małgorzata Pawłowska graduated from the University of Warsaw (MSc in Mathematics) and completed his PhD thesis and obtained habilitation in Finance at the Warsaw School of Economics. Currently, she heads the Traditional Banking Unit at the Institute of Risk and Financial Markets of SGH and is also employed as Advisor of the National Bank of Poland.

Carlos Salvador (PhD in Banking and Quantitative Finance) is Associate Professor at the University of Valencia. His research has been published in the *Journal of Financial Stability*, *Journal of International Money and Finance*, *Research in International Business and Finance* and *The North American Journal of Economics and Finance*, among others.

Sabrina Severini is a research fellow at the Università Politecnica delle Marche, Ancona, Italy. She holds a master's degree in Finance and PhD in Economics. Her primary research interests lie in the area of Financial Markets, with a focus on Sustainable Finance, ESG investing and climate-oriented behaviours. Her research studies are also aimed at the study of the Initial Public Offerings (IPOs) and Initial Coin Offerings (ICOs).

Aleksandra Staniszewska graduated from the Warsaw School of Economics and in 2008 defended her PhD thesis, after a research period in Columbia Business School, NY, in 2007 (Fulbright Scholarship). Currently she is an assistant professor in Traditional Banking Unit, Institute of Risk and Financial Markets, in Collegium of Management and Finance of SGH.

Nuria Suárez (PhD, University of Oviedo) is a researcher in the banking and corporate finance field. She has published her research in *Journal of Banking and Finance*, *Journal of Corporate Finance*, *Journal of Financial Stability*, *Journal of International Financial Markets, Institutions & Money*, *Journal of International Money and Finance*, among others.

Paul Wachtel is Professor Emeritus of Economics at the New York University Stern School of Business. He joined the faculty in 1972 after receiving a PhD from the University of Rochester. His numerous research publications are on monetary policy, central banking and financial sector reform in economies in transition.

Jacek Woźniak is Assistant Professor at the Military University of Technology in Warsaw. He is a graduate of the Warsaw School of Economics, where he obtained a doctoral degree (a risk management at the creative enterprises). He is deputy editor-in-chief of the quarterly *Modern Management Systems*.

1 Introduction by the editors

Paul Wachtel and Ewa Miklaszewska

Over the last 15 years, the global financial sector has seen a rapid rise in shocks, risks and sources of instability: the 2008 crisis and the post-crisis regulatory reform, technological revolution, ESG programs, the COVID pandemic and the Ukrainian war, to name but a few. They affected economic and financial trends around the world as one source of uncertainty negatively influences the others. The coronavirus crisis put the real economy and financial markets under extraordinary stress, not only during the pandemic in 2020 but also for subsequent years. Although the international economy and financial markets recovered from the initial impact of COVID shutdowns better and faster than expected, particularly in terms of GDP growth, its long-term impact is still to be observed. Similarly, the indirect effects of the global financial crisis of 2008 turned out to be long lasting. Hence, the motivation behind this volume is to present research that analyzes the possible long-lasting effects of the pandemic for the economy and financial and banking markets.

Despite the fact that the financial industry was not at the centre of the 2020 economic crisis, it has nevertheless been significantly affected. The COVID-19 pandemic which had a direct influence on the real economy also created a number of vulnerabilities for the banking sector. The pandemic triggered or strengthened structural changes in financial access and influenced consumer preferences. Additionally, bank business models were threatened by the low interest rate environment, as well as by the low demand for credit and tight regulatory and compliance requirements, which imposed new costs and reduced bank operational flexibility. Pandemic-related restrictions imposed burdens on enterprises, lowering GDP growth and investment, as well as threatening the growth of bank NPL portfolios. The low interest rate environment forced banks to look for non-interest-bearing sources of income. The supply shock was accompanied by a demand shock, as consumer preferences and habits were transformed by the pandemic. The supply shock might have been more devastating were it not for the substantial fiscal and monetary stimuli in all major countries, which stabilized the economies at the cost of a growing public debt.

The chapters in this volume analyze the impact of the pandemic on bank stability, performance and credit policies, as well as the extent of banks' and financial markets' strategic adjustments to the challenges brought about by the COVID-19

DOI: 10.4324/9781003310754-1

pandemic. This book concentrates on four related issues: the impact of the pandemic on macroeconomic policies (Chapters 2–4), on the enterprise sector (Chapters 5 and 6), on banking industry performance (Chapters 7 and 8) and on the nature and extent of the pressures coming from the FinTech sector (Chapters 9 and 10).

Chapter 2 by *P. J. Cuadros-Solas, C. Salvador and N. Suárez: Crisis interventions and sovereign risk ratings* examines whether and to what extent the different government interventions that were undertaken during the global financial crisis and the COVID-19 – bailouts, liquidity support, blank guarantees and nationalizations – affected changes in sovereign ratings as a synthetic measure of sovereign risk. The empirical research relies on data on all types of intervention measures undertaken by OECD countries from 2008 to 2016 from the IMF Fiscal Monitor Database that summarizes the key measures that governments have announced or taken in response to the COVID-19 pandemic. The empirical findings show that bank recapitalizations (bailouts) undertaken during the GFC were the main measure that negatively influenced changes in sovereign risk (risk-increasing effect). Although the OECD countries implemented a variety of measures aiming at supporting economies during this crisis period, sovereign risk does not seem to be affected, as most countries in the sample did not experience a significant change in their ratings. This result suggests that the COVID-19-related interventions were different from those undertaken to overcome the effects of the GFC in 2008. In the recent crisis, the responses were not interpreted as an indication of underlying weakness.

Chapter 3 by *G. Chesini, The impact of Covid-19 pandemic on European bank regulation and supervision: Lessons from the past crises* analyzes the consequences of exogenous events such as the global crisis, the sovereign debt crisis and recently the pandemic shock on the architecture of bank supervision in Europe. The chapter points out that the fiscal and monetary policies in many European countries have evolved towards more cross-border cooperation between supervisors and that the post-2008 architecture has empowered the ECB with new significant supervisory responsibilities, in particular regarding the largest banks in the Eurozone. Thus the chapter, analyzing the causes and the consequences of these changes, focuses on the new role played by the ECB, which has to find a new balance between independence and accountability, maintaining the effectiveness of its action as bank supervisor.

Chapter 4 by *M. Czaplicki, The countercyclicality of macroprudential policy in the EU. The case of the COVID-19 pandemic* analyzes changes in the restrictiveness of macroprudential requirements, using various measures such as capital requirement, surplus capital, or bank lending capacity. Additionally, the main reasons for changes in the restrictiveness of macroprudential policy have been identified, using qualitative and quantitative analyses. Consequently, the research sheds light on the positive impact of the loosening of macroprudential policy on the expansion of bank assets and on the macroeconomic benefits of the countercyclical macroprudential policy, conducted during the pandemic.

Chapter 5 by *P. Bongini, M. Iwanicz-Drozdowska and C. Liberati, Business continuity planning and management: A life jacket in the COVID-19 storm?* adopts the approach of enterprise risk management (ERM) to analyze problems of business continuity planning (BCP) and business continuity management (BCM). In the ERM process, business continuity results in a sub-process of risk mitigation which can guarantee crisis management in response to extreme events that could compromise normal organizational operations. In the last 20 years, ERM was put to test in many "tail" situations, including the pandemic. Tail events, due to their nature, occur very rarely and are therefore often regarded as an element of surprise. However, BCM as a part of ERM should protect businesses from disruption in case of such events. In this chapter, the authors investigate whether businesses of different sizes were more or less ready to withstand the consequences of the outbreak of the pandemic in 2020. They analyze the results of a global survey conducted during the major lockdown period (April–May 2020) using multiple correspondence analysis (MCA) and cluster analysis to detect whether business continuity planning and management were helpful in terms of the organization's readiness to respond to the pandemic scenario and the ability to implement protective measures and guarantee overall business continuity. The findings indicate that the financial sector was the best prepared for tail events, which may be attributed to regulations faced by most financial institutions.

Chapter 6 by *P. Brighi and S. Severini, The COVID-19 loan moratorium and SMEs' liquidity shortfall* analyzes the effectiveness of the financial measures introduced in Italy by Law Decree No. 18 of 17 March 2020, which aimed to mitigate the impact of COVID-19 on businesses. The study uses a proprietary quarterly database of lending decisions for small- and medium-sized enterprises (SMEs) to investigate how the financial measures introduced by the law, specifically the moratorium on interest payments, could have offset liquidity shortfalls during the COVID-19 outbreak. Findings suggest that a public measure of assessment works better in the case of low risk and large firms, as well as with a personal guarantee and a strong relationship lending environment.

Chapter 7 by *R. Karkowska, The influence of the COVID-19 pandemic on bank lending. Evidence from European countries* analyzes how the COVID-19 pandemic has affected bank lending activity in European countries, based on a panel data regression model carried out on 652 commercial banks in 36 European countries for the period 2018q3–2021q1. The results confirm the hypothesis that the pandemic resulted in declining bank lending. The chapter also analyses the impact of loosening bank regulatory requirements (i.e. cancelling some capital buffers) and finds out that it had different effects on low-capitalized versus high-capitalized banks. High-capitalized banks decrease their lending more, which is consistent with the literature on zombie lending, that banks with low capital ratios engage in excessive lending during crises in an attempt to write off fewer non-performing loans. The study also confirms that banks have reduced their lending significantly more in countries with a greater exposure to the COVID-19 outbreak.

Chapter 8 by *K. Krzysztof and E. Miklaszewska, The impact of the COVID-19 pandemic on bank stability and performance in the CEE region* aims at researching the impact of the pandemic on bank performance as shown by bank stability, bank profitability and credit accessibility in the CEE (Central and East European) region. The main research hypothesis is that although challenges were universal, bank resilience and sustainability was not, depending on country-specific factors and strategies. The methodology employed is a dynamic panel data model – generalized method of moment (GMM-SYS version), using an adjusted dataset from the BankFocus database for unconsolidated bank data for the 2016–2022(q2) period. The empirical analysis showed that the overall assessment of CEE banks' financial stability, from the regulatory point of view, is positive. However, banks tended to increase their capital adequacy ratios mostly due to reducing the value of risk-weighted assets (purchasing government securities), rather than by increasing the value of regulatory capital. The profitability and bank lending results vary – some banking sectors have exposed resilience to the external shocks, such as in the Czech Republic or Estonia, for some the shocks strengthen already detrimental trends, particularly in Poland and Hungary.

The last two chapters are devoted to the pandemic's impact on the digital transformation of the banking sector. Chapter 9 by *M. Pawłowska and A. Staniszewska, Relationship between banks and FinTechs: Does the pandemic have an impact on it?* investigates the impact of innovative financial technology on the performance of the EU banking. It stresses that the COVID-19 pandemic forced banking sector to implement innovations and catch up with advanced IT solutions. The research attempts to isolate the channels of the impact of new FinTech technologies on the financial market. The quantitative investigation is based on panel analysis of data from payments statistics from the European Central Bank, Eurostat and the Bloomberg. Additionally, FinTech variables for EU were taken from the study: Cornelli, Doerr, Franco, & Frost (2021). The findings show how the intensity and strength of accelerated FinTech implementation effect banking sector performance.

Chapter 10 by *S. Kasiewicz, L. Kurkliński and J. Woźniak, Competition between banks and FinTechs in the context of the COVID-19 pandemic* analyzes the ongoing digital transformation of the Polish banking sector, focusing on the consequences of the COVID-19 pandemic, particularly in respect to digital competition. The research tries to find the answers to the question whether the pandemic has changed the competitive position of the Polish banks versus the FinTech sector. Based on some empirical research, particularly the bank expert survey of June/July 2021, the research presents the directions and possible outcomes of the FinTech challenge.

To sum up, this monograph aims to present a comprehensive analysis of the impact of the COVID-19 pandemic on European banking, both at a macro and a micro level. The initial chapters analyze the various governmental responses; the scale and scope of implementation of a wide range of public policies undertaken to mitigate the consequences of the crisis, and their efficiency in limiting the negative impact of the pandemic on the economy. The results presented in Chapters 2–6 suggest that these public interventions have been largely successful in averting the possible disastrous consequences for the financial sector on a macro level.

However, at a micro scale, the COVID-19 pandemic has disrupted the restructuring and recovery of the banking industry after the 2008 crisis and had a significant negative impact on businesses, jobs and incomes around the world, which together with a possible economic downturn, could have a very negative long-lasting effect on sustainable development. Thus, the second part of this monograph (Chapters 7–10) focuses on the impact of the pandemic on bank lending policies, bank stability and performance and on their competitive position versus the FinTech sector. The assessment is mixed. The banking sector turned out to be resilient to the recent shock; however, the individual chapters point to many sources of vulnerability, particularly in respect to credit distribution and bank profitability. Moreover, the pandemic strengthened the role of the digital revolution, which has created a vast field of new unregulated or partially regulated players in financial markets, which forces banks to constantly adjust to an ever-changing environment.

2 Crisis interventions and sovereign risk ratings

Pedro J. Cuadros-Solas, Carlos Salvador and Nuria Suárez

2.1 Introduction

Governments respond to economic crises by implementing a number of public policies – fiscal, social, economic, and monetary – to limit the negative impact of turmoil periods on the whole economy. In the last two decades, there have been two global crises, with different origins and nature, but with a deep economic impact all over the world.

On the one hand, the GFC in 2008 led to a significant deterioration in the financial situation of the banking sectors around the world (ECB, 2017; Laeven & Valencia, 2018). During this period, the collapse of the financial markets led to a reduction in loan and credit quality and an increase in uncertainty, thereby contributing to an increase in financing costs. These circumstances caused serious problems for banks that had large liquidity needs or that were overly dependent on the wholesale markets or real estate assets. The effects were especially negative for those institutions that were heavily exposed to structured products and the sovereign debt of peripherical European countries. In response to these problems, and with the medium-term objectives of restoring confidence and stability in the banking sector and guaranteeing the provision of funding to firms and households (King, 2019), countries with financially distressed banks intervened in their banking sectors. Governments implemented several containment and resolution measures such as bank recapitalization packages, liquidity support, blank guarantees, and the nationalization of some banks, aiming at avoiding the negative real effects of the financial turmoil period.

On the other hand, the breakout of the COVID-19 pandemic in March 2020 has caused large economic damages to the global economy. The magnitude and speed of the economic collapse caused by the pandemic were unprecedented. The crisis has undermined global financial stability and large segments of the global economy ground to a standstill, including the informal economy (Barrett et al., 2021). As a consequence, the COVID-19 pandemic has led to a severe global economic recession with differential impacts within and across countries (Alberola et al., 2021; Barrett et al., 2021; Chudik et al., 2021; Elgin et al., 2020). In order to face the economic consequences of the pandemic, governments had to adopt policies to provide fiscal stimulus and relief to those affected by this global disaster (IMF, 2020).

DOI: 10.4324/9781003310754-2

The main objective of this chapter is to examine whether the different government interventions that were undertaken during the abovementioned crises – the GFC and the COVID-19 – may have caused a change in levels of sovereign risk. In doing so, this research focuses on the changes of sovereign ratings, as a synthetic measure of sovereign risk. Regarding the examination of the impact of government interventions during the GFC, while prior studies limited their analyses to the impact of public bailouts during the GFC on sovereign risk (Acharya et al., 2014; Beirne & Fratzscher, 2013; Cuadros-Solas et al., 2021), we contribute to the literature of government interventions by investigating whether and to what extent the different government interventions – *bailouts, liquidity support, blank guarantees, and nationalizations* – affected changes in sovereign risk. Then, we also examine to what extent the sovereign ratings issued by the three CRAs changed during the period corresponding to the pre-COVID-19 (December 2019) and after the COVID-19 episode (December 2020).

To examine the impact of the government measures during the GFC, our empirical approach relies on data on all the types of intervention measures undertaken by OECD countries from 2008 to 2016. In order to explore the government interventions during the COVID-19 pandemic, we rely on the Fiscal Monitor Database of Country Fiscal Measures in Response to the COVID-19 Pandemic (IMF, 2021) that summarizes the key measures that governments in our sample of OECD countries have announced or taken in response to the COVID-19 pandemic.

The effects of the different government interventions on sovereign risk may result in a priori contradictory predictions. On the one hand, as pointed out by Brůha and Kočenda (2018), Homar and van Wijnbergen (2017) and King (2019), among others, implementing measures to rescue and restructure the banking sector during and after turmoil periods could reduce financial frictions and restore financial stability, thereby contributing to reducing sovereign risk (*risk-reducing effect*). On the other hand, as argued by Acharya et al. (2014) or IMF (2009), among others, government interventions could lead to a transfer of default risk from the private sector to sovereigns. As Cuadros-Solas et al. (2021) demonstrate, the high fiscal costs associated with these government interventions would trigger an increase in public debt that provokes higher levels of sovereign credit risk (*risk-increasing effect*). In any case, since each measure is implemented with a different short-term goal (i.e. improving bank liquidity conditions or avoiding individual bankruptcies), their effects on sovereign risk may differ across countries.

Our empirical findings show that bank recapitalizations (bailouts) undertaken during the GFC are the main intervention measure that negatively influences changes in sovereign risk. In other words, we provide evidence on the role played by bailouts as the main intervention measure that provokes an increase in sovereign risk after its implementation (*risk-increasing effect*). As regards the impact of government measures as a result of the COVID-19 pandemic, although the OECD countries implemented different measures aiming at supporting economies during this crisis period, the sovereign risk does not seem to be enduringly affected, as most countries in our sample did not experience a significant change in their ratings. This result suggests that the nature of COVID-19-related intervention measures has been different from those undertaken to overcome the effects of the GFC in 2008.

The remainder of the chapter is organized as follows. Section 2.2 provides an overview of the existing literature on government interventions and sovereign risk. Section 2.3 describes how sovereign risk is measured. The analysis of the government interventions during the GFC is addressed in Section 2.4. Section 2.5 relates the sovereign ratings' adjustments during the COVID-19 with the measures that were undertaken. Finally, Section 2.6 concludes this chapter.

2.2 Related literature

Our research is related to the literature that has examined the effects of government interventions during and after periods of economic and banking crises. The implications of the public measures adopted to face crises periods – *bailouts, liquidity support, blank guarantees, and nationalizations* – have attracted the attention of the academic literature since the GFC episode. Particularly, a large body of literature has been devoted to examining the effects of bank bailouts on sovereign risk. Government bailouts increase national debt burdens and cause a deterioration in public finances (IMF, 2009), which, consequently, would increase the sovereign risk (*risk-increasing effect*). In this vein, Laeven and Valencia (2018) find that the median output loss of banking crisis episodes was large, accounting for about 25% of GDP. Acharya and Yorulmazer (2007, 2008) and Philippon and Schnabl (2013) investigate the relevance of taxation-related fiscal costs as the main costs related to bank bailouts. According to these authors, these costs would increase the quantity of bailout funding. Along these lines, Reinhart and Reinhart (2010) provide evidence that economic activity remains in a deep slump after the distressing episode, and that private debt shrinks significantly while sovereign debt rises. Acharya et al. (2014) show that bailouts triggered the rise of sovereign credit risk in 2008.

By contrast, other papers in the literature argue that implementing bank government interventions to reduce financial friction and restore financial stability may help to reduce sovereign risk (*risk-reducing effect*). In this line, Brůha and Kočenda (2018) and Aktug et al. (2013) find evidence that policy measures focused on reducing the vulnerability of the banking system could be beneficial for sovereign risk. Similarly, King (2019) and Homar and van Wijnbergen, (2017) point out that bailouts avoid the default of systemically important banks, restore confidence in the financial system, and ultimately promote the restarting of the credit flow to support the real economy.

Several papers have also examined the implications of the measures implemented as a result of the COVID-19 pandemic. Gourinchas (2020) underline that all the measures helped to flatten the economic curve and to limit the economic loss. During this crisis, although the measures were costly, without substantial, timely, and stimulative macroeconomic interventions, the output losses would have been amplified. Using a novel database of daily fiscal policy announcements, Deb et al. (2021) find that fiscal policy announcements have been effective in stimulating economic activity, boosting confidence, and reducing unemployment, but their effect varies by type of measure and country characteristics. Using firm-level financial data from 50 sectors in 27 countries, Gourinchas et al. (2021) find that without government support, the failure rate of SMEs would have increased by 9 percentage points. Moreover, these authors also find that fiscal policy helped offset about 8% of the economic downturn. Overall, these studies suggest that the COVID-19-related measures had a positive effect on alleviating the economic losses. Without these sizeable and prompt policies, the domestic economies would have faced a more difficult situation.

2.3 Measuring sovereign risk: Sovereign ratings

Sovereign ratings issued by the three main CRAs (Fitch, Moody's, and Standard and Poor's) are one of the most relevant indicators that investors, regulators, and governments consider to gauge risk (Aktug et al., 2013; Kaminsky & Schmukler, 2002). As a measure of sovereign risk, ratings play an important role in mitigating information asymmetries between insiders (governments) and outsiders (investors) (An & Chan, 2008; Bosch & Steffen, 2011; Sufi, 2009). The relevance of sovereign ratings is also explained by their implications for the rated countries and the economy as a whole. Sovereign ratings affect the funding costs of states (Afonso et al., 2012), non-financial firms (Chava et al., 2019; Kanno, 2020), and banks (BIS, 2011; Opoku Mensah et al., 2017). Moreover, the facto sovereign ratings represent a ceiling for the ratings assigned to financial institutions – mainly investment and commercial banks – corporates, and regional governments within a country (Borensztein et al., 2013).

The CRAs point out in their methodological reports that sovereign ratings are based considering both quantitative (economic and financial indicators) and qualitative (institutional quality) criteria (FitchRatings, 2014; Moody's, 2015; Standard and Poor's, 2014). Furthermore, sovereign ratings tend to focus on the long term and thus aim to respond only to the perceived permanent component of credit-quality changes (Altman & Rijken, 2004, 2006). In this sense, unlike other common measures of sovereign risk, such as sovereign bond yields and CDS spreads, sovereign ratings are not pure market-based measures but also include this type of information.[1]

Literature on modeling ratings has confirmed that sovereign ratings are based on both quantitative (macroeconomic factors) and qualitative (such as government effectiveness and institutional variables) determinants. Among the earlier studies that base their analyses on quantitative factors, Cantor and Packer (1996), for a sample of 49 countries, find evidence that the sovereign ratings issued by Standard and Poor's (S&P) and Moody's are affected by macroeconomic indicators, such as GDP growth, inflation, external debt, per capita income, the country's level of economic development, and default history. Similarly, Hu et al. (2002) find evidence that quantitative factors such as the debt-to-exports, debt-to-GNP, and reserves-to-imports ratios have a significant effect on the ratings issued by S&P. Subsequent studies find evidence that qualitative factors – such as political and institutional variables – are also important in explaining sovereign credit ratings (Afonso et al., 2009, 2011; Reusens & Croux, 2017; Vernazza & Nielsen, 2015).

Consequently, as the main proxy of sovereign risk, we use the long-term foreign currency sovereign ratings, issued by the three main credit rating agencies (CRAs): Fitch, Moody's, and Standard and Poor's. We examine the influence of the different intervention measures undertaken in country *i* on the change in sovereign ratings in year *t* ($\Delta SOVEREIGNRATING_{i,t}$), defined as the difference between each year's rating ($SOVEREIGNRATING_{i,t}$) and the sovereign rating before any of the post-GFC government interventions took place.[2] Information about sovereign ratings was obtained from Thomson Reuters database and checked against CRA publications. As is standard in the ratings literature, the categorical ratings scale was transformed to a numerical scale and grouped into 21 categories, so that higher values imply higher creditworthiness.

In particular, we examine the impact of the government measures by examining the changes on sovereign ratings of 35 OECD countries.[3] By focusing on the OECD countries, we examine the most relevant government interventions that resulted from the GFC as, according to Laeven and Valencia's (2018) database, the bulk of the government interventions undertaken during the GFC were implemented by developed countries. Furthermore, also during the COVID-19 pandemic, the size of the financial support has been much higher in advanced economies than in emerging market economies (Alberola et al., 2021). Moreover, since OECD countries represent a relatively homogeneous group in terms of the economic and democratic perspectives, the alternative cost of the different policies adoption will be similar across them.

2.4 Government interventions during the global financial crisis

2.4.1 Empirical findings

In order to capture the specific intervention measures implemented in a country in a particular year, we define individual qualitative variables, namely, *Bailout*, *Liquidity support*, *Blanket guarantees*, and *Nationalization*. To provide comparable results, these variables are defined following prior studies' methodology (Calderon & Schaeck, 2016; Homar & van Wijnbergen, 2017). Hence, *Bailout* is defined as a dummy variable indicating if the government injected public capital to the banking sector at year *t*. We define *Liquidity support* as a dummy that takes value 1 if at year *t* the ratio central bank claims on the financial sector-to-deposits and foreign liabilities exceeds 5% and is more than double relative to its pre-crisis level. *Blanket guarantees* is also a dummy variable that indicates if, at year *t*, the government has implemented measures consisting of a full protection of bank liabilities or instances in which the non-deposit liabilities of banks are protected. Finally, *Nationalization* takes value 1 if at year *t* the government has taken over systemically important financial institutions.

Table 2.1 Summary statistics

Variables	*Obs.*	*Mean*	*St. Dev.*	*25%*	*Median*	*75%*
	(1)	(2)	(3)	(4)	(5)	(6)
ΔFitch	315	−1.05	2.58	−1.00	0.00	0.00
ΔS&P	315	−1.10	2.59	−1.00	0.00	0.00
ΔMoody's	315	−1.48	3.37	−2.00	0.00	0.00
Bailout	315	0.25	0.43	0.00	0.00	1.00
Liquidity support	315	0.35	0.48	0.00	0.00	1.00
Blanket guarantees	315	0.25	0.43	0.00	0.00	1.00
Nationalizations	315	0.31	0.46	0.00	0.00	1.00
Log GDP per Capita	315	10.40	0.62	9.89	10.59	10.84
GDP Growth	315	1.28	3.46	0.20	1.69	2.90
Inflation	315	1.95	2.19	0.54	1.72	2.76
Fiscal Surplus/Deficit	315	−2.85	4.45	−4.54	−2.72	−0.63
Public Debt (%GDP)	315	66.69	43.39	37.80	54.71	85.38
Sovereign Default	315	0.22	0.41	0.00	0.00	0.00
Economic Freedom Index	315	71.30	6.34	66.80	71.50	76.00
Forecasted GDP growth	315	0.89	2.95	−0.36	0.45	1.54

This table shows the descriptive statistics – mean, standard deviation, 25th percentile, median (50th percentile), 75th percentile – of the main variables of interest. All the variables are defined in Table A.2.1 in the Appendix.

The main descriptive statistics are presented in Table 2.1. As can be seen, on average, during the sample period, sovereign ratings decreased by 1.05 notches for Fitch and 1.10 and 1.48 notches for S&P and Moody's, respectively. As for the intervention measures, 25% of country–year observations refer to bailouts, 35% to liquidity support measures, 25% to blanket guarantees, and 31% to nationalizations.

To investigate the impact of the different government interventions on changes in sovereign ratings, we estimate a random-effects ordered probit model with panel data for each CRA during the period 2008–2016. As Alsakka and ap Gwilym (2010) and Afonso et al. (2011) argue, random-effects ordered probit estimation is the best procedure for the analysis of panel data, as it considers the existence of an additional normally distributed cross-section error.[4] Specifically, the following equation is estimated:

$$\Delta SOVEREIGNRATING_{i,t} = \alpha + \beta_0 INTERVENTION_{i,t} + \sum_{z=1}^{8} \beta_z CONTROLS_{i,t} + \delta_t + \varepsilon_{it} \tag{2.1}$$

where the dependent variable $\Delta SOVEREIGNRATING_{i,t}$ is the annual change in the sovereign rating compared to the pre-crisis rating. $INTERVENTION_{i,t}$ is our main variable of interest and it refers to each type of intervention measure (*Bailout*, *Liquidity support*, *Blanket guarantees*, and *Nationalization*) implemented in our sample of countries and years. $CONTROLS_{i,t}$ is the vector of control variables that have been identified by previous literature (Afonso et al., 2011, 2012; Cuadros-Solas & Salvador, 2022; Reusens & Croux, 2017) as determinants of sovereign ratings. In particular, we include the natural logarithm of GDP per capita (*Log GDP per capita*), the annual GDP growth rate (*GDP growth*), the inflation level (*Inflation*), the fiscal balance (*Fiscal Surplus/Deficit*), the level of public debt as a percentage of GDP (*Public Debt [%GDP]*), the default history of the country (*Sovereign Default*), the level of institutional quality proxied by the economic freedom index (*Economic Freedom Index*), and the forecasted GDP growth (*Forecasted GDP growth*).[5] Furthermore, in all the estimates we include time fixed effects (δ_t), and the standard errors are clustered at the country level. As Calderon and Schaeck (2016) highlight, it is important to consider potential issues of collinearity with respect to alternative intervention measures, as some of these measures were adopted simultaneously. Following these authors, we estimate regressions separately for each intervention.[6]

The baseline results are reported in Table 2.2. In columns (1), (5) and (9), we present the results for the impact of the occurrence of a bailout (*Bailout*) on the change in sovereign ratings. As can be seen, the negative and statistically significant coefficient found for all three CRAs reveals that, on average, bailouts caused a downgrade of sovereign ratings. In other words, bailouts, as intervention measures in the banking system undertaken after the GFC, lead to relatively lower ratings (rating downgrades) and therefore higher sovereign risk. However, we do not find any significant coefficients for *Liquidity support, Blanket guarantees,* or *Nationalization*, revealing that none of these measures had a statistically significant effect on sovereign ratings changes.

These estimated parameters of this baseline regression [Equation 1] reflect the sign and whether the influence of each intervention measure is statistically significant in explaining rating changes (changes on sovereign risk). Therefore, marginal effects are also calculated to understand the economic significance and the change (increase or decrease) in the probability of experiencing a rating change if an intervention measure is implemented.

As can be seen in Table 2.2, bailouts increase significantly the probability of experiencing a downgrade by two or more notches. Specifically, bailouts increase the likelihood that Fitch, S&P, and Moody's would carry out a downgrade of two or more notches by 17.11, 17.91, and 25.16 percentage points (pp), respectively. In contrast, the implementation of liquidity support, blanket guarantees, or nationalizations measures implies only an increase in the probability of experiencing a downgrade of two or more notches between 5.66 pp and 8.49 pp in Fitch, 5.14 pp and 8.3 pp in S&P, and 7.5 pp and 8.36 pp in Moody's. Likewise, it is also noted that, compared to other measures, bailouts have the greatest effect on experiencing a one-notch downgrade.

Furthermore, Table 2.3 also reveals that the probability of carrying out an upgrade decreases after undertaking a government intervention. The probability of being upgraded decreases, particularly in the case of bailouts. Overall, a bailout implies a decrease in the probability that Fitch would carry out a one-notch upgrade by 10.39 pp, and around by 7.5 pp in S&P and Moody's. Meanwhile, the other interventions measures imply a reduction in the probability of being upgraded between 3.12 and 4.8 pp in Fitch, 1.9 and 2.9 in S&P, and 2.14 pp and 2.36 in Moody's.

Table 2.2 Effect of government intervention measures during the GFC on sovereign rating adjustments

Dependent variable:	*ΔFitch*				*ΔS&P*				*ΔMoody's*			
	Bailout	*Liquidity support*	*Blanket guarantees*	*Nationalization*	*Bailout*	*Liquidity support*	*Blanket guarantees*	*Nationalization*	*Bailout*	*Liquidity support*	*Blanket guarantees*	*Nationalization*
	(1)	(2)	(3)	(4)	(5)	(6)	(7)	(8)	(9)	(10)	(11)	(12)
Intervention measure	−0.848***	−0.366	−0.257	−0.400	−0.851***	−0.265	−0.305	−0.378	−1.283***	−0.327	−0.358	−0.417
	(0.274)	(0.285)	(0.284)	(0.302)	(0.290)	(0.249)	(0.268)	(0.334)	(0.296)	(0.288)	(0.270)	(0.490)
Log GDP per Capita	0.022	−0.176	−0.210	−0.140	−0.216	−0.794**	−0.434	−0.380	0.326	−0.020	−0.0335	−0.008
	(0.230)	(0.279)	(0.273)	(0.214)	(0.256)	(0.340)	(0.310)	(0.261)	(0.356)	(0.359)	(0.357)	(0.344)
GDP Growth	0.309***	0.338***	0.345***	0.378***	0.236**	0.240**	0.272***	0.308***	0.226*	0.277**	0.272**	0.184**
	(0.102)	(0.095)	(0.092)	(0.093)	(0.109)	(0.117)	(0.098)	(0.102)	(0.125)	(0.110)	(0.116)	(0.090)
Inflation	0.072	0.087	0.091	0.107	0.026	−0.016	0.043	0.059	0.053	0.075	0.078	0.015
	(0.110)	(0.111)	(0.105)	(0.101)	(0.089)	(0.114)	(0.084)	(0.079)	(0.115)	(0.108)	(0.104)	(0.0762)
Fiscal Surplus/ Deficit	0.015	0.023	0.027	0.024	0.034	−0.008	0.044*	0.042	0.027	0.038	0.039	0.014
	(0.028)	(0.024)	(0.026)	(0.027)	(0.026)	(0.019)	(0.024)	(0.027)	(0.033)	(0.026)	(0.028)	(0.033)
Public Debt (%GDP)	−0.011***	−0.010**	−0.010*	−0.010*	−0.011***	−0.014***	−0.010*	−0.010*	−0.012***	−0.010**	−0.010**	−0.016***
	(0.004)	(0.005)	(0.005)	(0.005)	(0.004)	(0.004)	(0.005)	(0.005)	(0.002)	(0.004)	(0.004)	(0.004)
Sovereign Default	−0.649**	−0.677*	−0.713**	−0.798**	−0.964***	−1.355***	−1.00***	−1.099***	0.096	−0.058	−0.082	−0.242
	(0.328)	(0.354)	(0.349)	(0.348)	(0.316)	(0.380)	(0.353)	(0.351)	(0.466)	(0.479)	(0.482)	(0.419)
Economic Freedom Index	0.006	0.010	0.018	0.024	0.006	−0.024	0.016	0.023	0.017	0.025	0.030	0.004
	(0.025)	(0.025)	(0.026)	(0.027)	(0.025)	(0.027)	(0.026)	(0.028)	(0.030)	(0.028)	(0.027)	(0.037)
Forecasted GDP growth	0.261**	0.285***	0.302***	0.329***	0.168	0.163	0.208**	0.240**	0.187	0.230**	0.235**	0.129
	(0.107)	(0.092)	(0.092)	(0.099)	(0.121)	(0.121)	(0.106)	(0.113)	(0.125)	(0.101)	(0.113)	(0.085)
Year Dummies	Yes	Yes	Yes	Yes	Yes	Yes	Yes	Yes	Yes	Yes	Yes	Yes
Clustered Standard Errors	Country	Country	Country	Country	Country	Country	Country	Country	Country	Country	Country	Country
Observations	315	315	315	315	315	315	315	315	315	315	315	315
Number of countries	35	35	35	35	35	35	35	35	35	35	35	35
Log pseudolikelihood	−437.46	−449.04	−450.64	−448.18	−470.08	−478.66	−483.87	−482.06	−454.41	−479.24	−479.54	−456.69
Pseudo R2	0.1957	0.1744	0.1715	0.1760	0.1919	0.1771	0.1682	0.1713	0.2024	0.1588	0.1583	0.1984
p−value (chi2)	0.00	0.00	0.00	0.00	0.00	0.00	0.00	0.00	0.00	0.00	0.00	0.00

This table shows the results for the impact of government interventions in the banking system on the change of sovereign risk (*ΔSOVEREIGN RATING*). Our dependent variables are the difference between each year's rating and the sovereign rating in 2007, before any of the government intervention occurred for each of the main CRAs: Fitch, S&P, and Moody's. Bailout takes the value 1 for those years in which the government injects public capital into its banking system, and 0 otherwise. Liquidity support takes the value 1 for those years in which the ratio of central bank claims on the financial sector to deposits and foreign liabilities exceeds 5% and more than doubles relative to its pre-crisis level, and 0 otherwise. Blanket guarantees takes the value 1 for those years in which the government has implemented blanket guarantees, and 0 otherwise. Nationalization takes the value 1 for those years in which the government has taken over systemically important financial institutions, and 0 otherwise. The rest of the variables are defined in Appendix . Year fixed effects are included but not reported. Clustered standard errors (at country-level) are reported in parentheses. ***, **, and * indicate significance at the 1%, 5%, and 10% levels, respectively.

Table 2.3 Marginal effects of the different government interventions measures implemented during the GFC

	Downgrade		*No Change*	*Upgrade*	
Government intervention measure	*=2 or more notches*	*=1 notch*	*0*	*=1 notch*	*=2 or more notches*
Fitch					
Bailouts	17.11	4.81	−8.9	−10.39	−2.62
Liquidity Support	8.08	1.08	−4.04	−4.39	−1.45
Blanket guarantees	5.66	1.21	−2.75	−3.12	−1.01
Nationalization	8.49	1.84	−4.02	−4.8	−1.51
S&P					
Bailouts	17.91	5.91	−10.96	−7.11	−5.74
Liquidity Support	5.14	1.63	−2.91	−1.98	−1.99
Blanket guarantees	6.95	1.75	−3.99	−2.4	−2.32
Nationalization	8.3	2.14	−4.55	−2.98	−2.89
Moody's					
Bailouts	25.16	5.42	−15.85	−7.53	−7.18
Liquidity support	7.5	1.15	−3.95	−2.14	−2.56
Blanket guarantees	8.32	1.21	−4.6	−2.29	−2.66
Nationalization	8.36	1.01	−4.39	−2.36	−2.63

This table shows the marginal effects in percentage points (pp) computed for the baseline model (Eq. 2.1) reported in Table 2.1. Specifically, it is shown the effect of each government intervention on the probability of rating change (Δ*SOVEREIGN RATING*) by one (=1 notch), no change (=0) and multiples notches (=2 or more notches).

Thus, the marginal effects add evidence that bailouts, compared to the other intervention measures, lead to a greater increase in the probability of being downgraded and the greater decrease in the probability of being upgraded. Thus, bailouts are the main intervention measures affecting the sovereign risk (*risk-increasing effect*). This larger impact of bailouts compared to other government intervention measures is also found by Calderon and Schaeck (2016) and Homar and van Wijnbergen (2017), when examining the effects of bailouts on competition and the real economy, respectively. In this sense, the provision of capital to distressed banks through bailouts has traditionally been considered one of the most severe intervention measures that a government can implement. As Laeven and Valencia (2018) underline, during the containment phase, governments tend to implement policies aimed at easing banks' access to funding (*Liquidity support*) and restoring public confidence (*Blanket guarantees*) to minimize the repercussions on the real sector. In contrast, the resolution phase involves the restructuring of financial institutions and corporations (*Bailouts*). These results suggest that, among all the intervention measures that governments usually implement in the banking system, the impact on sovereign risk arises mainly from bank bailouts and it is consistent with the existence of a *risk-increasing effect* associated with this intervention measure.

2.4.2 Robustness checks

In order to check the robustness of our results, we develop additional analyses. First, although for potential multicollinearity problems we have shown the baseline results running individual regressions for each of the intervention measures separately, we have also corroborated that the results are not driven by this approach. Hence, we run a regression for each CRA including all four intervention measures simultaneously. The results are reported in columns (1)–(3) of Table 2.3. As can be seen, the negative and statistically significant coefficient for the *Bailout* variable remains in all three cases, whereas none of the other intervention measures enters the regressions with a significant coefficient.

Second, we also demonstrate that the results do not change when an alternative dependent variable is defined. In particular, we consider *ΔAvg.rating*, defined as the difference between each year's average rating across the three CRAs and the average rating in 2007. The results reported in column (4) of Table 2.4 remain consistent with those previously reported.

Table 2.4 Effect of government intervention measures on sovereign rating adjustments: All measures

Dependent variable:	*ΔFitch*	*ΔS&P*	*ΔMoody's*	*ΔAvg.rating*
	(1)	(2)	(3)	(4)
Bailout	−0.997***	−0.990***	−1.312***	−1.908***
	(0.343)	(0.356)	(0.344)	(0.489)
Liquidity support	−0.0287	−0.0425	−0.0547	0.322
	(0.291)	(0.275)	(0.249)	(0.224)
Blanket guarantees	−0.198	−0.417	−0.103	−0.366
	(0.280)	(0.291)	(0.283)	(0.222)
Nationalization	0.269	0.309	0.089	0.057
	(0.409)	(0.433)	(0.445)	(1.059)
Log GDP per Capita	0.0405	−0.168	0.337	2.256**
	(0.240)	(0.271)	(0.365)	(0.880)
GDP Growth	0.272***	0.179*	0.203*	0.213
	(0.0977)	(0.105)	(0.115)	(0.152)
Inflation	0.056	0.005	0.045	−0.049
	(0.108)	(0.091)	(0.109)	(0.062)
Fiscal Surplus/Deficit	0.013	0.027	0.025	−0.044
	(0.0269)	(0.023)	(0.034)	(0.056)
Public Debt (%GDP)	−0.011***	−0.012***	−0.013***	−0.058***
	(0.003)	(0.004)	(0.002)	(0.015)
Sovereign Default	−0.558	−0.825**	0.139	−0.108
	(0.348)	(0.345)	(0.463)	(0.468)
Economic Freedom Index	−0.004	−0.011	0.012	0.011
	(0.027)	(0.028)	(0.031)	(0.053)
Forecasted GDP growth	0.221**	0.101	0.163	0.138
	(0.095)	(0.108)	(0.109)	(0.129)
Year Dummies	Yes	Yes	Yes	Yes
Clustered standard errors	Country	Country	Country	Country
Observations	315	315	315	315

(*Continued*)

Table 2.4 (Continued)

Dependent variable:	*ΔFitch*	*ΔS&P*	*ΔMoody's*	*ΔAvg.rating*
Number of countries	35	35	35	35
Log pseudolikelihood	−435.78	−465.35	−454.06	–
Pseudo R^2/R^2	0.1988	0.2000	0.2030	0.4327
p-value (chi^2)	0.00	0.00	0.00	0.00

This table shows the results for the impact of government interventions in the banking system on the change of sovereign risk (*ΔSOVEREIGN RATING*). Our dependent variables are the difference between each year's rating and the sovereign rating in 2007, before any of the government intervention occurred. Bailout takes the value 1 for those years in which the government injects public capital into its banking system, and 0 otherwise. Liquidity support takes the value 1 for those years in which the ratio of central bank claims on the financial sector to deposits and foreign liabilities exceeds 5% and more than doubles relative to its pre-crisis level, and 0 otherwise. Blanket guarantees take the value 1 for those years in which the government has implemented blanket guarantees, and 0 otherwise. Nationalization takes the value 1 for those years in which the government has taken over systemically important financial institutions, and 0 otherwise. The rest of the variables are defined in Appendix. Year fixed effects are included but not reported. Clustered standard errors (at country-level) are reported in parentheses. ***, **, and * indicate significance at the 1%, 5%, and 10% levels, respectively.

Third, in Table 2.5, we report the results obtained from additional robustness tests. In Panel A, we use an ordinal variable ranging from −2 (a downgrade of two or more notches since the GFC) to +2 (an upgrade of two or more notches since the GFC) as the dependent variable. In Panel B, the dependent variable is a dummy that takes the value 1 if at year *t* the country has experienced a downgrade since the GFC, and 0 otherwise. In Panel C, we exclude the GIPSI countries (Greece, Ireland, Portugal, Spain, and Italy), as they are traditionally seen as the European countries that were most affected by the GFC. Following a similar idea, in Panel D, and using data from Laeven and Valencia (2018), we exclude those countries with a GFC-induced output loss above the 90th percentile of the distribution of output losses for the OECD countries. As can be seen, in all the cases we corroborate that bailouts remain as the main intervention measure negatively affecting changes in sovereign ratings and thus sovereign risk.

2.5 COVID-19 intervention measures and sovereign ratings

Since March 2020, policymakers and governments around the globe saw themselves in the need of implementing a wide set of emergency actions aiming at giving response to the COVID-19 pandemic and the economic effects derived from it. This wide set of policies has included social distancing measures, public awareness programs or testing and quarantining policies to deal with the spread of the illness, as well as income support packages in order to alleviate the negative economic impact of the sanitary crisis.

As for the income support packages, according to the estimates of the International Monetary Fund (IMF), fiscal measures announced as of September 11, 2020, were estimated at $11.7 trillion globally, or close to 12% of global GDP (IMF, 2021). Nevertheless, the global fiscal response to the crisis has been unparalleled and it has highlighted the existence of major differences in the ability of countries

Table 2.5 Robustness checks

Dependent variable	*ΔFitch*				*ΔS&P*				*ΔMoody's*			
	Bailout	*Liquidity support*	*Blanket guarantees*	*Nationalization*	*Bailout*	*Liquidity support*	*Blanket guarantees*	*Nationalization*	*Bailout*	*Liquidity support*	*Blanket guarantees*	*Nationalization*
Panel A. Rating change (−2 to +2)	*(1)*	*(2)*	*(3)*	*(4)*	*(5)*	*(6)*	*(7)*	*(8)*	*(9)*	*(10)*	*(11)*	*(12)*
Intervention measure	−0.768***	−0.174	−0.055	−0.340	−0.815***	−0.434	−0.124	−0.325	−1.152***	−0.206	−0.137	−0.602
	(0.254)	(0.261)	(0.295)	(0.291)	(0.296)	(0.281)	(0.288)	(0.335)	(0.294)	(0.267)	(0.298)	(0.378)
Controls and Year Dummies	Yes	Yes	Yes	Yes	Yes	Yes	Yes	Yes	Yes	Yes	Yes	Yes
Clustered Standard Errors	Country	Country	Country	Country	Country	Country	Country	Country	Country	Country	Country	Country
Observations	315	315	315	315	315	315	315	315	315	315	315	315
Log pseudolikelihood	−296.24	−306.35	−306.83	−304.64	−329.15	−338.87	−342.00	−340.03	−267.25	−285.48	−285.96	−280.22
Pseudo R2	0.2424	0.2166	0.2153	0.2209	0.2214	0.1984	0.1910	0.1957	0.2841	0.2352	0.2340	0.2493
Panel B. Downgrade	(13)	(14)	(15)	(16)	(17)	(18)	(19)	(20)	(21)	(22)	(23)	(24)
Intervention measure	0.993***	0.404	0.182	0.456	0.699*	0.476	0.253	0.467	1.918***	0.279	0.357	0.442
	(0.402)	(0.259)	(0.373)	(0.438)	(0.367)	(0.295)	(0.376)	(0.446)	(0.425)	(0.288)	(0.389)	(0.522)
Controls and Year Dummies	Yes	Yes	Yes	Yes	Yes	Yes	Yes	Yes	Yes	Yes	Yes	Yes
Clustered Standard Errors	Country	Country	Country	Country	Country	Country	Country	Country	Country	Country	Country	Country
Observations	315	315	315	315	315	315	315	315	315	315	315	315
Log pseudolikelihood	−124.35	−123.67	−133.90	−131.73	−124.56	−120.21	−129.16	−127.04	−83.63	−103.83	−103.87	−93.11
Pseudo R2	0.3731	0.3765	0.3250	0.3358	0.4063	0.4270	0.3844	0.3944	0.5768	0.4746	0.4744	0.5288
Panel C. Excluding GIPSI	(25)	(26)	(27)	(28)	(29)	(30)	(31)	(32)	(33)	(34)	(35)	(36)
Intervention measure	−0.721***	0.223	0.275	−0.421	−0.847***	0.017	0.165	−0.553	−1.163***	0.127	−0.011	−0.420
	(0.268)	(0.202)	(0.320)	(0.297)	(0.285)	(0.213)	(0.291)	(0.315)	(0.305)	(0.222)	(0.328)	(0.486)
Controls and Year Dummies	Yes	Yes	Yes	Yes	Yes	Yes	Yes	Yes	Yes	Yes	Yes	Yes
Clustered Standard Errors	Country	Country	Country	Country	Country	Country	Country	Country	Country	Country	Country	Country
Observations	270	270	270	270	270	270	270	270	270	270	270	270
Log pseudolikelihood	−321.42	−329.44	−329.44	−327.07	−345.44	−358.07	−357.79	−352.53	−342.08	−361.16	−361.39	−354.74
Pseudo R2	0.1558	0.1347	0.1347	0.1410	0.1513	0.1203	0.1210	0.1339	0.1640	0.1173	0.1168	0.1330
Panel D. Excluding slightly affected	(37)	(38)	(39)	(40)	(41)	(42)	(43)	(44)	(45)	(46)	(47)	(48)
Intervention measure	−0.626**	−0.494	−0.336	−0.197	−0.634***	−0.343	−0.311	−0.149	−1.078***	−0.512	−0.386	−0.553
	(0.278)	(0.311)	(0.354)	(0.279)	(0.275)	(0.279)	(0.323)	(0.310)	(0.316)	(0.308)	(0.382)	(0.354)
Controls and Year Dummies	Yes	Yes	Yes	Yes	Yes	Yes	Yes	Yes	Yes	Yes	Yes	Yes
Clustered Standard Errors	Country	Country	Country	Country	Country	Country	Country	Country	Country	Country	Country	Country
Observations	279	279	279	279	279	279	279	279	279	279	279	279
Log pseudolikelihood	−338.00	−340.65	−343.22	−343.60	−384.50	−383.27	−390.61	−391.21	−347.88	−359.60	−362.10	−358.52
Pseudo R2	0.1975	0.1913	0.1852	0.1842	0.1627	0.1654	0.1494	0.1481	0.2235	0.1974	0.1918	0.1998

This table shows the results for the impact of government interventions on the change of sovereign risk (ΔSOVEREIGN RATING). Our dependent variables are the difference between each year's rating and the sovereign rating in 2007, before any of the government intervention occurred. The intervention measures are defined in Appendix. In Panel A, the dependent variable is an ordinal variable from −2 (two or more notches of downgrade since the GFC) to +2 (two or more notches of upgrade since the GFC). In Panel B, the dependent variable is a dummy taking the value if at year *t* the country has experienced a downgrade since the GFC. In Panel C, GIPSI countries (Greece, Ireland, Portugal, Spain, and Italy) are excluded. In Panel D, we exclude those countries with an output loss larger than the 90th percentile of the distribution of output losses for the OECD countries. The same set of quantitative and qualitative controls included in our baseline model are included. Year fixed effects are included. Clustered standard errors (at country-level) in parentheses. ***, **, and * indicate significance at the 1%, 5%, and 10% levels, respectively.

to finance emergency spending, thereby reflecting their countries' fiscal space and their financial health in terms of public and private debt (IMF, 2021). Hence, responses to the crisis vary across economies depending on country-specific circumstances, including the impact of the pandemic and other shocks, as well as the health of the country in terms of public finances. IMF's estimates for September 2021 reveal that the fiscal response in advanced economies increased during the second year of the sanitary crisis (IMF, 2021; Pappa & Vella, 2022). Hence, in terms of equity, loans, and guarantees, implemented measures represent on average around 11.38% of GDP. In emerging markets economies, these measures are close to 4.55% of GDP, whereas the percentage that these measures represent in the case of low-income countries is 0.85%. In terms of additional spending and forgone revenue, developed countries injected on average 11.68%. In emerging economies and low-income countries, this percentage is 5.67% and 3.20%, respectively.

Recent papers have examined the effects of COVID-19 economic support measures. Chudik et al. (2021) quantify the macroeconomic impact of fiscal actions undertaken by a sample of 33 countries and show that fiscal policy measures are playing a prominent role in mitigating the effects of the pandemic. In a similar vein, Deb et al. (2021) illustrate that fiscal policy announcements have been an effective countercyclical tool that has boosted confidence and reduced unemployment.

Given the relevance of this wide set of measures on countries' public finances, we now aim at exploring their potential relationship with sovereign ratings. We collect data for the 35 OECD countries that compose our dataset from the IMF Fiscal Monitor Database of Country Fiscal Measures in Response to the COVID-19 Pandemic.[7] It reports the information up to October 2020 on (i) *above the line measures* on additional spending and forgone revenue in the health sector, and on (ii) *below the line measures* such as equity injections, loans, asset purchase, or debt assumptions; guarantees and quasi-fiscal operations. We specifically focus on the latter as they could represent the set of measures that could be most directly affecting public debt finances and thereby sovereign ratings.

In columns (1)–(3) of Table 2.6, we report the share of GDP that each set of *below the line measures* represents on average on each of the countries composing our database. As can be seen, guarantees are the most frequent instruments to inject financial support. In our sample, Italy is the country with the highest percentage of guarantees over the GDP (32.8%), followed by Germany (24.79%), United Kingdom (16.52%), Czech Republic (15.4%), France (14.2%), and Spain (13.2%). In terms of equity injections, loans, asset purchase or debt assumptions, Germany is the country with the highest percentage of these support instruments (6%). As for the least frequent measure in our sample, quasi-fiscal operations, Japan is the country where these types of policies has been more relevant (20.07%).

Columns (4)–(6) report the change in sovereign ratings issued by the three CRAs during the period correspondent to the pre-COVID-19 sanitary crisis (December 2019) and after the COVID-19 episode (December 2020). As can be seen, few changes in ratings occurred during this period. In particular, 26 out of the 35 countries in our sample (74,29%) have not experienced any change in their ratings during this period.

Table 2.6 COVID-19 intervention measures and sovereign ratings

Country	*Equity injections, loans, asset purchase, or debt assumptions*	*Guarantees*	*Quasi-fiscal operations*	*ΔRating (Pre-COVID19 vs COVID19)*		
	(1)	*(2)*	*(3)*	Δ*Fitch* *(4)*	Δ*S&P* *(5)*	Δ*Moody's* *(6)*
Austria	–	2.4	–	0	0	0
Australia	0.8	1.0	–	0	0	0
Belgium	0.2	11.8	–	0	0	0
Canada	0.2	4.0	–	−1	0	0
Chile	–	–	2.3	−1	0	0
Czech Republic	0.02	15.4	–	0	0	0
Denmark	2.65	6.40	–	0	0	0
Estonia	3.22	1.13	–	0	0	0
Finland	1.03	5.51	0.43	0	0	0
France	0.90	14.8	–	0	0	0
Germany	6.00	24.79	–	0	0	0
Greece	2.00	1.69	–	0	0	1
Hungary	–	4.42	–	0	0	0
Iceland	0.00	4.42	0.00	0	0	0
Ireland	1.15	0.57	–	0	0	0
Israel	0.25	2.66	–	0	0	0
Italy	0.20	32.8	–	−1	0	0
Japan	–	2.98	20.7	0	0	0
Korea	–	3.67	6.60	0	0	0
Latvia	0.70	2.48	0.00	0	0	0
Luxembourg	–	4.17	1.83	0	0	0
Mexico	0.17	–	0.29	−1	0	−1
Netherlands	–	4.26	–	0	0	0
New Zealand	2.03	2.08	–	0	0	0
Norway	1.68	4.35	–	0	0	0
Poland	1.76	3.25	–	0	0	0
Portugal	–	6.70	–	0	0	0
Slovak Republic	0.00	4.50	–	−1	0	0
Slovenia	1.32	5.07	0.22	0	0	1
Spain	0.10	13.20	0.91	0	0	0
Sweden	0.24	5.14	–	0	0	0
Switzerland	0.14	6.24	–	0	0	0
Turkey	0.44	10.19	2.36	−1	1	−1
United Kingdom	0.05	16.52	–	0	0	−1
United States	0.27	2.18	–	0	0	0

This table shows the COVID-19 intervention measures – in the form of equity injections, loans, asset purchase, debt assumptions, guarantees and quasi-fiscal operations – that were implemented in each country during the period March 2020–October 2020, according to the IMF Database on Fiscal Policy Responses to COVID-19 (columns [1]–[3]). In columns (4)–(6), we report the change in sovereign ratings between December 2019 and December 2020 for each CRA.

In the case of S&P, there is only one change in ratings – Turkey (+1 notch). Fitch and Moody's have adjusted their ratings just for six and five countries, respectively. Interestingly, it does not seem to be a correlation between the rating adjustments and the magnitude of the measures undertaken as a result of the COVID-19 pandemic. Most of the countries that implemented the more sizeable measures – Germany, Japan, Czech Republic, France, or Spain – have not experienced any downgrade. Just Italy[8] and the United Kingdom[9] have experienced a one-notch downgrade. For these latter countries, in both cases, the CRAs acknowledged that besides the impact of the COVID-19, other factors were driving the downgrade. So, it cannot be argued that the rating adjustment was purely driven by the deterioration of the public finances as a result of the measures undertaken in response to the pandemic.

Taken together, this evidence may suggest that during the first year of the sanitary crisis, OECD countries in our sample implemented different intervention measures aiming at supporting economies and restoring confidence and normality. However, during this period sovereign risk does not seem to be permanently affected, as most countries in our sample did not experience a significant change in their ratings. Hence, the nature of COVID-19-related intervention measures has been different from those undertaken to overcome the effects of the GFC in 2008.

2.6 Conclusions

This chapter provides empirical evidence on the relationship between the most traditional government intervention measures undertaken during two crises periods – the GFC and the COVID-19 pandemic – and changes that occurred in sovereign ratings compared to the pre-crisis levels. In both cases, we focus on a sample of 35 OECD countries.

Our empirical findings reveal that bailouts were the most relevant intervention measure during the GFC and that they negatively influenced the change in sovereign ratings, providing evidence on the existence of a *risk-increasing effect* associated with this intervention mechanism. This result holds after controlling for other intervention measures and for the traditional determinants of sovereign ratings. During the COVID-19 crisis, despite the measures being sizeable, the sovereign risk does not seem to be permanently affected, as most countries in our sample did not experience a significant change in their ratings. The distinct nature of COVID-19-related intervention measures, compared to the measures undertaken during the GFC, might explain why the pandemic sovereign ratings were not affected.

Our findings may have implications, as they reveal that during global banking crises, the relationship between bank bailout programs and country-level characteristics in terms of their creditworthiness should be considered when governments are planning to intervene in the banking sector. In fact, bailout packages could help avoid the worst consequences of a late response to a financial distress period, especially in the case of countries characterized by higher sovereign ratings before the occurrence of the crisis. Future research could aim to further disentangle the effects of the various intervention measures that could have been undertaken simultaneously and to further explore the consequences of their implementation for sovereign risk and country-level financing costs.

Notes

1 For example, Moody's, in their "Procedures and Methodologies Used to Determine Credit Ratings," recognize that " . . . *we may use various other opinions on credit quality such as those implied by bond yields, CDS, and stock prices*" (Moody's, 2020).
2 For robustness purposes, as a pre-crisis rating, we also employed the average rating from 2005 to 2007. The results are qualitatively similar. The results are available upon request.
3 All the current OECD members are considered, with the exception of Lithuania, Colombia and Costa Rica as these countries were brought into the OECD in 2018, 2020 and 2021, respectively.
4 We test whether it is more appropriate to estimate these models using a fixed-effects or a random-effects model. The Hausman test shows that the random-effects estimators are efficient, and therefore the random-effects model is preferable. In further robustness tests, we checked that the results do not change when a fixed-effects estimator is used. The results are available upon request.
5 Appendix 1 reports the definitions of all of the variables and their sources.
6 In our sample, 51% of the OECD countries (18 out of 35) adopted three or more measures. In further robustness tests, we corroborated that results do not change when all the measures are included in the regression at the same time.
7 https://www.imf.org/COVID19policytracker.
8 In the case of Italy, as Fitch recognized in the rating announcement, the downgrade was also triggered by the political tensions. As part of these tensions were resolved, Italy recovered the pre-COVID-19 Fitch's rating (BBB) on December 2021.
9 In the case of United Kingdom, Moody's adjusted the United Kingdom's rating over the economic hit from the coronavirus crisis but also due to the uncertainty related to Brexit and the lack of clear budget plans from government.

References

Acharya, V., Drechsler, I., & Schnabl, P. (2014). A pyrrhic victory? Bank bailouts and sovereign credit risk. *Journal of Finance*, *69*(6), 2689–2739. https://doi.org/10.1111/jofi.12206

Acharya, V. V., & Yorulmazer, T. (2007). Too many to fail-An analysis of time-inconsistency in bank closure policies. *Journal of Financial Intermediation*, *16*(1), 1–31. https://doi.org/10.1016/j.jfi.2006.06.001

Acharya, V. V., & Yorulmazer, T. (2008). Cash-in-the-market pricing and optimal resolution of bank failures. *Review of Financial Studies*, *21*(6), 2705–2742. https://doi.org/10.1093/rfs/hhm078

Afonso, A., Furceri, D., & Gomes, P. (2012). Sovereign credit ratings and financial markets linkages: Application to European data. *Journal of International Money and Finance*, *31*(3), 606–638. https://doi.org/10.1016/j.jimonfin.2012.01.016

Afonso, A., Gomes, P., & Rother, P. (2009). Ordered response models for sovereign. *Applied Economics Letters*, *16*, 769–773.

Afonso, A., Gomes, P., & Rother, P. (2011). Short-and long-run determinants of sovereging debt ratings. *International Journal of Finance & Economics*, *16*, 1–15. https://doi.org/10.1002/ijfe

Aktug, R. E., Nayar, N. (Nandu), & Vasconcellos, G. M. (2013). Is sovereign risk related to the banking sector? *Global Finance Journal*, *24*(3), 222–249. https://doi.org/10.1016/j.gfj.2013.10.001

Alberola, E., Arslan, Y., Cheng, G., & Moessner, R. (2021). Fiscal response to the COVID-19 crisis in advanced and emerging market economies†. *Pacific Economic Review*, *26*(4), 459–468. https://doi.org/10.1111/1468-0106.12370

Alsakka, R., & ap Gwilym, O. (2010). A random effects ordered probit model for rating migrations. *Finance Research Letters*, *7*(3), 140–147. https://doi.org/10.1016/j.frl.2010.02.004

Altman, E. I., & Rijken, H. A. (2004). How rating agencies achieve rating stability. *Journal of Banking and Finance*, *28*(11), 2679–2714. https://doi.org/10.1016/j.jbankfin.2004.06.006

Altman, E. I., & Rijken, H. A. (2006). A point-in-time perspective on through-the-cycle ratings. *Financial Analysts Journal*, *62*(1), 54–70. https://doi.org/10.2469/faj.v62.n1.4058

An, H. (Hunter), & Chan, K. C. (2008). Credit ratings and IPO pricing. *Journal of Corporate Finance*, *14*(5), 584–595. https://doi.org/10.1016/j.jcorpfin.2008.09.010

Barrett, P., Das, S., Magistretti, G., Pugacheva, E., & Wingender, P. (2021). After-effects of the COVID-19 pandemic: Prospects for medium-term economic damage. *IMF Working Paper 21/203*.

Beers, D. T., & Mavalwalla, J. (2017). Database of sovereign defaults, 2017. In *Bank of Canada Technical Report* (Issue 101). https://doi.org/10.2139/ssrn.3000226

Beirne, J., & Fratzscher, M. (2013). The pricing of sovereign risk and contagion during the European sovereign debt crisis. *Journal of International Money and Finance*, *34*, 60–82. https://doi.org/10.1016/j.jimonfin.2012.11.004

BIS. (2011). *The impact of sovereign credit risk on bank funding conditions*. CGFS Papers. No 43. https://www.bis.org/publ/cgfs43.pdf

Borensztein, E., Cowan, K., & Valenzuela, P. (2013). Sovereign ceilings "lite"? The impact of sovereign ratings on corporate ratings. *Journal of Banking and Finance*, *37*(11), 4014–4024. https://doi.org/10.1016/j.jbankfin.2013.07.006

Bosch, O., & Steffen, S. (2011). On syndicate composition, corporate structure and the certification effect of credit ratings. *Journal of Banking & Finance*, *35*(2), 290–299. https://doi.org/10.1016/j.jbankfin.2010.08.002

Brůha, J., & Kočenda, E. (2018). Financial stability in Europe: Banking and sovereign risk. *Journal of Financial Stability*, *36*, 305–321. https://doi.org/10.1016/j.jfs.2018.03.001

Calderon, C., & Schaeck, K. (2016). The effects of government interventions in the financial sector on banking competition and the evolution of zombie banks. *Journal of Financial and Quantitative Analysis*, *51*(4), 1391–1436. https://doi.org/10.1017/S0022109016000478

Cantor, R., & Packer, F. (1996). Determinants and impact of sovereign credit ratings. *Economic Policy Review*, *6*(3), 37–54. https://doi.org/10.3905/jfi.1996.408185

Chava, S., Ganduri, R., & Ornthanalai, C. (2019). Do credit default swaps mitigate the impact of credit rating downgrades? *Review of Finance*, *23*(3), 471–511. https://doi.org/10.1093/rof/rfy033

Chudik, A., Mohaddes, K., & Raissi, M. (2021). COVID-19 fiscal support and its effectiveness. *Economics Letters*, *205*, 109939. https://doi.org/10.1016/j.econlet.2021.109939

Cuadros-Solas, P. J., & Salvador, C. (2022). Disentangling the sources of sovereign rating adjustments: An examination of changes in rating policies following the GFC. *Research in International Business and Finance*, *59*, 101535. https://doi.org/10.1016/j.ribaf.2021.101535

Cuadros-Solas, P. J., Salvador, C., & Suárez, N. (2021). Am I riskier if I rescue my banks ? Beyond the effects of bailouts. *Journal of Financial Stability*, *56*(100935). https://doi.org/10.1016/j.jfs.2021.100935

Deb, P., Furceri, D., Ostry, J., Tawk, N., & Yang, N. (2021). The effects of fiscal measures during COVID-19. *IMF Working Papers*, *2021*(262), 1. https://doi.org/10.5089/9781557754264.001

ECB. (2017). A new database for financial crises in European countries. *Occasional Paper Series*, *194*. https://doi.org/10.2849/119019

Elgin, C., Basbug, G., & Yalaman, A. (2020). Economic policy responses to a pandemic: Developing the COVID-19 economic stimulus index. In *COVID Economics*.

FitchRatings. (2014). *Sovereign Rating Criteria Effective from 13 August 2012 – 12 August 2014*. https://www.fitchratings.com/research/sovereigns/sovereign-rating-criteria-effective-from-13-august-2012-12-august-2014-13-08-2012.

Gourinchas, P.-O. (2020). Flattening the pandemic and recession curves. In *Mitigating the COVID Economic* Crisis: Act Fast and Do Whatever It Takes, ed. by R. Baldwin and B. Weder di Mauro, *CEPR Press. https://cepr.org/publications/books-and-reports/mitigating-covid-economic-crisis-act-fast-and-do-whatever-it-takes* (pp. 1–227).

Gourinchas, P.-O., Kalemli-Özcan, Ş., Penciakova, V., & Sander, N. (2021). Fiscal policy in the age of COVID. *NBER Working Paper* no. 29293. http://www.nber.org/papers/w29293

Homar, T., & van Wijnbergen, S. J. G. (2017). Bank recapitalization and economic recovery after financial crises. *Journal of Financial Intermediation, 32*, 1339–1351. https://doi.org/10.1016/j.jfi.2016.11.004

Hu, Y. T., Kiesel, R., & Perraudin, W. (2002). The estimation of transition matrices for sovereign credit ratings. *Journal of Banking and Finance, 26*(7), 1383–1406. https://doi.org/10.1016/S0378-4266(02)00268-6

IMF. (2009). Fiscal implications of the global economic and financial crisis. In *IMF Staff Position Note. SPN/09/13*. https://doi.org/10.5089/9781462374755.004

IMF (2020). IMF Annual Report: A year like no other. *IMF – Annual Reports*, https://www.imf.org/external/pubs/ft/ar/2020/eng/downloads/imf-annual-report-2020.pdf

IMF (2021). *Fiscal monitor: Database of Country fiscal measures in response to the COVID-19 Pandemic*. https://www.imf.org/en/Topics/imf-and-covid19/Fiscal-Policies-Database-in-Response-to-COVID-19.

Kaminsky, G., & Schmukler, S. L. (2002). Emerging market instability: Do sovereign ratings affect country risk and stock returns? *The World Bank Economic Review, 16*(2), 171–195.

Kanno, M. (2020). Credit rating migration risk and interconnectedness in a corporate lending network. *Research in International Business and Finance, 54*(October 2019), 101282. https://doi.org/10.1016/j.ribaf.2020.101282

King, M. R. (2019). Time to buy or just buying time? Lessons from October 2008 for the cross-border bailout of banks. *Journal of Financial Stability, 41*(April 2019), 55–72. https://doi.org/10.1016/j.jfs.2019.03.003

Laeven, L., & Valencia, F. (2018). Systemic banking crises revisited. *IMF Economic Review, 61*(2), 225–270. https://doi.org/10.1057/imfer.2013.12

Moody's (2015). Moody's Global Credit Research: Moody's Country Credit Statistical Handbook. http://www.alacrastore.com/moodys-credit-research/Moody-s-Country-Credit-Statistical-Handbook-May-2015-PBC_181421.

Moody's Investors Service (2021). *Procedures and methodologies used to determine credit ratings*. https://www.moodys.com/sites/products/ProductAttachments/Exhibit2.pdf

Opoku Mensah, M., Agbloyor, E. K., Harvey, S. K., & Fiador, V. O. (2017). Sovereign credit ratings and bank funding cost: Evidence from Africa. *Research in International Business and Finance, 42*(October 2016), 887–899. https://doi.org/10.1016/j.ribaf.2017.07.024

Pappa, E., & Vella, E. (2022). Phase out of the crisis support measures: How successful are Member States in moving from broad support measures towards more targeted support? *Economic Governance Support Unit (EGOV), January*.

Philippon, T., & Schnabl, P. (2013). Efficient recapitalization. *The Journal of Finance*, vol. 68, issue 1, 1–42.

Reinhart, C. M., & Reinhart, V. R. (2010). After the Fall. In *NBER Working Paper Series*.

Reusens, P., & Croux, C. (2017). Sovereign credit rating determinants: A comparison before and after the European debt crisis. *Journal of Banking and Finance*, *77*, 108–121. https://doi.org/10.1016/j.jbankfin.2017.01.006

AU: Please provide report number for this reference.

Standard and Poor's. (2014). *Sovereign Rating Methodology*. https://enterprise.press/wp-content/uploads/2017/05/Sovereign-Rating-Methodology.pdf

Sufi, A. (2009). The real effects of debt certification: Evidence from the introduction of bank loan ratings. *Review of Financial Studies*, *22*(4), 1659–1691. https://doi.org/10.1093/rfs/hhm061

Vernazza, D. R., & Nielsen, E. F. (2015). The damaging bias of sovereign ratings. *Economic Notes*, *44*(2), 361–408. https://doi.org/10.1111/ecno.12037

Appendix

Table A.2.1 Variables and data sources

Variable	*Definition*	*Source*
Panel A. Sovereign risk and bank bailouts		
ΔSOVEREIGN RATING	Difference between each year's rating (SOVEREIGN RATING$_{i,t}$) and the sovereign rating in 2007, before any of the government interventions occurred (*SOVEREIGN RATING*$_{i,2007}$). The long-term foreign currency sovereign credit ratings issued by the three main CRAs – Fitch (Δ*Fitch*), S&P (Δ*S&P*) and Moody's (Δ*Moody's*) – are employed.	Thomson Reuters
Panel B. Intervention measures		
Bailout	Dummy variable taking the value 1 if at year *t* the government injects public capital into its banking system, and 0 otherwise.	Laeven and Valencia (2018), Homar and van Wijnbergen (2017), the IMF Country Reports and the World Bank
Liquidity support	Dummy variable taking the value 1 if at year *t* the ratio of central bank claims on the financial sector to deposits and foreign liabilities exceeds 5% and is more than double relative to its pre-crisis level, and 0 otherwise.	
Blanket guarantees	Dummy variable taking the value 1 if at year *t* the government has implemented blanket guarantees (full protection of bank liabilities or instances in which the non-deposit liabilities of banks are protected), and 0 otherwise.	
Nationalization	Dummy variable taking the value 1 if at year *t* the government has taken over systemically important financial institutions, and 0 otherwise.	

(*Continued*)

Table A.2.1 (Continued)

Panel C. Control variables		
GDP Growth	Annual percentage growth rate of GDP.	World Bank
Log GDP per Capita	Natural logarithm of GDP over total population.	IMF
Inflation	Annual percentage change of end-of-period consumer prices.	IMF
Fiscal Surplus/Deficit	General government net lending/borrowing, calculated as government revenue minus total government expenditure, as a % of GDP.	IMF
Public Debt (%GDP)	Total debt of the public sector as a % of GDP.	World Bank
Sovereign Default	Dummy variable taking value 1 if the country has experienced a sovereign default in the last 10 years, and 0 otherwise.	(Beers & Mavalwalla, 2017)
Economic Freedom Index	The Heritage Foundation's Economic Freedom Index ranks countries' policies and performance in terms of the extent to which they provide economic freedom. Economic freedom is based on 12 quantitative and qualitative factors, grouped into four broad categories: rule of law (property rights, government integrity, judicial effectiveness), government size (government spending, tax burden, fiscal health), regulatory efficiency (business freedom, labor freedom, monetary freedom) and open markets (trade freedom, investment freedom, financial freedom).	Heritage Foundation
Forecasted GDP growth	Difference between the average of the IMF staff's analysis and projections of economic development for the following two years ($t+1$, $t+2$) and current GDP growth (GDP at market prices based on constant local currency, 2010 U.S. dollars)	IMF

This table describes the variables used in the chapter and indicates the sources from which the data were retrieved.

3 The impact of the COVID-19 pandemic on European bank regulation and supervision

Lessons from past crises

Giuseppina Chesini

3.1 Introduction

Banking crises are recurrent and, after a crisis, a more effective regulatory and supervisory framework is usually developed to avoid, or at least mitigate, the effects of another crisis. Thus, the improvements of bank regulation and supervision tend to proceed in tandem with the most robust revisions subsequent to crisis events (Masciandaro and Romelli, 2018). Consequently, it is possible to say that if we now have a quite effective set of regulatory measures and supervisory practices, it is due essentially to what we have learned from past crises.

Preventing crises is not an easy task because the system of banking regulation and supervision should be capable of identifying and managing excesses before they lead to crises without repressing too much financial innovation and related risk-taking (Yellen, 2011). Consequently, it is necessary to maintain an equilibrium point between the prevention of catastrophe and keeping too tight a hold on the financial system throughout business cycles (Fiechter and Zamorski, 2016). Furthermore, prevention is a difficult task because crises are always triggered by different drivers. Throughout the period of 2007–2008, banks were one of the causes of the global financial crisis (GFC) and its key catalyst. Recently a pandemic – a public health problem – has been the main cause of a global crisis, and the banking sector has been required to operate as part of the solution and help the real economy escape the crisis.

The impact that the COVID-19 pandemic could have on banks and on their capacity to support the economy is analyzed in this chapter, by considering the regulation and supervision evolutionary steps developed until now after the recent crises. The main research question is the following: "Do the lessons learnt by regulatory and supervisory authorities during the previous crises enable European banks to both avoid the negative effects of the pandemic shock on their balance sheets and continue lending to households and businesses?"

At a first sight, during the COVID-19 pandemic, European banks seem to have emerged relatively unharmed from another severe crisis; one that has originated from the exogenous shock that primarily hit the commercial and productive sectors of the economy.

DOI: 10.4324/9781003310754-3

The current strengthening of the European banking sector in aggregate terms, particularly in comparison to the years following the GFC, together with an unprecedented unanimous policy response to the crisis by central banks, supervisors, and governments, has enabled banks to support the real economy through the most difficult time of the coronavirus (COVID-19) crisis without encountering relevant worries. This suggests the following research hypotheses:

1 regulatory reforms of the 2010s prepared banks to withstand the economic consequences of the pandemic;
2 supervisory responses during the pandemic – only possible because of the earlier reforms – enabled banks to preserve the financial stability and the soundness of their balance sheets while effectively supporting the economy.

The chapter is organized as follows. The first section describes the role of European regulation and supervision after the creation of the European Monetary Union (EMU). The second section tackles the changes introduced after the GFC. The third section outlines what happened after the European sovereign debt crisis. The fourth section discusses the research hypotheses concerning the economic consequences of the COVID-19 pandemic. The chapter ends with the conclusions.

3.2 European regulation and supervision before the global financial crisis (GFC)

Since the mid-1990s, efforts have been undertaken to improve domestic financial regulation and supervision. At that time, financial systems were barely international, and the effectiveness of the regulatory and supervisory settings was focused mainly on their micro-capacity to design and implement the correct interest alignment of all players involved in the banking and financial industry (Masciandaro et al., 2013).

In particular, before the outbreak of the GFC, we can distinguish four main characteristics of European regulation and supervision that contributed to spreading the GFC:

- The Basel II Capital Accord in 2004 replaced the first innovative but too simple Accord of 1988, after many years of discussions and analyses. Although the Basel II Capital Accord has considered market and operational risks in addition to credit risk, the set of prudential regulatory standards that major global banks were required to meet permitted these banks to maintain low levels of capital and liquidity and excessively high levels of leverage on their balance sheets (Giese and Haldane, 2020). In fact, no internationally agreed standards for minimum levels of leverage ratio and of liquid assets had yet been set. In Basel II banks' capital requirements were still calibrated based on the idiosyncratic risk of that institution failing, not on the risk that an institution posed to the financial system as a whole, because of size or complexity or interconnectivity with others in the system (Cukierman, 2021). Consequently, the largest and most systemically important banks proportionally had smaller capital buffers than the small banks. Considering financial stability, this had two negative side effects. First, it increased perceptions that these large, interconnected institutions would be bailed out in the event of a potential crisis, i.e., that they were too big to fail. Second, those perceptions lowered the cost of borrowing for these institutions, and in this way, they encouraged further growth in their size, complexity and connectivity, which is a dangerous 'doom loop' of risk-taking (Giese and Haldane, 2020).

- The Basel Core Principles for Effective Banking Supervision (BCPs) were issued in 1997 with the objective of promoting best practices; they were used for peer reviews as part of the Financial Sector Assessment Programs (FSAPs) jointly conducted by the IMF and World Bank. The principles themselves were subject to a major revision in 2006 (BCBS, 2006).
- European banking supervision was still organized on a national basis, while the banking sector had become international (De Grauwe, 2016; Heisenberg, 2014). This divergence did not consider international contagion risk because banks were becoming highly interconnected. The pre-crisis regulation was focused on the insolvency of individual institutions and not on the stability of the banking sector. The probability and costs of systemic risk were greatly underestimated.
- The identification of the most effective national supervisory architecture was a very relevant issue at that time. In particular, given the demarcation lines blurring between several types of financial institutions and the formation of financial conglomerates, unifying all financial supervisors under one roof was increasingly considered the most effective solution (Abrams and Taylor, 2002).
- The UK was the first country that unified all financial supervisors under one authority in 1997 – the Financial Services Authority (FSA) (Llewellyn, 1998). In 2002, following the same trend, the German Financial Services Authority (BAFIN) was established to serve as the primary regulator of Germany's financial markets and institutions. Following that, many countries reformed their supervisory architecture, even though not all countries opted for a complete unification, but configurations with different levels of integration emerged with a consequent lower involvement of central banks in the supervisory processes (Masciandaro et al., 2013).

3.3 The evolution of European financial regulation and supervision following the GFC

When the GFC erupted, the lack of resilience of European banks was immediately evident, imposing huge costs on the economy. In fact, banks reacted by cutting lending to households and businesses to protect their balance sheets. Those banks with the lowest levels of capital and liquidity restricted lending most sharply, imposing the largest costs on the economy (Cukierman, 2021). Even if cutting lending seemed sensible for less resilient banks individually, the collective consequence of these individual lending decisions constricted aggregate credit, which imposed an externality on aggregate demand that was both large and lasting and fed back to raise losses for the banking system in a vicious cycle.

Searching for the causes of the crisis, in addition to macroeconomic factors, a number of studies (Moshirian, 2011; Čihák et al., 2012; Barth et al., 2013; Meier et al., 2021) have pointed to weaknesses in financial regulation and supervision as one of the factors spreading the GFC in Europe; this awareness prompted regulators and supervisors to begin to devise an overhaul of the entire system (Fiechter and Zamorski, 2016; Masciandaro et al., 2013).

The focus of the revision became systemic risk management because in any of the countries stricken by the crisis, there was no institution in charge of macro-prudential or systemic supervision, and even from the regulatory point of view, systemic risk had not yet been properly considered.

Consequently, concerning the global regulatory framework, extensive work started on behalf of the Basel Committee on Banking Supervision. A revision of the Basel II Capital Accord started soon after the crisis because it had become fully operational only in 2007, clearly demonstrating its inability to avoid any crisis; in addition, a new version of the Basel Core Principles for Effective Banking Supervision was issued in 2012.

The new version of the Basel Capital Accord – Basel III – was released in November 2010 proposing a set of new measures to address main problems exposed by the GFC in the financial system. In principle, new regulatory minimum requirements concerning bank liquidity and leverage ratio were introduced. In addition, a system-wide approach to financial sector risks was proposed by introducing a so-called macro-prudential perspective that aims to promote financial stability and mitigate systemic risk (BIS, 2020). Although the voluntary implementation deadline for the new rules was originally 2015, the date has repeatedly been pushed back and, after the outbreak of the COVID-19 pandemic, the deadline was further extended to the beginning of 2023.

More specifically, a minimum leverage ratio has been introduced, and banks must have enough high-quality liquid assets to meet 30-day liquidity needs – namely, the liquidity coverage ratio (LCR) – while a net stable funding ratio (NSFR) guarantees that banks' funding profiles are sustainable.

Moreover, banks must hold a capital conservation buffer (CCoB), which aims to ensure that banks have an additional layer of usable capital that can be drawn down to absorb losses during periods of financial and economic stress.

Considering the necessity to properly manage systemic risk, beyond the cover of idiosyncratic risk, new requirements that focus on risks across the financial system and on enabling banks have been set to maintain lending in periods of stress. Consequently, under Basel III, all banks are now required to hold a countercyclical capital buffer (CCyB). The latter aims to protect the banking sector from periods of excess aggregate credit growth that have often been associated with a build-up of system-wide risk; it can be imposed and released by macro-prudential authorities to build resilience during the upswing of a financial cycle and released during stress.

Finally, a new systemic risk buffer (SIB) has been introduced that applies only to globally systemically important banks (G-SIBs), i.e., banks designated by the

Financial Stability Board considering a set of objective criteria such as size and connectivity.

The new capital regulation provided both the global financial system with greater insurance against extreme events and global regulators with extra degrees of policy freedom when dealing with such stressful events.

Passing from regulation to supervision, after the outbreak of the GFC, it was immediately recognized that the failure of European banking supervision also depended on the fact that it had been organized on a national basis, while the banking sector—through the activity of cross-country banking groups—had become international. In fact, until then, the supervision performed by individual central banks, or other specific supervisors, on their national banking system was not planned to prevent international crises (Recine and Teixeira, 2009).

Consequently, the GFC highlighted that the existing architecture for financial services supervision in the European Union (EU) was lacking (Quaglia, 2013), and to avoid a repeat of such a crisis, the principles of supervision should have been revised, and the architecture of financial supervision at the national level should have been changed.

Regarding the architecture of national banking supervision, some flaws were immediately recognized and solved; in 2008, the German grand coalition government expressed its willingness to dismantle its sole financial supervisor (BAFIN), and banking supervision returned to the Bundesbank. In June 2010, the UK government also unveiled the reform of the bank supervisory system. The key functions of the Financial Services Authority (FSA) concerning the UK banks moved within the Bank of England, specifically in the Prudential Regulatory Authority. In the summer of 2010, the Irish Financial Services Regulatory Authority was legally merged with the central bank. Finally, in the summer of 2012, the Italian government proposed increasing the role of the Bank of Italy in monitoring financial stability across banking, insurance and pension fund markets.

Synthetically, regarding banking supervision, three new trends were observable because of the GFC:

1 A growing attention to macro-prudential supervision. The neglect or lack of understanding of systemic risks in the financial system in the run-up to the GFC made it clear that it was crucial to monitor and assess the threats to financial stability arising from microeconomic as well as macrofinancial developments (Cukierman, 2021; Quaglia, 2013).
2 Central banks tended to be more involved in supervision (Masciandaro and Romelli, 2018), especially in some countries belonging to the EMU, where the monetary policy responsibilities were no longer in their hands after the advent of the Euro. This is particularly the case for those central banks that have chosen the route of specialization in surveillance. The most emblematic cases are Belgium, Germany, Ireland, the Netherlands and the Slovak Republic.
3 The opacity of European banking supervision came to light. In particular, it was evident that cross-border banks contributed positively to the integration of European financial markets, but supervision was fragmented and remained at

the national level. The supervisory framework was based on cooperation and information exchange between national supervisors, but this worked badly in times of crisis where national interests obviously tended to prevail (Ferrarini and Chiodini, 2009).

From an institutional point of view, it emerges that the GFC hit all European countries, and the answer should have been a European one. Considering this, very soon in October 2008, the European Commission (EC) set up a high-level group of experts chaired by Jacques de Larosière, an internationally renowned banker (and former governor of the Bank of France), to formulate a report containing proposals to strengthen the European regulatory framework across all financial sectors.

In February 2009, a report was published (De Larosière, 2009), indicating the following concerns:

- the absence of macro-prudential supervision;
- the lack of early warning mechanisms; and
- the differences among the national micro-prudential supervisory systems (structures, rules, powers, sanctioning systems).

The de Larosière report was very innovative in that it proposed regulatory arrangements in which micro- and macro-prudential supervision were jointly deployed and interactions with economic policies were also taken into account (Ferrarini and Chiodini, 2009). Specifically, the expert group identified a new European System of Financial Supervision (ESFS) to be applied to all European countries, which finally became operational at the beginning of 2011. In the ESFS, the ECB began to act as an important player, even if it was still not a protagonist.

The ESFS is based on a two-pillar framework for macro- and micro-prudential supervision working together (Ferrarini, 2015):

- The European Systemic Risk Board (ESRB), which was set up under the auspices and with the support of the ECB, is responsible for macro-prudential oversight of the financial system (based in Frankfurt) (Ferrarini and Chiodini, 2009); the scope of the activity of the ESRB is not limited to the banking system because it has control over insurance, asset management companies, shadow banking entities, financial market infrastructure, and other financial markets and institutions. In pursuing its macro-prudential mandate, the ESRB monitors and assesses systemic risks and issues reports and recommendations (European Parliament, 2013).
- A network of European supervisors coordinated by three new European Supervisory Authorities (ESAs), which are sector-specific with micro-prudential supervisory tasks, representing the heirs to the "level three Committees" already operating (same offices); more precisely, the ESAs are the following:
    - the European Banking Authority (EBA), based in London and now in Paris as a consequence of Brexit;

- the European Securities and Markets Authority (ESMA), based in Paris; and
- the European Insurance and Occupational Pensions Authority (EIOPA), based in Frankfurt.

The ESAs represent a new type of EU agency having legal character, represented by their respective presidents. They develop regulatory and implementation technical standards, which are then adopted by the Commission; they also issue guidelines and recommendations and intervene when there are breaches of EU law by national supervisory authorities and in the case of emergency situations and disagreements between national competent authorities. The ESAs cooperate through a Joint Committee of European Supervisory Authorities, composed of the chairpersons of each authority. In this way, supervisory consistency across sectors has been guaranteed. Moreover, the linkage between the ESAs and the ESRB is very relevant, and it represents an attempt to establish a more coherent institutional framework aimed at a more harmonized implementation.

The de Larosière report recognized that the ECB (more precisely the ESRB, which is closely linked to the ECB) was best positioned to exercise macro-prudential supervision. As far as micro-prudential supervision, it acknowledged that if it were attributed to the ECB, it might have conflicted with its role in monetary policy or might have been exposed to excessive political pressures (Masciandaro et al., 2009). The result was the creation of different authorities, and in such a supervisory architecture, information sharing has become crucial. Unfortunately, in a complex supervisory structure such as the one proposed in the de Laroisière report, the exchange of information was not assured, and a loss of information was possible (Ferrarini and Chiodini, 2009).

In the words of the de Larosière report, the new "European System of Financial Supervision (ESFS) would be a largely decentralized structure, fully respecting the proportionality and subsidiarity principles of the Treaty". Therefore, existing national supervisors, who were the closest to the markets and institutions they supervised, would continue to carry out day-to-day supervision and would preserve the majority of their present competences.

In summary, the ESFS was mainly based on cooperation among national supervisory authorities. It enhanced coordination mechanisms without changing the allocation of powers and responsibilities among national (lead home) authorities. It is considered a step toward centralization and a considerable political compromise (Ferrarini and Chiarella, 2013). In this framework, the ECB acquired relevance in the supervisory structure that it did not have, but micro-supervision remained substantially decentralized (De Rynck, 2014); decentralization proved to be dramatic during the following sovereign debt crisis because it induces the misalignment of incentives between national supervisors given the threat to the countries' financial stability and possible fiscal responsibilities.

Finally, it is worth mentioning that post-GFC, banking authorities, in several countries, began conducting regular, comprehensive stress tests of their banking systems to ensure that large banks would remain adequately capitalized even after the losses arising from adverse macroeconomic scenarios (Garel and Petit-Romec, 2021).

This was not something completely new because large international banks started using internal stress tests in the 1990s. In fact, in 1996, the first Basel Capital Accord was amended to require banks and investment firms to conduct stress tests to determine their ability to respond to market events, and properly manage market risk.

In 2009, the Committee of Banking Supervisors (CEBS) – the ancestor of the European Banking Authority (EBA) – started its first EU-wide stress test. The purpose of the test was to assess the EU banking industry in aggregate, leaving the individual bank assessment with each national supervisor.

Later, the EBA was given powers to initiate and coordinate EU-wide stress tests in a bottom-up fashion using consistent methodologies, scenarios and key assumptions developed in cooperation with the ESRB, the ECB and the EC. The results are publicized to provide an added degree of market discipline on banks' risk-taking. In principle, doing these stress tests simultaneously across banks allows feedback effects (both between banks and between banks and the economy) to be taken into account in assessing banks' resilience and lending capacity.

Even if the efforts in revising the European regulatory and supervisory structures were consistent and timely, it is argued that the framework for financial regulation and supervision resulting as a response to the GFC was still poorly equipped to deal with (or to prevent) future financial crises mainly because of the political constraints encountered during the reform process. In fact, it is evident that political factors were as important as (if not more important than) economic factors in shaping financial services regulation and supervision (Quaglia, 2013).

3.4 What happens after the European sovereign debt crisis (2010–2012)

The new ESFS had to be capable of averting other financial crises, but it lacked a centralized mechanism of supervision. In fact, very soon, in 2010, the fears for keeping the Monetary Union highlighted the need to intervene to break the vicious circle between banks and the sovereign debt caused by the fragmentation of domestic markets and supervisory authorities in several countries.

It was thus evident that banks, from an operational point of view, were the most integrated financial institutions in the single market, but the controls on their activity were held by the individual states. The latter were no longer able to rescue a large banking group with their debt if they entered into a crisis. It became clear that individual countries had to accept the delegation of elements of their sovereignty to more solid supranational supervisory institutions (Chesini and Fauri, 2020). Moreover, it clearly emerged that while cross-border cooperation could sufficiently work for ongoing supervision of multinational groups, fully centralized mechanisms for supervising and resolving banking crises were the only way to prevent the national bias of local supervisors and cut the link between banks and sovereigns.

Consequently, in June 2012, the euro area heads of state and government set up the European Banking Union (EBU) and, in this way, they made the Eurozone banking systems less tied to sovereign debt and also made banking supervision more centralized. This ambitious project includes, in addition to single rulebook uniform regulation, the following pillars: (1) a single supervisory mechanism (SSM), (2) a single resolution mechanism (SRM), and (3) a common deposit guarantee scheme.

The EBU, commonly considered the most important integration project after the single currency, has developed rapidly regarding the implementation of the first two pillars but has had more difficulties with the third, and hence it remains an incomplete project.

At the end of 2013, it was clear that the ECB had become indirectly in charge of macro-prudential supervision, through the ESRB, and in charge of micro-prudential supervision in significant banks, through the SSM. Furthermore, it must be recognized that the ECB also conducts the monetary policy. The separation between monetary policy and supervisory tasks within the ECB was reinforced by a specific requirement to ensure the organizational separation (a sort of Chinese walls) of both the staff involved and their reporting lines (Alexander, 2014).

Although the ECB is given considerable responsibility together with powers of direction and substitution with respect to national supervisors, the whole system of micro-prudential supervision involves national competent authorities (NCAs), both in the decision-making processes and in the supervisory enforcement phase, achieving an adequate balance between the unitary system and operational decentralization (Chang, 2015).

The SSM is not based simply on enhanced cooperation with respect to the previous form of European supervision because the ECB and the NCAs are subject to a duty of both cooperation and the exchange of information: Even if the ECB holds the responsibility for the entire system, the NCAs constitute an integral part of the SSM (Gortsos, 2015).

The sharing of responsibilities between the ECB and the NCAs is based on the concept of significance, which allows a distinction to be made between more significant banks and less significant banks in the euro area. The two-level supervision is the result of a compromise because the German government itself was opposed to the transferring of supervisory responsibilities of the country's regional public savings and cooperative banks to the ECB (Gren et al., 2015).

The criteria by which the significance of a credit institution is determined are the following: the size of the bank, the importance of the bank for the EU economy or for any participating member country, and the relevance of its cross-border activities.[1]

The SSM became operational in November 2014. Since then, the ECB through the SSM has become responsible for the direct supervision of "significant banks" (in 2021, a total of 114 banking groups in the 19 Eurozone countries accounted for almost 82% of total bank assets).

The national competent authorities (NCAs) are delegated the direct supervision of the other "less significant" institutions, of which the ECB can, however, acquire direct surveillance. In any case, the NCAs adhere to the guidelines issued by the ECB.

In the new framework, the ECB is also responsible for authorizing credit institutions and ensuring compliance with regulatory and prudential requirements

(Ferrarini, 2015). In addition, the ECB cooperates closely with the other authorities that make up the ESFS, and in particular with the European Banking Authority (EBA), whose duties were partly redefined to avoid possible conflicts with those of the ECB.

Cooperation between the ECB and the NCAs, as well as any relationship with supervised entities, is achieved through the establishment of ad hoc structures – the so-called Joint Supervisory Teams (JSTs) – which are composed by both the ECB staff and by the national supervisors of the countries where the banks are located.

For each significant bank supervised, a special JST has been formed, and the size, nature and risk profile of the bank determines the organizational structure of the relative JST. At the head of each JST is an ECB coordinator (usually of different nationality with respect to the country of registration of the bank), who is responsible for the implementation of supervisory activities (Wissink, 2017).

The single supervisory mechanism (SSM), the first pillar of the Banking Union, was implemented rapidly, not having encountered significant internal conflict in the euro area; however, a single supervisory function could not cope with the countless fragmentations and multiple systemic contagions that the long years of crisis had brought to light.

The SSM had to be assisted by another supranational instrument of the same scale to be able to standardize the models for the reorganization and resolution of those banks in which the ECB had recently become responsible for supervisory purposes (Boccuzzi, 2016).

In fact, if the funding of bank resolutions had remained with national governments, it would not have been possible to break the vicious circle between sovereign debt and those of the banks. Therefore, for banks controlled directly by the ECB, the remedy to this situation was thought of in the aforementioned second pillar of the EBU, the Single Resolution Mechanism (SRM).

Basically, with the EBU, a unitary structure was created that was able to strengthen crisis prevention and, second, to change the impact these crises had on stakeholders. In particular, they wanted to avoid the generalized form of sharing costs due to the insolvency of a bank, which in some way placed the debt burden of its bankruptcy on the community of taxpayers.

The first step toward the definition of the new mechanism was carried out by the Bank Recovery and Resolution Directive (BRRD). Although the latter has harmonized procedures, it has retained discretionary power at the national level. Accordingly, the various states maintained a wide margin of decision-making, which could accentuate differences in administrative practices. Since 2016, this gap has been filled with the creation of the Single Resolution Mechanism (SRM), which has made it possible to reduce the burden of damage to taxpayers and to greatly reduce the pressure on public budgets (Howarth and Quaglia, 2014).

The SRM operates with the assistance of the national competent authorities (NCAs) as well. In particular, a single resolution authority (the Single Resolution Board, or the SRB) was established, and as a complement to it, a Single Resolution Fund (SRF) was set up to finance resolution programs.

For banks that are not under the direct supervision of the ECB, resolution responsibilities shall be referred to the national resolution authorities, except in cases where it is necessary to resort to the SRF; in such cases, the SRB is responsible for the resolution, regardless of the significance of the bank.[2]

In summary, following the sovereign debt crisis, the ECB has been given direct responsibility for the micro-prudential supervision of the most important banks in the euro area. It also actively collaborates with the NCAs in the supervision of less relevant banks. Furthermore, the ECB is an important player in the resolution mechanism as well, operating within the SRB with its own representatives as permanent observers, as well as in the decision-making mechanism concerned with the use of the SRF, in this case together with the European Council, the EC and the SRB.

The important role currently performed by the ECB in European banking supervision had already been envisaged in 2008 with the work of de Larosière, but the final report did not support a role of the ECB in micro-prudential supervision (Ferrarini and Chiodini, 2009). Evidently, the European countries were not yet ready for such a great change (De Rynck, 2014), but a few years later, the ECB emerged as a single micro-prudential supervisor. Even though the SSM is largely grounded on cooperation and delegation mechanisms among the ECB and national authorities, the system is more than simply a system of enhanced cooperation considering the power vested by the ECB, which has the power of direction and substitution with respect to national supervisors. Indeed, the SSM can be defined as a system of semi-strong centralization of supervision, which can surely be improved with its operation (Ferrarini, 2015).

Moreover, regarding international regulation, the Basel Capital Accord has become a sort of construction site that is going to remain open. In fact, in December 2017, the Basel Committee on Banking Supervision unveiled the new rules revising Basel III (BCBS, 2017a).

A key objective of the revisions was the reduction of the excessive variability of risk-weighted assets (RWAs) among different banks and jurisdictions and the improvement of the comparability of risk-based capital ratios (Feridun and Ozun, 2020). In practical terms, the revisions were manifold, and the industry sometimes refers to them as Basel IV (KPMG, 2018).

Even if with the press conference announcing the endorsement of the Basel III reforms, Mario Draghi presented this achievement as "the end of the game" (BCBS, 2017b), for sure he only intended the completion of the global reform of the regulatory framework following the global financial crisis. It remains highly probable that the COVID-19 pandemic shock would induce other revisions of the Accord.

3.5 The COVID-19 pandemic and the lessons learned from previous crises

Following the GFC and the sovereign debt crisis, the entire system of European financial regulation and supervision was revamped and strengthened (Lautenschläger, 2018).

The onset of the COVID-19 pandemic makes it rapidly evident that this shock represented a sort of real test for the Basel III Capital Accord and for the ECB Banking Supervision. It also presented the set of circumstances in which the financial reforms put in place over the past decade would be expected to yield a reward in terms of improved financial sector resilience and consequent banks' effective role in offering credit at low cost and great availability to businesses and households.

Preliminarily, it must be said that even if the pandemic shock originated in the real economy and was totally unanticipated, it caused extreme uncertainty in financial markets, and there were fears that banks on their own could aggravate the situation and amplify the downturn as a consequence of cash-flow short-falls of households and businesses (Schularick et al., 2020).

Even though the uncertainty was deep, banks' balance sheets, from the beginning, appeared very different from the previous crises. Banks started to face the pandemic with much stronger capital and liquidity positions because in the previous six years they were obliged to comply with the stronger requirements imposed by the supervisory authorities; for example, they had built up different kinds of capital buffers that could be used in crisis situations (Af Jochnick, 2021).

The measures that supervisors can adopt during a crisis event such as a pandemic can be summarized as follows (Ozili, 2022): (1) temporarily, approve a more flexible supervisory framework; (2) modify bank supervisory examinations; (3) use ad hoc stress tests; (4) let banks release the countercyclical capital buffers; and (5) increase the use of regulatory forbearance.

Supervisory authorities in Europe have utilized all these measures and have learned from the previous crises that the answer to uncertainty must be immediate. The ECB Banking Supervision reacted very soon by allowing banks to draw on regulatory capital and liquidity buffers, and in this way gave them more leeway to support lending and absorb losses. Furthermore, immediate extraordinary monetary and fiscal policy measures provided support to the economy, mitigating risks of financial instability and making the situation less problematic even for banks themselves.

As a result, the deepest European recession after the GFC did not trigger numerous corporate insolvencies, and the rise in unemployment was contained as well. The economic consequences of the pandemic, due to lockdowns and curfews, have been huge, but keeping previous crises in mind, the monetary and fiscal policy response has been equally large, even at the cost of a large budget deficit and a substantial increase in debt/GDP ratios (Cukierman, 2021).

Consequently, the yields in sovereign debt markets have remained substantially stable, and adverse feedback loops between the real economy and the financial system were averted. Soon, it became clear that, contrary to what occurred in the aftermath of the previous crises, the COVID-19 shock had not been associated with a deeply procyclical reaction by the banking sector.

In summary, the positive results observable two years after the onset of the pandemic can be ascribed to three concomitant processes related to banking regulation and supervision (Af Jochnick, 2021):

1 After the GFC, banks were pushed by the Basel III Capital Accord to build greater capital and liquidity buffers, and the latter could be used to withstand

the COVID-19 crisis. Furthermore, one of the key lessons of the GFC was that the deterioration in asset quality, if not actively managed at the early stages of a crisis, leads to a serious impairment of the banking sector lending capacity, with severe adverse macroeconomic effects (European Parliament, 2021). For this reason, the ECB Banking Supervision devolved great attention to banks' credit risk management.

2 After the sovereign debt crisis, with the SSM, a new system of banking supervision was created where the ECB, the National Competent Authorities (NCAs) and the Joint Supervisory Teams (JSTs) are jointly able to manage banks' riskiness in an effective and timely way. This has resulted in greater integration of bank supervision in the Eurozone.
3 Upon the onset of the pandemic shock, different authorities (monetary, supervisory, regulatory and fiscal) immediately recognized the importance of a rapid intervention that was unprecedented in scale and complementary in nature (Gortsos and Ringe, 2021) and in this way were able to stabilize the banking sector and keep the credit channel to the real economy open.

Looking specifically at the ECB Banking Supervision, after the onset of the pandemic shock, a new trend of sensitivity and incisiveness was manifested by continuous instructions given to European banks to make them fulfill their role of support to the economy (ECB, 2022):

- Immediately in March 2020, the ECB allowed banks to operate below the level of capital defined by the Pillar 2 Guidance and use their full capital buffers. Later, in July 2020 and in February 2022, the ECB announced that banks could maintain this full buffer flexibility until the end of 2022.
- In September 2020 – because of exceptional macroeconomic circumstances – the ECB allowed banks to exclude certain central bank exposures from the denominators of their leverage ratios. In June 2021, the ECB extended that measure until the end of March 2022, and in February 2022, this deadline was confirmed.
- In February 2022, ECB Banking Supervision communicated that European banks – despite the pandemic – still had ample headroom above capital and leverage ratio requirements.

Another important measure taken by the ECB Banking Supervision was a recommendation inviting banks not to pay dividends and share buy-backs until at least October 2020 and subsequently to refrain from or limit them until September 2021. This measure aimed to bolster banks' capacity to absorb losses and support lending to businesses and households (Enria, 2021). Even if some banks criticized this recommendation to be too general which sent negative signals to investors, most of them recognized the necessity to maintain the safety and soundness of their activity in a period of stress and uncertainty. The national competent authorities (NCAs) issued the same recommendation to the banks they directly supervised. In the summer of 2021, the ECB declared that this restriction would have expired at the end of September as initially scheduled.

After these general measures contemplating all banks in the European Banking Union, the ECB Banking Supervision concentrated its efforts on the identified deficiencies in every single bank through the Supervisory Review and Evaluation Process (SREP). In addition, a more detailed and granular understanding of exposures based on sectors and subsectors became critical, and the ECB started to perform a deep-dive analysis into certain sectors which were more adversely affected by the economic impacts of the pandemic (vulnerable business sectors). One of the first sectors analyzed was the "accommodation and food service sector".

These supervisory measures – and in particular a very different approach by bank supervisors with respect to the previous crises – seem to have avoided further adverse economic consequences to banks and to the overall economy. Although there is still some uncertainty regarding the impact of the pandemic, at the beginning of 2022, banks still maintain ample levels of their capital requirements and leverage ratio requirements.

Finally, in this regard, it is worth mentioning the outcomes of the stress tests of the European Banking Authority (EBA) around a year after the manifestation of the pandemic shock.

The EBA stress test was initially scheduled for 2020, but it was postponed by one year as part of the temporary relief measures due to the pandemic. The EBA published the results of its 2021 EU-wide stress test at the end of July 2021; the test involved 50 banks from 15 countries, covering 70% of the EU banking sector assets. The EBA verified that since the previous EU-wide stress test in 2018, banks have continued building up their capital base, and at the end of 2020, they had the highest capitalization (CET1) since the EBA has been performing stress tests. This result was achieved despite an unprecedented decline in the EU's GDP and the first effects of the COVID-19 pandemic in 2020.

The 2021 EBA stress test has allowed to assess the excellent resilience of EU banks over a three-year horizon (2021–2023) under both a baseline and an adverse scenario.

In parallel, the ECB conducted its own stress test for 51 banks it supervises directly but that were not included in the EBA-led stress test sample. Moreover, the results of the latter stress test have indicated an increased banking sector resilience and suggested that euro area banks could cope with further adverse economic developments should they materialize in the period ahead.

Another way to consider these achievements is to examine data shown in Figure 3.1 which, in aggregation for the banks in the Eurozone, give an account of the Capital tier 1 ratio, the solvency ratio, the leverage ratio and the percentage increase from one year to another of the amount of loans to non-financial companies and households. It is possible to note that all these ratios have maintained their values till the end of 2021. Differently we can notice the adverse effects of the GFC and of the sovereign debt crisis particularly for the value of the leverage ratio and for the growth of the amount of loans.

Synthetically, together with a huge and unprecedented response from the fiscal and monetary authorities, the Basel III Capital Accord implementation and the SSM full operation have permitted European banks not to adversely encounter another crisis, demonstrating the greater resilience acquired by the banking system.

3.6 Conclusions

The GFC highlighted that regulation and supervision were inadequate and that systemic risk factors were neglected, leading to substantial regulatory reforms and the creation of an ESFS where macro- and micro-prudential authorities started to operate together.

After the sovereign debt crisis, the SSM was created, and the ECB assumed the role of a micro-prudential supervisor, integrating Eurozone financial supervision, which is no longer simply domestic.

In Europe, strong collaboration among monetary policy, macro-prudential supervision and micro-prudential supervision has been created, and a pivotal role in the banking system is played by the ECB.

As a consequence of all these changes, banks entered the pandemic with capital and liquidity levels well above minimum requirements and buffers, which helped them remain resilient. Furthermore, financial policies by both fiscal and monetary authorities have bolstered market confidence through government credit guarantees and support for the restructuring of loans. Under these conditions, banks were easily able to absorb the sizeable impact of the COVID-19 pandemic. Certainly, the banking system would have faced greater stress had the Basel reforms not been adopted.

Therefore, even with the general outcome being quite satisfactory, new issues have emerged during the pandemic, and obviously, it would be irrational for regulators and supervisors not to properly consider them.

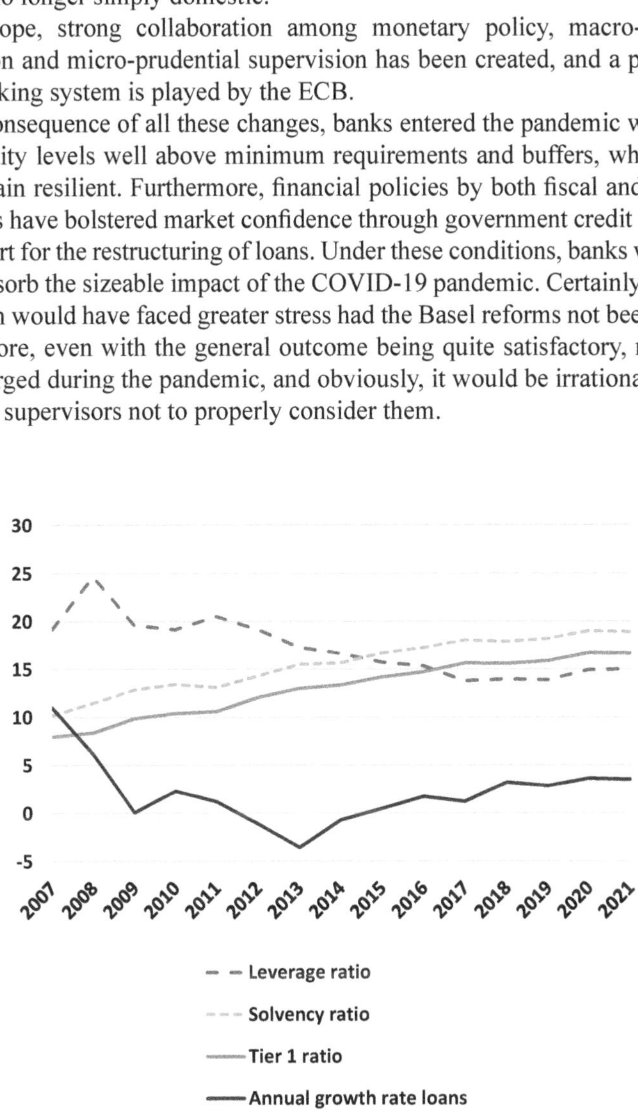

Figure 3.1 Eurozone banks' ratios

Source: Our elaboration from ECB Statistical Data Warehouse

First, capital buffers are an important feature of the Basel reforms, but very few banks used them. Banks generally need not use buffers to meet loan demand in the pandemic given their capital headroom and the support of governments and European institutions; however, several disincentives seem to exist that might have made banks reluctant to use them even as they were facing significant capital pressures. In fact, buffer use could be seen by financial markets as a sign of weakness, a sort of stigma, which negatively affects a bank's share price, credit rating and access to low-cost funding. A remarkable design feature of the Basel buffer regime is the automatic distribution restrictions imposed on banks that draw down on their buffers. This feature was introduced partly to avert behaviors manifested during the GFC, when banks with weak capital positions maintained generous distributions to shareholders, other capital providers and management. Considering this reluctance, the functioning and utilization of buffers might need a revision.

Second, many interventions on behalf of different institutions were enacted during the pandemic in a simultaneous and joint effort to sustain the economy. Perhaps it is possible to plan a separate crisis policy framework that will be automatically implemented when certain environmental, epidemic or similar events occur involving notable impacts on people's lives, the operation of the economies and the functioning of the financial system.

In this regard, the possibilities of new potential crises must be identified, and lessons learned till now must be properly considered to further improve the regulatory and supervisory framework. Among the most likely crisis events that require a proper evaluation of the related risks are cyber threats and climate change or environmental events. Indeed, the COVID-19 shock has accelerated the shift toward digitalization. This is a positive outcome, but it could also accelerate the potential vulnerability of the banking sector to operational outages and cyber threats that must be properly analyzed by regulators and supervisors. The impacts of climate change and environmental degradation, as well as the transition to a low-carbon economy, must be considered and evaluated to understand the exposure of banks to climate risk and its implications for financial stability.

Notes

1 A credit institution is considered "significant" if at least one of the following conditions is met:

- the total value of its assets exceeds € 30 billion;
- the ratio between its total assets and the GDP of the member country within which the institution is established exceeds 20%, with the exception of entities whose total asset value does not exceed € 5 billion;
- it is considered one of the three most significant credit institutions in a member state;
- it can receive direct assistance from the European Stability Mechanism, and the total value of its assets exceeds € 5 billion, and the ratio between its cross-border assets (or liabilities) held in more than one member country and its total assets (or liabilities) is more than 20%.

2 National resolution authorities are significantly involved in the resolution of a credit institution, as they assist the SRB in defining and implementing resolution plans. In the

event that the individual national authority does not act in accordance with the decisions of the SRB, the Regulation provides that the same SRB can take the resolution action itself to replace the national authorities.

References

Abrams R.K. and M.W. Taylor (2000). Issues in the unification of financial sector supervision. IMF Working Paper, WP/00/213.

Af Jochnick K. (2021). European banks – How have they coped with the crisis and what lies ahead? Speech at the Handelsblatt Banking Summit 2021, September.

Alexander K. (2014). The ECB and banking supervision: Building effective prudential supervision? *Yearbook of European Law*, 33, 1, 417–432.

Bank for International Settlement (2020). Governors and Heads of Supervision announce deferral of Basel III implementation to increase operational capacity of banks and supervisors to respond to COVID-19, Press release, 27 March.

Barth J.R., G.J. Caprio and R. Levine (2013). Bank regulation and supervision in 180 countries from 1999 to 2011. *Journal of Financial Economic Policy*, 5, 111–219.

Basel Committee on Banking Supervision (2006). Core principle for effective banking supervision, October.

Basel Committee on Banking Supervision (2017a). Basel III: Finalising post-crisis reforms, December.

Basel Committee on Banking Supervision (2017b). Governors and Heads of Supervision finalise Basel III reforms. Press release, 07 December.

Bank for International Settlement (2020). Governors and Heads of Supervision announce deferral of Basel III implementation to increase operational capacity of banks and supervisors to respond to COVID-19, Press release, 27 March.

Boccuzzi G. (2016). *The European Banking Union. Supervision and Resolution*, Palgrave Macmillan, Houndmills.

Chang, M. (2014). The rising power of the ECB: The case of the Single Supervisory Mechanism, *Five years of crisis — lessons learned and paths towards a resilient European Monetary Union*, Conference, Trier, 9–10, October.

Chesini G. and F. Fauri (2020). La Banca Centrale Europea: baluardo contro le crisi finanziarie e motore di integrazione. Calandri E., Laschi G., Paoli S. (Eds), *L'Europa adulta.* Attori, ragioni e sfide dall'Atto Unico alla Brexit, Il Mulino.

Čihák M., Demirgüç-Kunt A., Soledad M., Pería M., and A. Mohseni-Cheraghlou (2012). Bank Regulation and Supervision around the World. A Crisis Update. Policy Research Working Paper 6286, December.

Cukierman A. (2021). Reflections on the shifting consensus about monetary and fiscal policies following the GFC and the COVID-19 crisis. In: Ferri G. and D'APice V. (eds.), *A Modern Guide to Financial Shocks and Crises*. Edward Elgar, Cheltenham, 180–198.

Garel, A., Petit-Romec A. (2021). Investor rewards to environmental responsibility: Evidence from the COVID-19 crisis, Journal of Corporate Finance: Contracting, Governance and Organization, vol. 68, pp. 1–20.

De Grauwe P. (2016). *Economia dell'integrazione europea*, Bologna, Il Mulino.

De Larosière J. (2009), Report of the High-Level Group on Financial Supervision in the EU, 25 February.

De Rynck S. (2014). Changing Banking Supervision in the Eurozone: The ECB as a Policy Entrepreneur. Bruges Political Research Papers No. 38.

ECB (2022). ECB will not extend capital and leverage relief for banks, Press release, February.

Enria A. (2021). European banks in the post-COVID-19 world. Speech of the Chair of the Supervisory Board of the ECB at the Morgan Stanley Virtual European Financials Conference, Frankfurt am Main, 16 March.

European Parliament (2013). The various roles of the ECB in the new EMU architecture. Monetary Dialogue, September.

European Parliament (2021). Directorate-General for Internal Policies of the Union, Resti, A., When and how to unwind COVID-support measures to the banking system?: The quest for safe landing place, European Parliament.

Feridun M. and A. Ozun (2020). Basel IV implementation: A review of the case of the European Union. *Journal of Capital Markets Studies*, 4, 1, 7–24.

Ferrarini G. (2015). Single supervision and the governance of banking markets: Will the SSM deliver the expected benefits? *European Business Organization Law Review* 16, 513–537.

Ferrarini G. and L. Chiarella (2013). Common Banking Supervision in the Eurozone: Strengths and Weaknesses. ECGI Law Working Paper N.223.

Ferrarini G. and F. Chiodini (2009). Regulating cross-border banks in Europe: A comment on the Larosière report and a modest proposal. *Capital Markets Law Journal*, 4, 123–140.

Fiechter J.L. and M. Zarmoski (2016). Improving the effectiveness of bank supervision. *SEACEN Financial Stability Journal*, 6, 21–35.

Garel A. and A. Petit-Romec (2021). Financial reforms. In Ferri G. and D'APice V. (Eds.) *A Modern Guide to Financial Shocks and Crises*. Edward Elgar, Cheltenham, 262–287.

Giese J. and A. Haldane (2020). COVID-19 and the financial system: A tale of two crises. *Oxford Review of Economic Policy*, 36, N.S1.

Gortsos C.V. (2015). Competence sharing between the ECB and the national competent supervisory authorities within the single supervisory mechanism (SSM). *European Business Organization Law Review*, 16, 401–420.

Gortsos C.V. and W. Ringe (eds) (2021). *Financial Stability amidst the Pandemic Crisis: On Top of the Wave*. European Banking Institute, https://ssrn.com/abstract=3877946.

Gren J., D. Howarth and L. Quaglia (2015). Supranational banking supervision in Europe: The construction of a credible watchdog. *Journal of Common Markets Studies*, 53, 181–191.

Heisenberg D. (2014). From the Single Market to the Single Currency. In D. Dinan (Ed.) *Origins and Evolution of the European Union*, Oxford University Press. 233–259.

Howarth D. and L. Quaglia. (2014). The steep road to European Banking Union: Constructing the single resolution mechanism. *Journal of Capital Markets Studies*, 52, 125–140.

KPMG, 2018. Basel 4: The way ahead, March. https://assets.kpmg.com/content/dam/kpmg/xx/pdf/2018/03/basel-4-the-way-ahead.pdf

Lautenschläger S. (2018). Banking regulation and supervision – you can't have one without the other. Speech at 9th Annual EFR Stakeholder Round Table on "Financial Fragmentation or Integration", Brussels, 22 March.

Llewellyn D.T. (1998). A prospectus from the FSA: Its approach to regulation. *Journal of Financial Regulation and Compliance*, 6, 4, 305–312.

Masciandaro D., M.G. Quintyn and M. Nieto (2009). "Will they Sing the Same Tune? Measuring Convergence in the new European System of Financial Supervisors." IMF Working Papers, 142.

Masciandaro D., R.V. Pansini and M. Quintyn (2013). The economic crisis: Did supervision architecture and governance matter? *Journal of Financial Stability*, 9, 578–596.

Masciandaro D. and D. Romelli (2018). Central bankers as supervisors: Do crises matter? *European Journal of Political Economy*, 52, 120–140.

Meier S., M. Rodriguez Gonzales and F. Kunze (2021). The global financial crisis, the EMU sovereign debt crisis and international financial regulation: Lessons from a systematic literature review. *International Review of Law and Economics*, 65, 105945.

Moshirian F. (2011). The global financial crisis and the evolution of markets, institutions and regulation. *Journal of Banking & Finance*, 35, 3, 502–551.

Ozili P.K. (2022). Financial Regulation and Bank Supervision during a Pandemic. In: Grima S., Özen E. and Gonzi R.E.D (eds.), *Insurance and Risk Management for Disruptions in Social, Economic and Environmental Systems: Decision and Control Allocations within New Domains of Risk*. Emerald Publishing Limited, Bingley, pp. 29–37.

Quaglia L. (2013). Financial regulation and supervision in the European Union after the crisis. *Journal of Economic Policy Reform*, 16(1), 17–30.

Recine F. and P.G. Teixeira (2009). The new financial stability architecture in the EU, Paolo Baffi Centre Research Paper No. 62.

Schularick M., S. Sascha and T.H. Tröger (2020). Bank capital and the European recovery from the COVID-19 crisis. SAFE White Paper No. 69, June.

4 The countercyclicality of macroprudential policy in the EU

The case of the COVID-19 pandemic

Marcin Czaplicki

4.1 Introduction

The most characteristic feature of macroprudential policy is its focus on the two dimensions of the systemic risk: time and cross-sectional one. The former refers to the inherent procyclicality of the financial sector, while the latter to the linkages between financial institutions that make them vulnerable to the problems of their peers. That said, the introduction of the macroprudential policy framework following the Global Financial Crisis (GFC) has been focused on strengthening the countercyclical, as well as structural capabilities of banking sector regulations. As such, the second half of last decade, which followed the introduction of the CRD IV – CRR[1] regulatory package in the European Union, has witnessed a costly process of the build-up of several buffers that were intended to safeguard the banks and to curb the build-up of systemic risk at the time, when the European economy finally started to recover from the long-lasting balance-sheet recession that followed the GFC and European Debt Crisis. The build-up of capital buffers was all the more desirable because the monetary policy of the European Central Bank, and other smaller central banks, remained fairly accommodative, targeting the (less-than) moderate inflationary pressure, but at the same time fueling the accumulation of systemic risk on some local markets.

As the macroprudential regulation was intended to prevent the European (and global) financial sector from the crisis scenario, the blow has been delivered from the least expected direction, which (to some extent) is one of the few things that should be expected from a crisis. With the outbreak of a global pandemic, the economic and financial crisis that followed did not result from irresponsible actions of financial institutions nor a materialization of risks that had been accumulating in the time preceding its outbreak. The introduction of the national sanitary restrictions including full-scale lockdowns that were intended to curb the mobility of the population has led to a sudden and unusually deep collapse of economic activity. As a result, many enterprises have discontinued their business, whereas the economic safety of many employees has been put under threat. The grave situation was faced by an unprecedented (both in scale and timing) reaction by the authorities that used both fiscal and monetary policy to stabilize the situation. These interventions did not manage to save the economies from the recession of a scale comparable to

DOI: 10.4324/9781003310754-4

the darkest hours of the GFC (2008–2009). However, they protected the financial sector that was inevitably falling into a crisis, as suggested by the month-long turbulence that started in late February 2020.

The macroprudential policy did not remain idle either. For the first time in the EU's history, it joined the fiscal and monetary policy, becoming the third force of the macrostabilizing apparatus. The first measures were taken as early as in March 2020. In the majority of European Union member states, the capital as well liquidity requirements have been loosened. On the central, European level, the CRR Quick Fix has been introduced,[2] along with some temporary measures intended to enhance credit flows to companies and households. The banks were also encouraged to build up their own funds at the time of weaker credit demand. As a result, from the regulatory standpoint, some few quarters after the outbreak of the pandemic, the capital position of the majority of the banks was stronger than in February 2020, that is, before the outbreak of the COVID-19 pandemic.

This chapter focuses on the macroprudential capital buffers (that is capital conservation buffer, countercyclical capital buffer, systemic risk buffer, as well as capital buffers for globally and other systemically important institutions)[3] and their changes during the pandemic. Moreover, it introduces an additional analysis of the changes of macroprudential policy restrictiveness during this time, with a focal point being the banks' capital surplus over regulatory requirement, as well as banks' potential to expand lending. That said, the drivers of changes in macroprudential policy restrictiveness are identified, basing on a premise similar to monetary policy, where despite rate cuts the policy may become more restrictive, if inflationary expectations decline to a bigger extent. The macroprudential policy is not that much different, because not only the combined capital requirement matters, but also the changes to the overall capital adequacy. The difference between the two above factors determines the lending capacity of the banks, and their overall eagerness to expand lending.

The chapter is structured as follows. As a first step, the methods of the measurement of macroprudential policy restrictiveness are presented with the focus on bank capital requirements. Second, the data used in the empirical analysis is introduced, as well as its sources. The empirical study starts with the enumeration of the changes to macroprudential capital buffers in the European Union during the pandemic. It is followed by the qualitative and quantitative analysis of the above changes. The last section concludes.

4.2 Measuring the stringency of bank capital regulations: A literature review

The increasing standardization (through the popularization of the Basel Agreements), as well as the usage of capital buffers present a promising field for research that aims at the measurement and assessment of the efficacy of these prudential tools. The capital requirements are in the spotlight of academic research for at least 30 years, when Bernanke and Lown (1991) pointed out the relation between the equity to assets ratio and bank credit expansion, suggesting that falling equity capital might have deepened the 1990 recession in the US. Hancock and Wilcox (1993) showed that lending expansion slowed down in 1990 due to a too low level of bank equity capital that has forced some of the banks to limit the volume of credit to fulfill capital requirements. Heid, Porath and Stolz (2003) stipulated that reaction by banks on changes to capital requirements depends on their surplus capital, i.e., the difference between the capital adequacy ratio and the regulatory requirement. This approach has been utilized before the GFC, as indicated by Fonseca, González, and Pereira da Silva (2010), who presented a thorough review of economic literature from that period. Indeed, as the required capital level remained (most of the time) flat at 8%, the surplus capital was a simple way to assess the binding strength of the regulations.

The use of surplus capital as a determinant for the credit action gained in importance following the GFC (see e.g., Berrospide and Edge [2010]; Borio and Gambacorta [2017], Catalán, Hoffmaister, and Harun [2017] and Gambacorta and Shin [2018]). De Jonghe, Dewachter and Ongena (2020) admittedly did not use this approach, but they modelled various measures of credit expansion using simultaneously the capital ratio and capital requirement as explanatory variables. Imbierowicz, Löffler, and Vogel (2021) extended the surplus capital approach by adding the risk density (i.e., ratio of risk weighted assets to total assets). They underlined that banks with lower average risk weight are less exposed to changes in capital requirements. The issue of risk weighting has been (much earlier) indicated as one of the crucial factors behind the severity of the GFC (see e.g., Blundell-Wignall and Atkinson [2010], who showed that simple leverage ratio had been a better predictor of bank losses than the capital adequacy ratio). Finally, Czaplicki (2021) utilized the ratios of surplus capital to both capital adequacy ratio, as well as capital requirement to show the impact of changing restrictiveness of capital regulations on bank lending in Poland.

Regardless of which measure of the regulatory restrictiveness has been utilized, the studies found that it has a statistically significant impact on bank behavior. Gambacorta and Shin (2018) showed that apart from credit dynamics, they also impact the bank financing cost, which, in their view, links the capital adequacy with bank lending. European Banking Authority (2015) found in a pan-European study that the higher level of capital positively impacts the supply side of credit market. Taking it all into consideration, the actions aimed at increasing the capital surplus of European banks after the outbreak of the pandemic and subsequent crisis were actually taken to soften credit conditions on the pandemic-hit lending market.

4.3 Data description and methodological issues

The study of the changes in the restrictiveness of European macropudential policy has been conducted with the utilization of four variables: capital requirement, capital adequacy ratio, surplus capital, as well as its ratio to the capital requirement indicating the potential for lending expansion. The latter indicator has been measured both in absolute (bn EUR), as well as relative (percentage of assets) terms. That said, any conclusions drawn from this study refer to the regulatory capital buffer (the actual buffer), whereas the internal capital buffer, i.e., the desired capital surplus over the regulatory requirement has not been estimated.

The analysis of the combined buffer requirement has been limited solely to the macroprudential capital buffers. As indicated earlier, the so-called II Pillar buffers has not been included in the study. The research study covered all 27 states of the EU. The values of capital requirements have been calculated based on the dataset offered by the ESRB.[4] The measures of capital adequacy, balance sheet, and risk weights have been downloaded from the ECB Statistical Data Warehouse. Table 4.1 contains the description of the utilized data.

As the combined buffer requirement varies not only for different economies but also for individual banks, the data has been aggregated on a country level. As a result, the requirements for each country represent the weighted average of requirements for local banks, weighted by the size of their own funds.[5] In contrast to the predominant (interval) presentation method of the capital requirements on a country level (e.g., 10.5–12.0%), the method utilized in this study lets us calculate a point measure of restrictiveness, thus allowing for a more precise analysis and conclusions.

That said, the data for 200 individual banks (banking groups from the European Union) has been collected, whereas the banks have been selected on the basis of the ESRB database (being distinguished either due to their systemic importance or participation in an activity regarded by the local authorities as posing systemic risk). If there was a merger or acquisition transaction in any of the period under study, the historical data has been aggregated in order to get a uniform data series.

Apart from presenting a precise measure of capital requirements in each country, the causes of changes in the restrictiveness of macroprudential policy have also been analyzed. That said, the study provides the decomposition of changes to the surplus capital starting from distinguishing the changes to capital adequacy ratio and capital requirement, as the two most important determinants of the surplus itself, as well as the lending potential of a bank. Second, the reasons behind changing capital adequacy have been investigated, including the changes to the own funds, total assets, as well as their risk density, i.e., the average risk weight. Due to

Table 4.1 Data used in the study

Data	*Source*
Capital buffers	ESRB
Capital adequacy ratios	ECB
Own funds (for the sector)	Own calculations based on the data on assets, average risk weight of assets, as well as capital adequacy ratio (all from the ECB)
Own funds (for individual institutions)	Consolidated financial statements
Average risk weight of assets	ECB
Loans and securities	ECB
Total assets	ECB
Exchange rates	stooq.pl

the missing data, further disaggregation of own funds, as well as bank assets (e.g., into different sources of credit risk exposure) has not been performed but could be a source of value added in future studies. So does the further identification of reasons behind changing risk weights (either regulatory, e.g., the introduction of CRR Quick Fix in June 2020 with the SME and infrastructure-supporting factors or a favorable treatment of certain loans backed by pension or salaries; or bank-related, leading to changing asset structure along with their risk density) or own funds (equity or subordinated debt issuance, dividend payments/retained earnings, accounting profits or losses on debt securities revaluation, etc.).

Nonetheless, the approach utilized in this research study allows us to make one step further (than previous studies) in explaining the changes to the restrictiveness of regulatory policy (assuming that the capital requirement itself is only the second-best measure of regulatory stringency, whereas the first best is the distance from the actual to the required level of capital). That said, one further (and final) adjustment is made to the data. As the values from the ECB are presented in euro, they may artificially inflate or deflate the balance sheet values from non-Eurozone member states (due to changes in the FX rate). Therefore, the EUR-denominated numbers are transformed into local currency before conducting the analysis including changes in own funds and total assets.

4.4 Changes to the macroprudential capital buffers during the pandemic

The COVID-19 pandemic provided a testing ground for the assumptions behind various macroprudential tools that have been implemented over some years preceding its outbreak. The global spread of the coronavirus pandemic and the resulting recession hit the economies of the European Union with unprecedented speed. The response of many governments and central banks in monetary and fiscal as well as macroprudential policy was immediate. In France, Ireland and Lithuania, the countercyclical buffer was reduced to zero. In Belgium, Germany, and Slovakia, previously announced increases in this buffer were canceled (Slovakia later made an additional reduction of the buffer to 1%). The Estonian and Finnish authorities have lifted the systemic risk buffer and in the Netherlands its amount has been reduced from 3% to 1.5% –2.5% depending on the institution. The buffers of other systemically important institutions (O-SII) in Cyprus, Finland, Lithuania and the Netherlands were also lowered or the period for the implementation of previously planned requirements (Portugal and Greece) was extended. In addition, the European Central Bank (2020) encouraged euro area banks to use the available capital buffers, including the second pillar.

Outside the euro area, the supervisory and regulatory authorities took measures aimed at reducing the burden of capital requirements for banks too. Czech Republic lowered the countercyclical buffer twice, from 1.75% to 0.5% in total, while Denmark and Sweden have fully lifted the buffer. In Bulgaria, the previously adopted increase was suspended. In Poland, the systemic risk buffer was abolished. In Hungary, the buffers of other systemically important institutions were fully released. By June 30, 2020, all macroprudential measures taken in the euro area countries freed €30.9 billion of own funds, and in the European Union as a whole, €46.8 billion.

Some countries started to reverse their policy later that year (e.g., Ireland did not waive nor postpone the increase of the O-SII buffer planned for July 1, 2020). Luxembourg increased the countercyclical capital buffer as early as the end of 2020. At that time, Italy increased the buffers for other systemically important institutions, Ireland implemented similar changes a quarter earlier. Overall, the combined buffer requirements remained well below the pre-pandemic levels (see the last section of this chapter) during the whole of 2021, despite a change to the approach of macroprudential authorities visible in the fourth quarter (increases in O-SII buffers as well as decisions on the increase of countercyclical capital buffers in some countries). Table 4.2 presents the macroprudential capital buffers used before and during the pandemic in the European Union.

Table 4.2 shows that 20 out of the 27 European Union countries took actions regarding the macroprudential capital buffers at the early stage of the pandemic. The action was more than swift. The European Systemic Risk Board (2021, p. 83) shows that Denmark lowered the CCyB as early as on March 8 with Sweden and Bulgaria to follow on March 15. On that same day, Poland, Finland and Hungary reduced/released the SRB (Finland additionally lowered the O-SII buffer for one institution). Further 11 countries followed in March/early April. As a result, within less than a month from the outbreak of the crisis, 17 European Union countries took accommodative macroprudential policy actions as capital buffers are concerned. Figure 4.1 shows that the average capital requirement in the EU initially fell by approximately 0.4 pp., whereas in the Eurozone by approximately 0.3pp. It remained fairly stable in the Eurozone by the end of 2021. Outside of the Eurozone, however, it started to increase in 2021, mostly due to increased requirements in Romania and Hungary.

Interestingly, Figure 4.2 also shows that on average, the Eurozone countries have lower capital requirements than the rest of the European Union. Figure 4.2 provides a closer look, both on the level of capital requirements (8% + macroprudential capital buffer, as defined earlier) on a country-by-country basis, as well as on their changes during the pandemic. Several things stand out (apart from the visibly higher requirements in non-Eurozone countries with Sweden, Bulgaria, Poland, and Denmark at the forefront). First, Poland and Sweden were the countries with the biggest drop in capital requirement. Second, Hungary released all of the buffers apart from the (technically unreleasable) capital conservation buffer. Third, countries like Croatia, Romania, Cyprus, Malta, Slovenia, Greece, Italy, and Portugal had a bigger required buffer at the end of 2021 than they had just before the outbreak of the pandemic.

Most of the decisions tackled the countercyclical capital buffer (either its reduction or cancellation of the earlier announced increase). In fact, only 15 out of 27 EU countries actually lowered the already existing buffers. As it is shown in Figure 4.3, many of the countries that did not lower the macroprudential capital buffers were prohibited from this decision by the lack of capital buffers that actually

Table 4.2 Macroprudential capital buffers in the EU before, during and after the pandemic crisis

	Before the pandemic			*Lowered or lifted during the pandemic crisis (2020)*	*Lowered or lifted during the pandemic crisis (2021)*	*Raised the buffer´*
Country	*Countercyclical capital buffer (CCyB)*	*Systemic risk buffer (SRB)*	*Other systemically important institution buffer (O-SII)*			
Austria		x	x	SRB	1	
Belgium	x^		x	CCyB*		
Bulgaria	x	x	x	CCyB*		CCyB (4q22, 1q23)
Croatia		x	x			SRB[2] (4q20)
Cyprus			x			O-SII (4q21)
Czechia	x	x	x	CCyB*, CCyB	SRB[3]	CCyB (3q22, 4q22, 1q23)
Denmark	x	x	x[4]	CCyB*, CCyB		O-SII[5]
Estonia		x	x	SRB		CCyB (4q22)
Finland		x	x	SRB, O-SII[6]		
France	x		x	CCyB*, CCyB	O-SII[7]	
Germany	x^		x	CCyB*, O-SII	O-SII[8]	O-SII[9]
Greece			x	O-SII		O-SII (4q21)
Hungary		x[10]	x	O-SII		O-SII (4q21)
Ireland	x		x	CCyB		O-SII[11]
Italy			x			O-SII (4q20)
Latvia			x			
Lithuania	x		x	CCyB		O-SII (4q21)
Luxembourg	x		x	O-SII[12]		CCyB[13], O-SII[14]
Malta			x			O-SII (4q21)
Netherlands		x	x	SRB, O-SII[15]		
Poland		x	x	SRB		O-SII (4q21)
Portugal			x	O-SII		O-SII (4q21)
Romania		x	x	O-SII[16]	O-SII (1q22)	

(*Continued*)

Slovakia	x	x	x	CCyB*, CCyB, O-SII[17]		O-SII (4q21)
Slovenia			x			O-SII[18]
Spain			x			O-SII[19]
Sweden	x	x	x	CCyB		O-SII[20]
Total	11	13	27	CCyB: 14 SRB: 5 O-SII: 9	SRB: 1 O-SII: 3	CCyB: 4 SRB: 1 O-SII: 16

Source: ESRB. ^Belgium and Germany were awaiting the introduction of CCyB in 2020; *Cancellation of decisions regarding the increase of the CCyB later in 2020; Postponement of the introduction of higher O-SII buffers; [1]Austria lowered the SRB and O-SII buffers in 2q21 but changed the rules of the calculation of combined buffer (from "the highest of the two" to "the sum of the two"). As a result, the combined capital buffer did not change; [2]Croatia actually lowered the SRB buffer in 4q20, but similarly to Austria changed the rules of the calculation of the combined buffer (from "the highest of the two" to "the sum of the two"). As a result, the combined buffer increased; [3]Czechia replaced the SRB with (lower) O-SII in 4q21. [4]Denmark identified O-SII before the pandemic but did not impose any buffer until 4q20, when the SRB was replaced; [5]In Denmark, one more bank (Arbejdernes Landsbank) has been identified as O-SII (with a buffer); [6]In Finland, the O-SII buffer for OP Bank has been reduced in 1q20; [7]In France, one more bank (HSBC France) has been identified as O-SII (with a buffer); [8]In Germany, one bank (Landesbank Hessen-Thüringen Girozentrale) has seen its O-SII buffer lowered in 4q21; [9]One more bank (Goldman Sachs Bank Europe SE) has been identified as O-SII (with a buffer) in 4q21; [10]There were two banks with an institution-specific systemic risk buffer, but its level was set at 0; [11]Ireland increased the O-SII buffer as early as in 3q20. They subsequently raised the buffer in 2q21; [12]Deutsche Bank Luxembourg has been withdrawn from the O-SII list (thus, its 0.5% buffer has been released in 4q20); [13]Luxembourg raised (as planned) the CCyB as early as in 4q20; [14]J.P. Morgan Bank Luxembourg has been withdrawn from the O-SII list (thus, its 0.5% buffer has been released in 1q22); [15]The Netherlands lowered the O-SII buffer for ABN Amro in 2q20. Later that year the SRB buffer has been released, but the combined buffer did not change, as "the highest of the two" rule has been used previously; ^{16}O-SII buffer in Romania has been released only for Garanti Bank in 4q20; [17]O-SII buffer in Slovakia has been released only for Poštová banka in 4q20; ^{18}O-SII buffer in Slovenia has been increased only for Nova Kreditna Banka Maribor in 4q21; [19]O-SII buffer in Spain has been increased only for CaixaBank in 4q21; [20]Sweden lowered the O-SII buffer in 4q20 but changed the rules of the calculation of combined buffer (from "the highest of the two [SRB and O-SII]" to "the sum of the two"), resulting in overall higher combined buffer requirements.

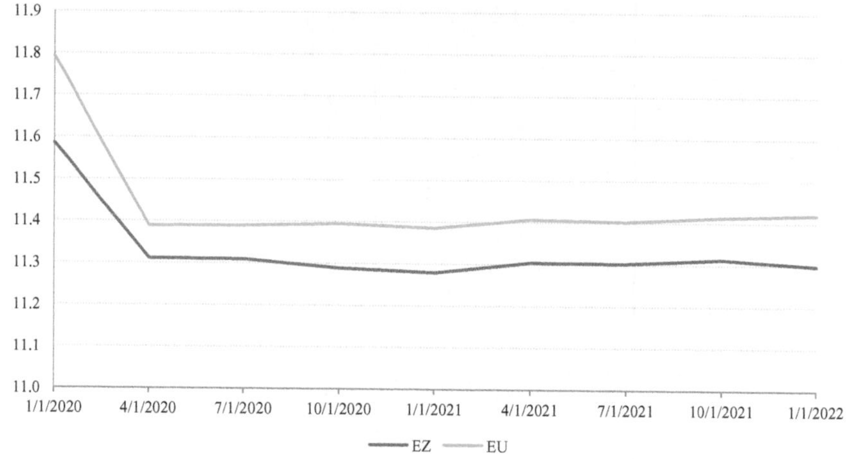

Figure 4.1 The weighted average* capital requirement (no Pillar II buffers were included) in the European Union and Eurozone (the overall requirement for each country [group] equals the weighted average of requirements for individual banks in that countries, with own funds as weights. If the size of heavier regulated institutions increases relative to others, so does the weighted average, that is the country-level [group-level] requirement)

Source: ESRB, ECB, banks consolidated financial statements. Author's own calculations

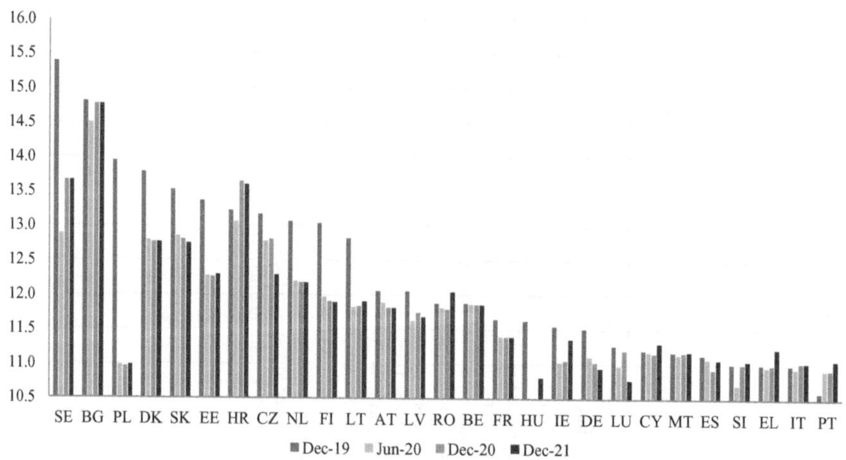

Figure 4.2 The weighted average capital requirement in the European Union countries

Source: ESRB, ECB, banks consolidated financial statements. Author's own calculations

could have been cut.[6] Being more precise, countries like Cyprus, Greece, Italy, Portugal or Spain were all struck by the European debt crisis earlier in the last decade. That said, their banking sectors have been recovering from the damages

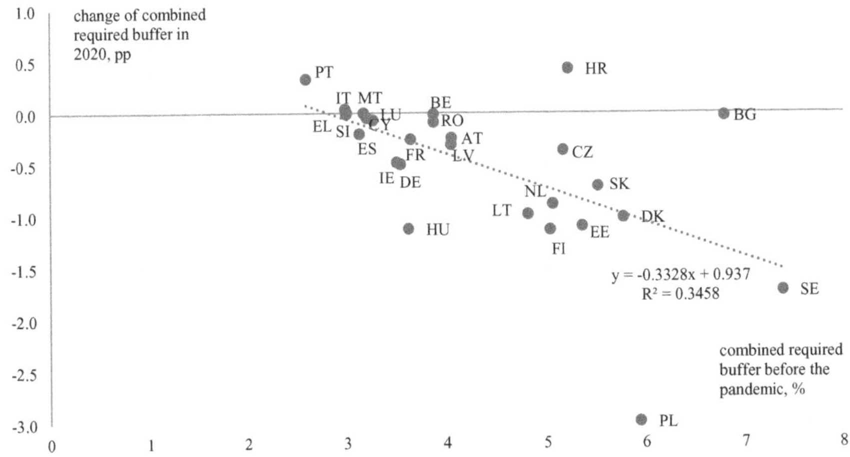

Figure 4.3 The pre-pandemic combined capital buffer versus its changes in 2020

Source: ESRB, ECB, banks consolidated financial statements. Author's own calculations

caused by the crisis making the regulatory authorities and supervisors reluctant to impose new regulatory burdens. As a result, no or only few capital buffers have been accumulated (apart from the capital conservation buffer), providing much less room (than in the case of other countries) to reduce them during the pandemic and to conduct a countercyclical macroprudential policy.

4.5 Early literature on the effects of macroprudential policy actions during the pandemic

There is already a number of studies that have analyzed the impact of macroprudential policy actions on the European Union's banking sector, with the credit action at the forefront. Casanova, Hardy, and Onen (2021) studied various ways of increasing bank lending and confirmed that the expansion of bank lending capacity had a positive impact on lending growth. Those banks that improved their capital position at the beginning of the pandemic showed a higher increase in the volume of loans in the remainder of 2020. Hardy (2021) showed, based on a sample of 133 large banks, that restrictions on dividend payments led to an increase in the capital base in 2020 and resulted in higher lending. Dicanio and Montesi (2021) analyzed aggregated data for France, Spain, Germany, United Kingdom, Italy, and USA. They compared the banks' loss absorption potential (capital surplus against the requirement, taking into account the increase in potential losses as a result of the pandemic) before the GFC (in 2007) and the pandemic crisis (in 2019). They concluded that banks had much higher buffers before the pandemic crisis, which allowed them to increase their assets by 10–20% while maintaining the potential of the space to absorb potential crisis-related losses. The Financial Stability Board (2021, p. 10) indicated that banks generally increased their capital surpluses during the first months of the pandemic. Riksbank (2020, p. 75) estimated that the lowering of capital requirements by the Swedish supervisor at the start of the pandemic released ca. SEK 900 billion in lending capacity of Swedish banks.

The analysis of Budnik, Dimitrov, Groß, Jancokova, Lampe, Sorvillo, Stular, and Volk (2021) showed that supervisory, regulatory, as well as other public actions (in particular loan guarantees) taken in the first phase of the crisis (in the first half of 2020) allowed the preservation of a 5% higher loan portfolio for the private non-financial sector (including 12% higher for non-financial enterprises) than in a counterfactual scenario with the absence of such interventions. Moreover, these actions had a positive impact on both the level of nonperforming loans, as well as the profitability of banks. Avezum, Oliveira, and Serra (2021) showed that the loosening and/or lifting of capital buffers (the countercyclical systemic risk buffer in particular) had a positive impact on lending to households (primarily in the form of mortgage loans) and small businesses. Bergant and Forbes (2021) conducted an international study and found out that countries that tightened macroprudential policy more aggressively before COVID-19 pandemic, as well as those that eased more during the pandemic, experienced less financial and economic stress. Moreover, they emphasized that the space to use the macroprudential tools during the crisis depended on the earlier tightening.

Finally, Czerniak, Czaplicki, Mokrogulski, Niedziółka, and Szelągowska (2021, pp. 289–290) estimated that the change in capital requirements, along with an increase in capital adequacy ratios in the banking sector, allowed the increase of the credit potential of banks in Central and Eastern Europe belonging to the European Union by 41.7%, i.e., by a total of €148.7 billion (in 2020). They also examined the difference between the level of restrictiveness of capital regulations in a wide group of countries (11 countries of Central and Eastern Europe) and stated that banks in the region were perfectly equipped to support the government in anti-crisis activities, with a credit potential varying between 33.5% (in Slovakia) and 54.9% (in Estonia) of the value of their volume of loans at that time.

4.6 The restrictiveness of capital requirements in the EU during the pandemic

The macroprudential capital buffers were released in most of the European Union countries at the outbreak of the pandemic. Figure 4.4 shows the scale of these releases providing the cumulative change to the combined required capital buffer in 2020.

Only three countries: Italy, Portugal and Croatia saw their capital requirements increasing in 2020. Croatia actually lowered the requirements at the initial stage of the pandemic crisis, but later on, increased them during the change of the methodology of the calculation of combined capital requirement. Italy increased the O-SII buffer at the end of that year, whereas Portugal kept the buffers flat. However, as the banks that were burdened with higher capital requirements grew faster than others, the weighted average capital buffer increased (with them).

"Higher" or "lower" capital buffers do not necessarily mean that the macroprudential policy is "more" or "less" restrictive (see Czaplicki, 2021). In fact, what

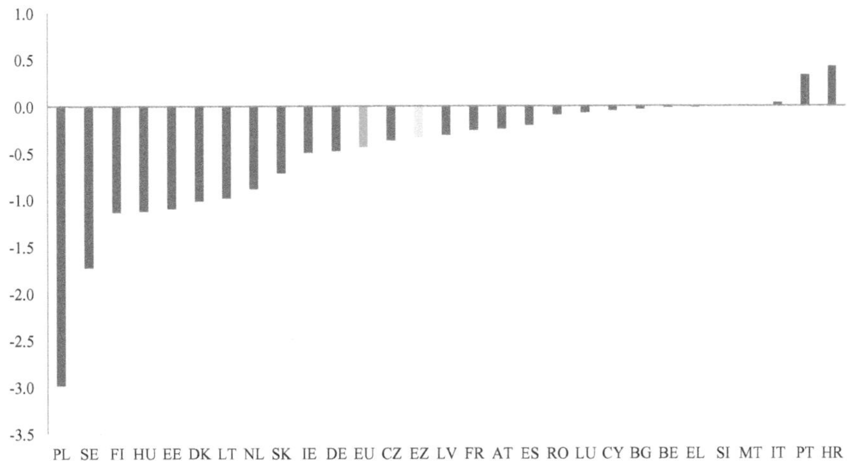

Figure 4.4 Change to the combined (macroprudential) capital buffer in the European Union in 2020

Source: ESRB, ECB, banks consolidated financial statements. Author's own calculations

matters is the capital surplus (i.e., the distance from the actual capital adequacy ratio to the requirement), as well as the lending potential it creates. That said, the level of capital adequacy is derived from the size of own funds, total assets, as well as their risk density (average risk weight). As follows, these characteristics are going to be scrutinized. The actual capital adequacy ratio increased (in 2020) in the vast majority of the EU countries (apart from Finland, Greece, and Slovenia). That said, rising capital adequacy has been yet another factor that was making the macroprudential policy more accommodative during the COVID-19 pandemic. Figure 4.5 shows the decomposition of the change to capital surplus in 2020.

Figure 4.5 shows that Poland remained at the top of the list of countries with the most accommodative macroprudential policy during the pandemic. What has changed is its followers. Interestingly, in many Central and Eastern European countries, the increase of the capital adequacy has been sufficient enough to multiply the effects of cuts in capital requirements (Bulgaria, Latvia, and Romania stand out, as the change to the restrictiveness of macroprudential policy results overwhelmingly from the sounder capital position of the banks). Furthermore, countries like Italy, Portugal, and Croatia saw decreasing restrictiveness of macroprudential policy despite increasing capital requirements. Finally, Slovenia and Greece experienced tighter macroprudential policy, due to the weakening situation of their banks.

Figure 4.6 provides a detailed decomposition of changes to the capital surplus of European banks in 2020. It shows that in all countries (except for Luxembourg), the banking sectors expanded during the first year of the pandemic (by 9% in the entire EU, i.e., €2.758 trillion). As supervisors encouraged banks not to pay out dividends, the retained earnings (along with 2020 profits) boosted their own funds (which altogether grew by €121.3 billion in 2020). Finally, banks actively reduced

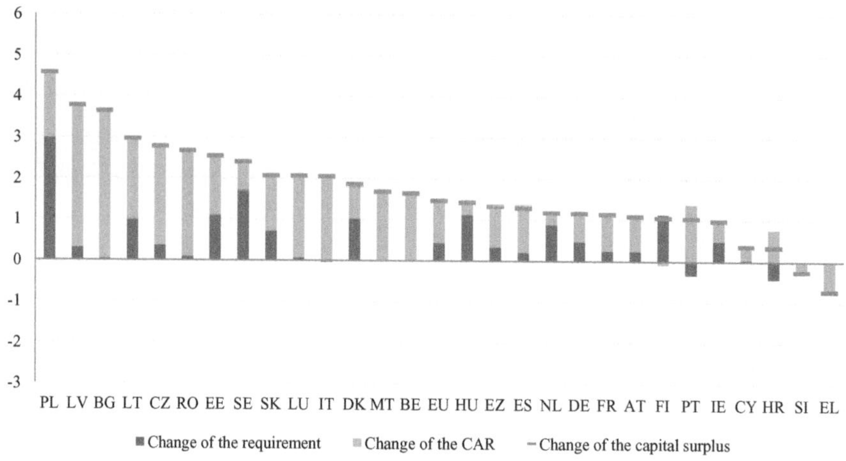

Figure 4.5 Change to the capital surplus in the European Union countries in 2020

Source: ESRB, ECB, banks consolidated financial statements. Author's own calculations

Figure 4.6 Detailed decomposition of change to the capital surplus in the European Union countries in 2020

Source: ESRB, ECB, banks consolidated financial statements. Author's own calculations.

the risk density of their portfolio (by 3.26 pp. to 35.9% at the end of 2020) via the expansion of sovereign bond purchases and retail loans. It should also be noted that the governments expanded the loan guarantee programs, which might have also helped to reduce the average risk weight of the credit portfolio.

Interestingly, the overall effect of increasing capital adequacy was over 2.3 times larger than of the decrease of capital requirement (the latter released €49.8 billion in the EU in 2020). It shows that banks have actively strengthened their capital position. However, in the case of eight countries (Finland, Hungary, Netherlands, Sweden, Poland, Denmark, Slovenia, and Greece), the impact of a reduced capital buffer requirement was prevalent. In total, EU banks increased their lending capacity (capacity to expand assets) by almost 15% during 2020, as shown in Figure 4.7.

The loosening of macroprudential capital requirements added 4.47 pp (€1.490 trillion) to this potential, whereas higher capital adequacy: 10.45 pp (€3.487 trillion). On top of that (as already mentioned), European banks expanded their assets by 9% (€2.758 trillion). Out of the overall €4.977 trillion additional lending capacity, €4.059 trillion (81.6%) has been contributed by the Eurozone. That said, the non-Eurozone countries that had 9.2% of EU banking sector assets at the end of 2020 were contributing twice that to the newly created lending capacity. Among these economies Poland, Sweden, and Denmark stood out, adding approximately 13.2% to the EU's overall additional lending capacity in that year.

Finally, Figure 4.8 shed light on a potential effectiveness of the changes to the restrictiveness of European macroprudential policy, as discussed earlier in this chapter. It points to quite a visible correlation (causation has not been analyzed, though) between the change to capital surplus (induced by three out of four sources: the impact of the growth of total assets has been excluded for obvious reasons) and growth of total assets in 2020. The simple qualitative analysis suggests that the bigger the increase of the surplus during the pandemic, the faster the growth of banking sector assets. That said, banks seem to have well utilized the space for expansion created by looser macroprudential policy, as they increased their funding for the economy.

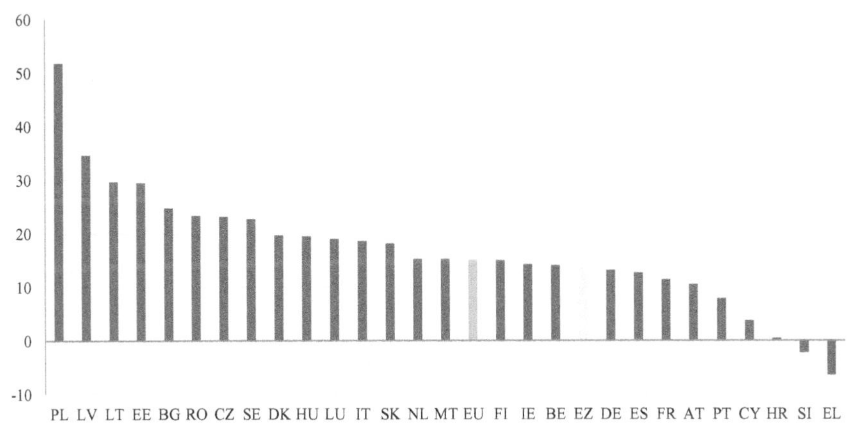

Figure 4.7 Change to the (capital induced) lending capacity (how much [in percent of initial total assets] could a bank[ing sector] expand given its increased capital surplus, and assuming constant risk density) in the European Union countries in 2020

Source: ESRB, ECB, banks consolidated financial statements. Author's own calculations

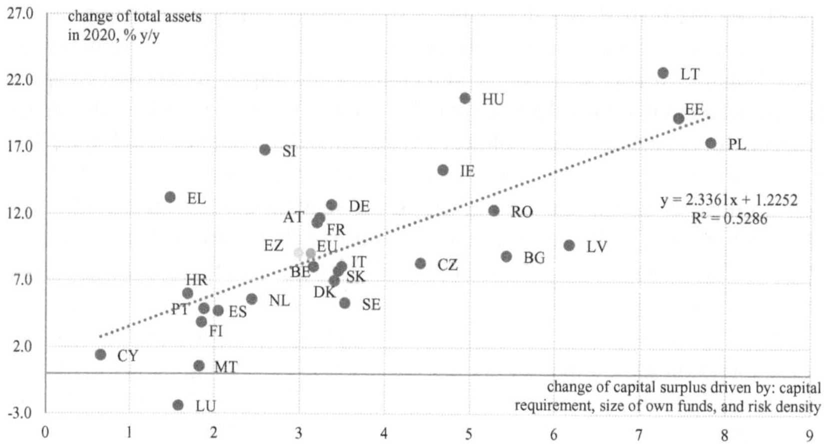

Figure 4.8 The change of bank capital surplus in 2020 versus change of bank's total assets in 2020 (measured in local currency)

Source: ESRB, ECB, banks consolidated financial statements. Author's own calculations

4.7 Conclusions

Among all the financial crises, the COVID-19 crisis distinguished itself with the pace of its spread, as well as the speed of response of public and monetary authorities. The priority was to ensure access to financing and maintain the liquidity of business entities, as well as their solvency. The authorities took steps to maintain the production capacity of enterprises during the period of anti-pandemic restrictions. A set of measures has also been targeted at the banking sector, which would have been the first to be affected by a wave of possible bankruptcies of its clients. In order to ensure its efficient operation during and after the pandemic, the monetary and supervisory authorities decided to implement an unprecedented accommodation of monetary and macroprudential policy.

The study showed that the majority of European Union countries have been conducting the macroprudential policy in a countercyclical fashion. After rising the capital requirements before the pandemic, they delivered a swift accommodation at the time of the outbreak of a crisis. Over a year and a half later, many of them decided to tighten macroprudential policy, as the economy started to recover from the pandemic. However, two years after the outbreak of the pandemic, most of the national macroprudential policies in the European Union countries remained less restrictive than before the outbreak (at least in terms of capital requirements). In addition, it has been indicated that larger changes to the requirements were introduced in countries where the supervisory authorities had applied stricter macroprudential policies before the crisis. That is, the more space (higher capital requirements) there had been in good times, before the pandemic, the bigger accommodation was delivered after its outbreak.

The empirical results of the study may be interesting from a theoretical standpoint too. It has been emphasized that the capital requirement (combined capital buffer) may be a second-best measure of the restrictiveness of capital regulations. Indeed, the extreme case of Portugal indicated that even in the face of the reduction of requirements, the overall macroprudential policy (on a country level) may turn out to be more restrictive, due to the increase in the share of banks subject to higher requirements. Furthermore, the article showed that the increase in the capital adequacy ratio, including an increase in own funds (e.g., as a result of retained profits), was 2.3 times more important for the decrease in the restrictiveness of macroprudential policy in the European Union countries, than loosening the requirements. As a result, despite the increase in assets, additional credit expansion potential was obtained. However, this general conclusion does not mean that there were no specific cases. For example, in Poland, the loosening of regulations was the largest in the EU, and the increase in own funds was (relatively) small. Finally, the analysis points to a correlation between the growth of banks assets in 2020 and the change of their capital surplus implying that the loosening of macroprudential policy might indeed have been beneficial from the macroeconomic point of view, as it provided banks with additional space to expand assets. That said, the conduct of macroprudential policy during the pandemic crisis proved to be countercyclical.

This study is not free from flaws or simplifications. As the analysis of the scope of changes in supervisory and regulatory instruments was limited to macroprudential capital requirements, it did not cover, for example, the so-called second pillar requirements. In addition, the supervisory measures taken in this regard were included only indirectly (in the form of changes in the level of asset risk weights). Having said this, the impact that, for example, the introduction of CRR Quick Fix had on risk weights could not be distinguished from the sovereign decisions of banks to change the structure of their trading/hedging portfolio. Finally, the study does not take into account other supervisory actions, such as inducing banks to retain profits generated in 2019. The analysis also does not answer the question regarding the impact of higher lending capacity on (actual) bank lending.

Notes

1 Capital Requirements Directive IV and Capital Requirements Regulation are the main source of post-GFC regulation for European Union's banking sector (they have been amended in 2019 by CRD V – CRR II package). They have implemented (among others) the Basel Capital Accord III to the European law.

2 It was a part of a series of measures taken by the EU institutions to mitigate the impact of the pandemic on the European banking sector. It introduced certain adjustments to the Capital Requirements Regulation including some temporary measures that were intended to strengthen the capital position of banks and enhance their ability to provide credit.

3 That said, the 2nd Pillar requirements are not included in the analysis, as they are considered to be microprudential, due to their establishing process, with a prominent role of stress tests, and case-by-case assessment of the supervisor.

4 "Overview of national capital-based measures" published with a quarterly frequency on the webpage of the ESRB that presents the local regulatory and supervisory measures (https://www.esrb.europa.eu/national_policy/html/index.en.html), as well the notifications of local macroprudential authorities.

5 For example, if a banking sector consists of two banks only, with capital requirements of 12% and 15% each and own funds of €1 billion and €3 billion, respectively, the weight of the first bank is 25%, and of the second is 75% giving a weighted average capital requirement for the entire sector of 14.25%, that is, 12% × 25% + 15% × 75%.

6 The small changes to the combined buffer visible on this figure result from changing structure of the banking sector (and individual institution's weights in the total). The overall requirement for each country equals the weighted average of requirements for individual banks in those countries, with own funds as weights. As the size of more heavily regulated institutions increases relative to others, so does the weighted average, that is the country-level requirement.

References

Avezum L., Oliveira V., Serra D. (2021), Assessment of the effectiveness of the macroprudential measures implemented in the context of the COVID-19 pandemic, SUERF Policy Brief No. 165, August.

Bergant K., Forbes K. (2021), Macroprudential Policy during COVID-19: The Role of Policy Space, NBER Working Paper No. 29346, October.

Bernanke B.S., Lown C.S. (1991), The Credit Crunch, *Brookings Papers on Economic Activity* 22 (2), pp. 205–247.

Berrospide J.M., Edge R.M. (2010), The Effects of Bank Capital on Lending: What Do We Know, and What Does It Mean? *International Journal of Central Banking* December, pp. 5–54.

Blundell-Wignall A., Atkinson P. (2010), Thinking Beyond Basel III: Necessary Solutions for Capital and Liquidity, *OECD Journal: Financial Market Trends* (1), pp. 9–33.

Borio C., Gambacorta L. (2017), Monetary policy and bank lending in a low interest rate environment: Diminishing effectiveness? *Journal of Macroeconomics* 54 (B), pp. 217–231.

Budnik K., Dimitrov I., Groß J., Jancoková M., Lampe M., Sorvillo B, Stular, A. Volk M. (2021), Policies in support of lending following the coronavirus (COVID-19) pandemic, ECB Occasional Paper No. 257, May.

Casanova C., Hardy B., Onen M. (2021), COVID-19 policy measures to support bank lending, *BIS Quarterly Review*, September, pp. 45–59.

Catalán M., Hoffmaister A.W., Harun C.A. (2017), Bank Capital and Lending: An Extended Framework and Evidence of Nonlinearity, IMF Working Paper No. WP/17/252.

Czaplicki M. (2021), Measuring the restrictiveness of (macro)prudential policy. The case of bank capital regulation in Poland, *Journal of Banking Regulation* (online first).

Czerniak A., Czaplicki M., Mokrogulski M., Niedziółka P., Szelągowska A. (2021), Wpływ pandemii COVID-19 na sektor bankowy w Polsce i innych krajach Europy Środkowo-Wschodniej, in: A. Chłoń-Domińczak, R. Sobiecki, M. Strojny, B. Majewski (eds.), Raport SGH i Forum Ekonomicznego 2021, Oficyna Wydawnicza SGH, Warsaw, pp. 269–295.

De Jonghe O., Dewachter H., Ongena S. (2020), Bank capital (requirements) and credit supply: Evidence from pillar 2 decisions, *Journal of Corporate Finance* 60, 101518. https://www.sciencedirect.com/journal/journal-of-corporate-finance/vol/60/suppl/C

Dicanio A., Montesi G. (2021), Banks in Time of COVID-19: Loss Absorption Capacity, Lending and Market Valuation, Bancaria 2/2021, February, pp. 31–58.

European Central Bank (2020), ECB Banking Supervision provides temporary capital and operational relief in reaction to coronavirus, https://www.bankingsupervision.europa.eu/press/pr/date/2020/html/ssm.pr200312~43351ac3ac.en.html.

European Banking Authority (2015), Report – 2015 EU-wide transparency exercise, November25,https://www.eba.europa.eu/sites/default/documents/files/documents/10180/1280458/106bdfd6-8c0f-4251-ba57-7cd0d97d8174/2015%20EU-wide%20Transparency%20Exercise%20Report%20FINAL.pdf?retry=1

European Systemic Risk Board (2021), A Review of Macroprudential Policy in the EU in 2020, July.

Financial Stability Board (2021), Lessons Learnt from the COVID-19 Pandemic from a Financial Stability Perspective, FSB Interim Report, 13 July.

Fonseca A.R., González F., Pereira da Silva L. (2010), Cyclical effects of Bank Capital Buffers with Imperfect Credit Markets: international evidence, Banco Central do Brasil Working Paper No. 216.

Gambacorta L., Shin H.S. (2018), Why bank capital matters for monetary policy, *Journal of Financial Intermediation* 35 (B), pp. 17–29.

Hancock D., Wilcox J.A. (1993), Has There Been a "Capital Crunch" in Banking? The Effects on Bank Lending of Real Estate Market Conditions and Bank Capital Shortfalls, *Journal of Housing Economics* 3 (1), pp. 31–50.

Heid F., Porath D., Stolz S. (2003), Does capital regulation matter for bank behaviour? Evidence for German savings banks, mimeo.

Imbierowicz B., Löffler A., Vogel U. (2021), The transmission of bank capital requirements and monetary policy to bank lending in Germany, *Review of International Economics* 29 (1), pp. 144–164.

Riksbank (2020), Financial Stability Report, 11 November.

5 Business continuity planning and management

A lifejacket in the COVID-19 storm?[1]

Paola Bongini, Małgorzata Iwanicz-Drozdowska and Caterina Liberati

5.1 Introduction

Business continuity planning (BCP) and business continuity management (BCM) are concepts rooted in the broader discipline of enterprise risk management – ERM (Shimpi, 2001; AIRMIC, 2002; Nocco & Stulz, 2006; Roggi, 2015). ERM is the process of methodically identifying and addressing potential events that represent risks to the achievement of strategic objectives or to opportunities for gaining a competitive advantage. In the last 20 years, ERM has gained relevance in business management and three main international standards have been developed: AIRMIC (2002), ISO31000-2017, and COSO (2017). These standards have underlined the relevance of an enterprise's risk philosophy or strategy, risk culture, and risk appetite as expressions of the attitude to risk in an organisation and the amount of risk that an organisation is willing to take.[2] Once risks are identified, measured, and evaluated, risk responses include acceptance or tolerance of risk, avoidance or termination of risk, risk transfer or sharing via insurance, a joint venture, or other arrangements, and reduction or mitigation activities.

In the ERM process, business continuity results in a sub-process of risk mitigation able to guarantee crisis management in response to extreme events that could compromise normal organisational operations. The idea is that companies should prepare and implement a plan intended to ensure that the organisation's critical functions continue to operate during a major disaster, such as an earthquake, pandemic, terrorist attack, war, system failure, disruption of supply chains, an economic crisis such as a deep recession, or reputational crises, and that they are able to recover and return to business as usual in the shortest possible time once the disaster is over (Hiles, 2007; Clark, 2016).

According to Herbane (2010), BCP/BCM started attracting the attention of experts in the 1970s with the advent of new information technology and the related awareness of the vulnerability of their electronic data processing (EDP) activities. The technology focus within the disaster recovery plan (DRP) characterised the subsequent decades, and it was not before the mid-1990s that scholars started to see BCP as an essential means to maintain customer services, revenue generation, essential support services, and the confidence of customers, shareholders and employees, as well as the public image of the company (Smith & Sherwoord, 1995).

DOI: 10.4324/9781003310754-5

Indeed, although a disaster recovery plan is vital, it should be noted that it is primarily a reactive approach, while a BCP is a comprehensive plan that seeks to eliminate or reduce the impact of a disaster condition before the condition occurs (Cerullo & Cerullo, 2004). According to the US Federal Emergency Management Agency, among all the businesses damaged by Hurricane Andrew in 1992, 80% of those lacking a BCP failed within two years after the storm.

However, it was only after the 9/11 attack on the World Trade Center that academics and practitioners' interest in BCPs grew exponentially, leading to holistic plans that contain every aspect of the business that might be affected, including business processes, assets, human resources, and business partners (IBM Services, 2019).

Several studies have confirmed that preparation for tail risk events pays off (Corey & Deitch, 2011; Mitroff & Alpaslan, 2003; Pearson & Clair, 1998; Runyan, 2006) and that planning and preparation are central to the well functioning of a risk mitigation framework. While these studies argue that all firms should have a business continuity plan, many do not, and they tend to differ quite significantly among those that have one. Although the main technical standard, i.e., ISO 22301–2019,[3] is intended to be applicable to all organisations, or parts thereof – regardless of the type, size, and nature of the organisation – business continuity regulations vary between countries and industries/sectors. They are particularly developed in the highly regulated financial sector.

Notwithstanding the lesson learned in the many tail situations recently experienced, starting with the SARS outbreaks in 2003 up to the global financial crises and global COVID-19 pandemic, *prima facie* this global pandemic seems to have caught businesses off guard both in advanced and emerging economies. The COVID-19 pandemic has not only presented an extraordinary health and social emergency but also meant a major threat to the continuity and long-term survival of many businesses.

Against this backdrop, our main research question is whether business continuity planning and management have reached the maturity to make a difference in extreme environments like that experienced in 2020, helping well-prepared organisations to withstand the storm.

To answer this question, we launched a global survey through digital channels during a period of major lockdown in many countries (April–May 2020). The data collected was first presented in a report available online (https://papers.ssrn.com/sol3/papers.cfm?abstract_id=3764401) in which we analysed: (i) the main features of the business continuity plans (BCPs) in our sample, (ii) the readiness of the BCPs in reaction to the pandemic, (iii) the features of the organisations' crisis management committee, and, finally, (iv) how the organisations' reacted to tail risk.

This chapter analyses the results of the survey by applying multiple correspondence analysis (MCA) and cluster analysis to detect whether business continuity planning and management were helpful in terms of the organisation's readiness to respond to the pandemic scenario and the ability to implement protective measures and guarantee overall business continuity in the longer term.

Few studies have so far been published on the relationship between BCP and COVID-19, and most of the research has a local focus; the only study with international coverage we are aware of is that of Margherita and Heikkila (2021), which concentrates on the top 50 world-leading companies according to the 2019 Fortune Global ranking. As in their study, we have an international scope, but we also include micro-businesses and SMEs as well as public sectors such as health and education. For this reason, we believe our study advances extant knowledge on the relevance of business continuity in weathering unexpected storms.

The remaining part of this chapter is organised as follows. In Section 5.2, we present the survey and the sample. In Section 5.3, we briefly describe our global survey results (for high-income and middle-income countries). Section 5.4 focuses on methodology, while Section 5.5 presents the results and a discussion. The final section provides conclusions.

5.2 Survey and sample

The survey consisted of 28 questions, divided into 5 sections referring to (i) the features of the BCP and principles of business continuity management (BMC), (ii) the use of remote work and the efficiency of coping with the COVID-19 pandemic, (iii) financial and operational responses to the crisis, (iv) the characteristics of the crisis management committee, and (v) socio-demographic questions.

The questionnaire was translated into nine languages and the survey was conducted using digital channels, particularly social networks such as LinkedIn, Facebook, and Twitter. With the use of our international social networks, we distributed the link to the questionnaires and reached various groups of respondents (snowball sampling). The survey questionnaires were opened online from 7 April to 13 May 2020. More statistics are presented in the annex.

In total, around 950 responses were obtained from 45 countries, and, after assessing the data quality, 924 responses were used for the analyses of this study (Figure 5.1).

Respondents mainly came from high-income countries (731) and, in particular, from Europe (79% of the sample). Brazil was particularly represented in middle-income countries (107 answers out of 192) and only one response came from a low-income country. The number of replies from Italian, Polish, Swedish, and Brazilian organisations was 125 (14%), 244 (26%), 177 (19%), and 107 (12%), respectively. These four countries represented 71% of the sample.

The questionnaire was mainly answered by senior management of the sample organisations (67%), aged 36–50 years (45%), male (64%), and with a higher educational status (92%).

As far as the characteristics of the organisations are concerned, 43% of the sample comprised large organisations, while the rest of the sample was almost equally divided between medium, small, and micro-organisations. These entities are mainly independent national organisations (68% of the total), and this is particularly true for respondents from middle-income (MI) countries.

The organisations that took part in the survey come from various sectors: around 24% of responses were from the financial sector, followed by "other services" (19%) and "education" (13%). Next were "manufacturing" (10%) and "other" (10%), "IT" (8%), "commerce" (8%), "state/public admin" (5%), and "healthcare" (4%).

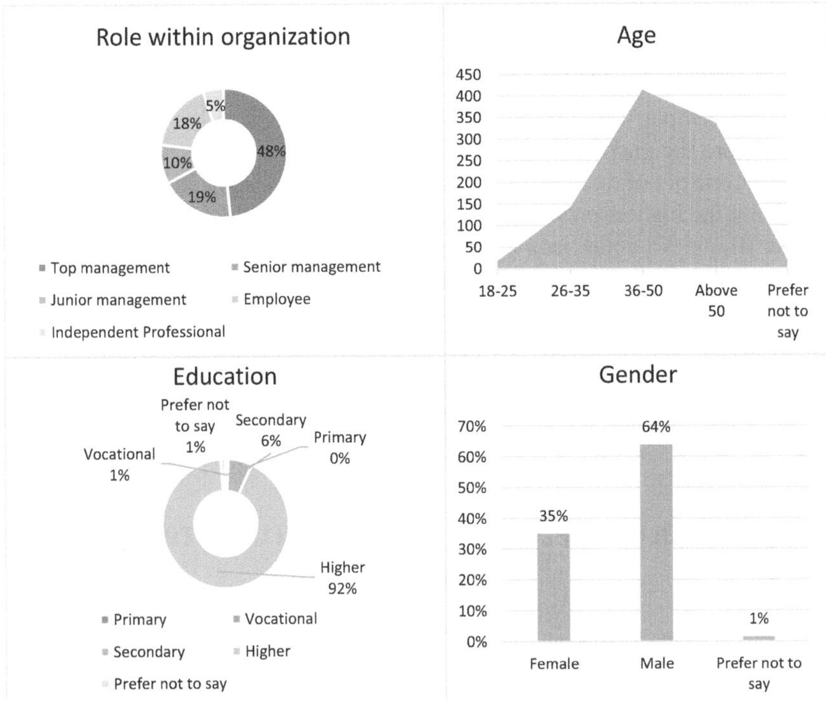

Figure 5.1 Socio-demographic characteristics of respondents

Source: Own work based on our survey

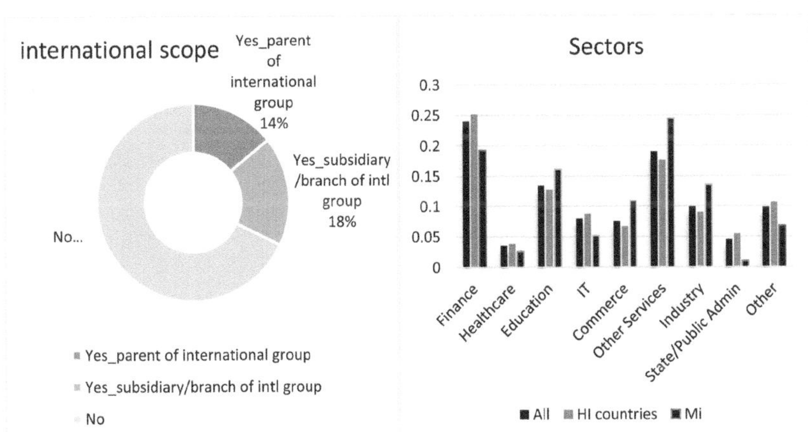

Figure 5.2 Sector, size, and international outreach of the responding organisations

Source: Own work based on our survey

5.3 Business continuity plan and management – Survey results

5.3.1 BCP and crisis management

Our global sample was almost equally divided between organisations that had a BCP before the pandemic (53%) and those that did not possess a BCP (47%). Moreover, one out of three had a plan that was regularly updated (Figure 5.3). The sector with the highest presence of organisations with BCPs in force was finance (both in HI and MI countries), followed by IT, especially in MI countries. On the contrary, healthcare, education, and services were the least prepared in general.

In our sample, most organisations realised that the pandemic would affect their activities in March 2020 (almost 52%), but, notably, firms with BCPs became aware of the problem around February 2020 (about 21.5% of the total). This shows that a BCP helps identify potential issues faster and gives further room for adequate preparation.

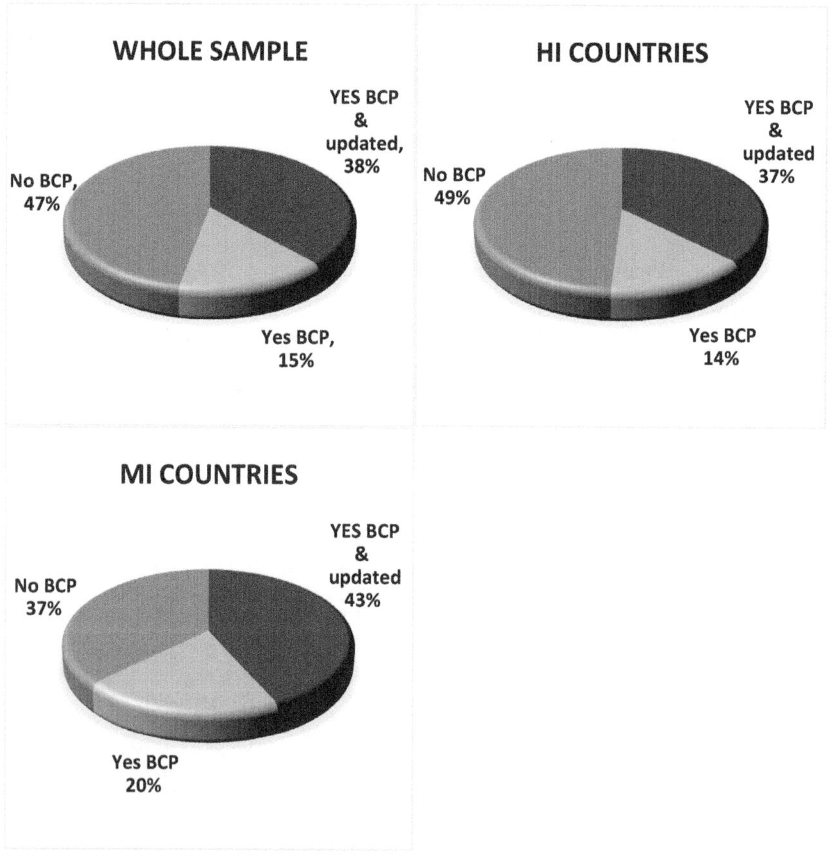

Figure 5.3 Existence of a BCP within organisations

Source: Own work based on our survey

However, since the pandemic scenario was considered by a little more than one-quarter of organisations with a BCP in force, most respondents admitted the need to change the plan after the outbreak of the COVID-19 pandemic. Organisations without a BCP increased their awareness, and many (40%) reported the need to develop one. In the case of entities having BCPs, most organisations from HI countries declared the need for a few changes in their extant plan. In contrast, organisations from MI countries required significant changes in their BCPs. This may be treated as a sign that BCPs in MI countries were not adequate for the scale of the problems caused by the COVID-19 pandemic.

5.3.2 *Readiness to react to the pandemic scenario*

One of the critical changes that organisations had to meet starting from March 2020 was the switch to remote work. Due to the pandemic, the existence of remote work has significantly increased in the whole sample and both groups of countries. At the start of 2020, 79% of organisations had not resorted to smart working or were using it to a limited extent, while this figure dropped to 22% in the first quarter of 2020. The higher current use of smart working in HI countries compared to MI countries replicates the differences before the pandemic (Table 5.1).

Considering the sectors of respondents, the use of remote work before the outbreak of the pandemic was less frequent in healthcare, education, commerce, manufacturing and state/public administration. During the pandemic, healthcare and commerce, due to the characteristics of the services provided by these two sectors, were less likely to switch to this new mode of work. The switch to remote work is considered one of the long-lasting consequences of the pandemic.

Although differences in the use of smart working before the pandemic were not seemingly directly linked to the presence of a BCP (see Figure 5.4), having a BCP could potentially be an important factor for an efficient adjustment to unexpected events. We, therefore, checked how the presence of a BCP facilitated an efficient switch to crisis mode. As shown in Table 5.2, organisations without a BCP more frequently declared that their adjustments to the new conditions were not efficient;

Table 5.1 The use of remote work

Remote work used before the pandemic	*Whole sample (%)*	*HI countries (%)*	*MI countries (%)*
To a large extent	21	23	14
To a limited extent	58	58	60
Not used	21	20	26
Currently remote work is used:			
To a large extent	60	62	52
To a moderate extent	18	18	18
To a limited extent	16	14	24
Not used	6	5	6

Source: Own work based on our survey.

however, organisations with BCPs from MI countries also declared non-efficient switches more often than the ones from HI countries.

A similar situation may be observed in the case of critical processes (Table 5.3). Organisations without BCPs more frequently declared that a minority of essential processes were functioning correctly during the period under investigation (first quarter of 2020). For most organisations with BCPs from HI countries, all critical processes were working properly, while for those from MI countries it was the majority of critical functions.

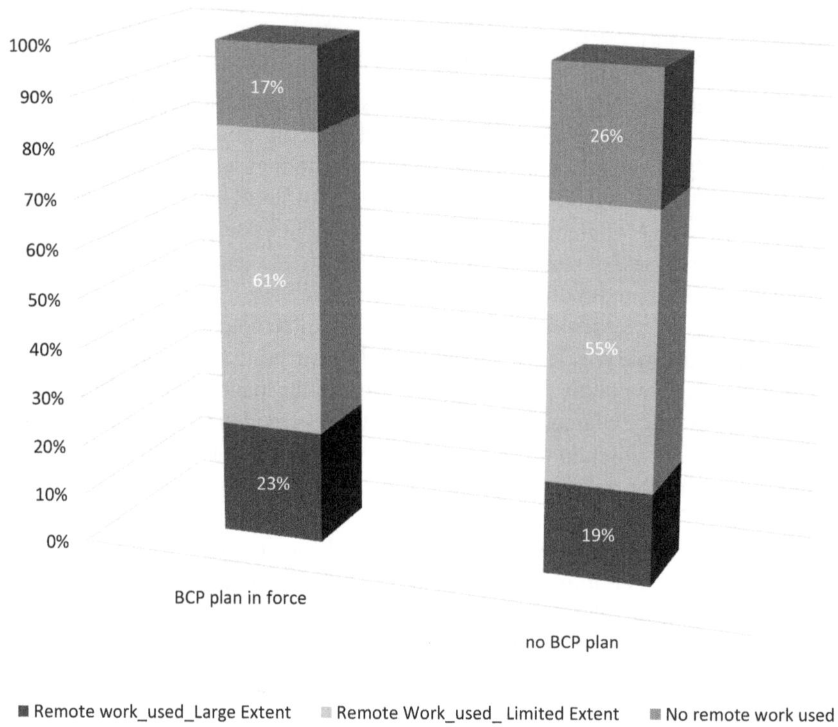

Figure 5.4 Remote work before the pandemic and BCPs

Source: Own work based on our survey

Table 5.2 BCP and an efficient switch to smart working

Organisations with	*Whole sample*		*HI countries*		*MI countries*	
	Yes	*No*	*Yes*	*No*	*Yes*	*No*
BCP before COVID & updated	92%	8%	93%	7%	87%	13%
BCP before COVID	92%	8%	94%	6%	87%	13%
No BCP	80%	20%	80%	20%	77%	23%
Pandemic event in BCP	88%	22%	89%	11%	83%	17%

Source: Own work based on our survey.

Table 5.3 BCP and critical processes

Organisations with	*HI countries*			*MI countries*		
	Critical processes managed			*Critical processes managed*		
	All	*Majority*	*Minority*	*All*	*Majority*	*Minority*
BCP before COVID & updated	70%	28%	1%	39%	54%	7%
BCP before COVID	55%	40%	5%	37%	53%	11%
No BCP	50%	40%	10%	20%	65%	15%

Source: Own work based on our survey.

We may conclude that although organisations from MI countries more frequently had BCPs, these were probably not adequate for the scale or type of problems that had arisen and, therefore, organisations from MI countries were less efficient in adjusting to the pandemic conditions.

5.3.3 Crisis management committee

Since crisis management requires coordination of the work of many individuals or teams in an organisation, it is good practice to create a crisis management committee (CMC) that coordinates and manages critical situations (see, for example, Williams et al., 2017). CMCs were established in 53% of organisations with BCPs in force (50% of organisations in HI countries and 63% in MI countries) and in 47% of organisations without a BCP (50% in HI countries and 37% in MI countries).

The setup of the crisis committee within the organisation is a recent phenomenon; more than 50% of the whole sample created it to face and manage the pandemic crisis, while only 43% of organisations had it in place since at least 2018. In most cases, the committee comprises between three and nine members, of which few are independent (16%), while typically CFOs, CROs, and the chair of the board of directors sit on the committee. An established crisis management committee helped anticipate the potential impact of the pandemic on the organisation before March 2020.

The presence of a CMC seems to increase the effectiveness of the organisation's response to the crisis. Data provided in Table 5.4 shows that the presence of a CMC coupled with a BCP increased the effectiveness of the organisation's response to the crisis, in terms of the efficient switch of operations into the remote mode of working and smooth continuation of all or the majority of critical processes.

In the following paragraphs, we analyse the measures undertaken by our sample organisations in order to react to the initial period of the crisis. Actions were distinguished between protective measures, aimed at protecting the cash position of the organisation given a potential or immediate stop of cash inflows with fixed cash outflows, and measures aimed at guaranteeing overall business continuity in the long run.

Table 5.4 CMC and crisis management

Organisations	*HI countries*						*MI countries*					
	%	*Efficient switch*		*Critical processes managed*			%	*Efficient switch*		*Critical processes managed*		
		Yes	*No*	*All*	*Majority*	*Minority*		*Yes*	*No*	*All*	*Majority*	*Minority*
No BCP, but CMC	16%	83%	17%	53%	41%	6%	20%	84%	16%	21%	63%	16%
No BCP, No CMC	34%	79%	21%	49%	40%	12%	17%	70%	30%	18%	67%	15%
BCP & CMC	34%	94%	6%	69%	29%	3%	39%	86%	14%	39%	53%	8%
BCP, no CMC	16%	92%	11%	59%	37%	4%	24%	87%	13%	36%	55%	9%

Source: own work based on our survey

5.3.4 Protective measures

With regard to the possible measures undertaken to protect the cash position of the organisation (Table 5.5), the most popular one in the two geographical subsamples was the revision of variable costs (i.e. cutting non-fixed costs). It is noticeable that organisations in MI countries were less prone to do nothing (7%) compared to their peers in HI countries (21%), which at the same time enjoyed greater state support – 30% of this subsample declared resorting to public help to avoid liquidity tensions. The availability of public financing may have reduced the need to search for new financing sources from alternative finance providers, which was used by a mere 8% of organisations in HI countries, compared to 26% in MI countries.

Focusing on those organisations that did not take any specific action to protect their cash position (18% of the sample), Figure 5.5 highlights that these are mainly large, national groups belonging to the finance sector (HI countries) or education/ other services (Figure 5.6). For instance, among those in the financial sector, only 24% of respondents who did not take any action were in fact without a BCP in force. A large group (36%) of small corporations in MI countries did not react to the COVID-19 liquidity constraint. This might be due to the lack of bargaining power against their counterparts, mainly banks and large suppliers.

5.3.5 Actions implemented to guarantee business continuity

Respondents could choose among several different actions that could have been implemented to guarantee the continuity of their business (Figure 5.7). These differ somewhat between organisations depending on whether they belong to HI or MI countries. The latter preferred renegotiation with suppliers (56% of MI sample used it) followed by other actions. In fact, the majority of respondents of MI countries (49%) belong to manufacturing, commerce, or services, which explains the preference for renegotiation with suppliers as it represents the quickest response to a systemic problem. The most representative sector of HI countries' organisations,

Table 5.5 Cash protection measures*

Actions	*Whole sample (%)*	*HI countries (%)*	*MI countries (%)*
Revision of variable costs	74	48	66
Conversion cycle renegotiation (credit terms)	27	21	51
Revisiting capital investment plan	37	35	46
Inventory management	19	17	27
New Financing Source from alternative finance providers	12	8	26
Public support	26	30	22
Other	22	24	23
None	18	21	7

*Figures in columns do not sum to 100 because respondents could choose more than one answer.
Source: Own work based on our survey.

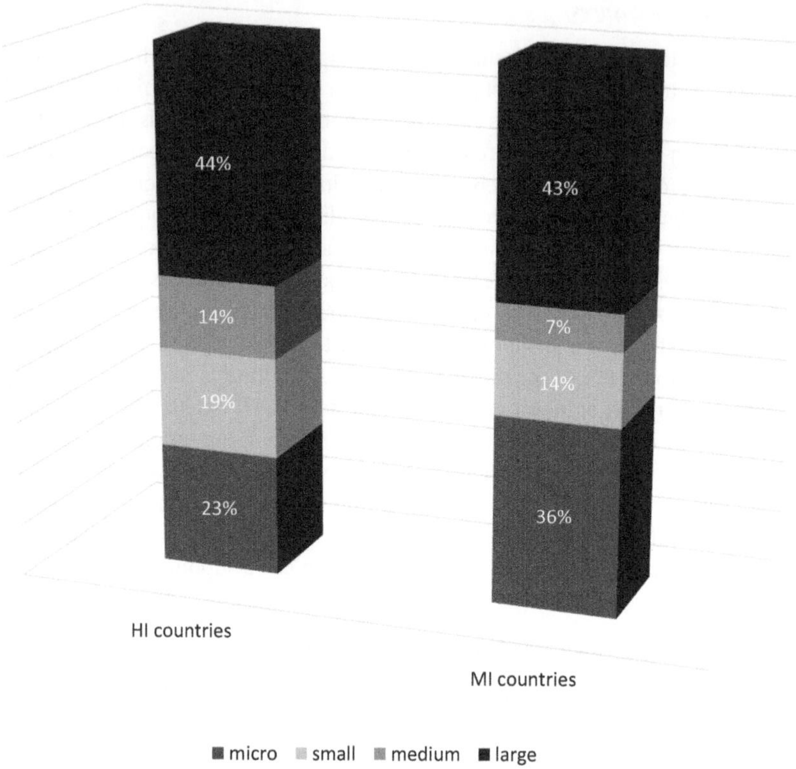

Figure 5.5 Size and non-cash protection measures

Source: Own work based on our survey

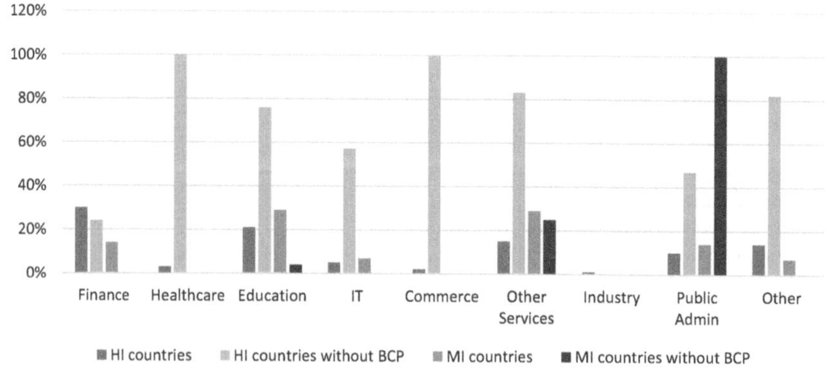

Figure 5.6 Sectors, geographical location, and presence of a BCP in organisations with no protective measures

Source: Own work based on our survey

on the other hand, is the financial sector, for which the term "renegotiation" does not represent the most viable (or quickest) action.

In MI countries, the actions implemented to guarantee business continuity were mainly directed to a generalised term "renegotiation" with a lower frequency in the finance and education sectors. Instead, the term "negotiation" was primarily used in the public sector, followed by manufacturing companies and the commerce sector. This action was often associated with other unidentified measures and product redundancy. The healthcare sector largely recurred to post-sales outsourcing. Moreover, the healthcare industry intensively used production outsourcing due to the increased demand for health services during the COVID-19 pandemic and the relative inelasticity of UTI beds offered in existing hospitals.

Finally, we focused on those organisations that declared not to undertake any action or protective measures to face this exceptional situation (Figure 5.8). Specifically, we investigated whether such inaction was linked to the absence of a BCP and related management readiness; in fact, the lack of action only partly supports our hypothesis. Most likely the decision depends on the occurrence in the whole sample of the financial and educational sectors, for which the measures and actions proposed in the questionnaire were probably less relevant.

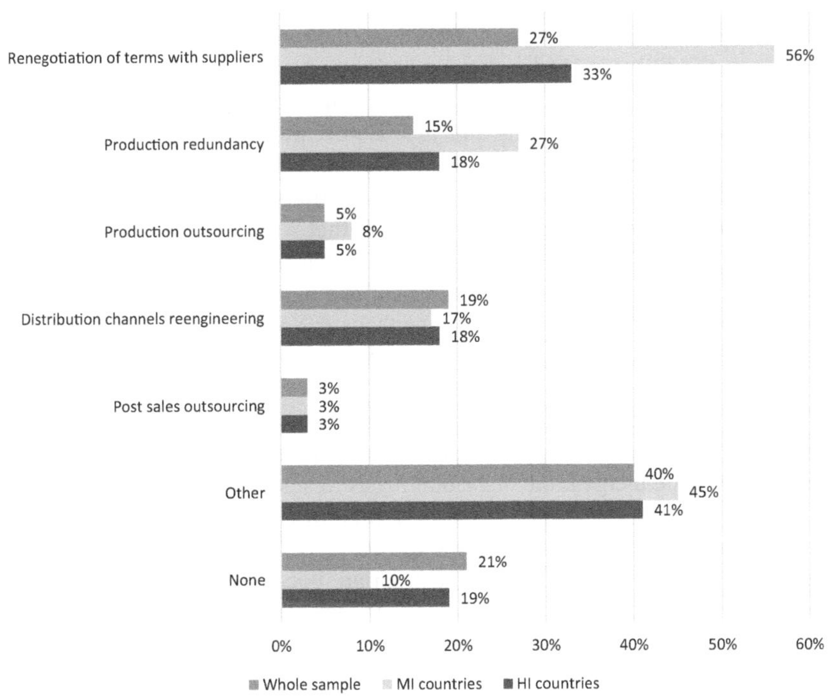

Figure 5.7 Actions to guarantee business continuity

Source: Own work based on our survey

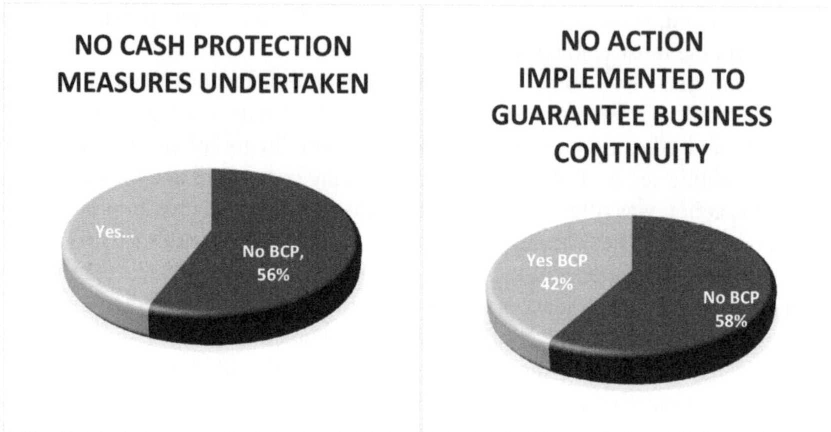

Figure 5.8 Inaction during the crisis and a BCP

Source: Own work based on our survey

5.4 Methodology

To investigate the relevance of BCP/BCM, we explored the behaviour of businesses from multiple aspects, e.g., from how they managed employees' remote working to the financial and operative actions taken to face the pandemic. To recognise similar patterns, we employed an unsupervised statistical approach based on the usage of clustering analysis. Before performing the classification, we carried out a pre-processing step. Using multiple correspondence analysis (MCA) (Benzècri, 1973; Greenacre, 1984), we transformed the monitored categorical variables[4] into numerical dimensions that we used as input for our segmentation. The MCA is a factorial technique that aims to summarise a set of categorical variables into a small number of orthogonal variables called principal components (Lebart et al., 1984; Tenenhaus & Young, 1985). In our case, we retained 25 axes, accounting for approximately 98% of the total variance (also called inertia).

We then performed a hierarchical clustering – an iterative algorithm that groups similar instances into groups, seeking a hierarchy of the clusters.[5] To decide which clusters should be merged, the algorithm needs to select a measure of dissimilarity between sets of observations. As it is well known, the choice of the metrics is critical because it influences the shape of the clusters. In our case, we used the Euclidean distance. The choice was appropriate because the input variables we used did not show any correlation problem, thanks to the application of the MCA that produced orthogonal axes. Finally, the hierarchy is designed utilising a criterion (linkage). In our case, we employed Ward's objective function (Ward, 1963), which groups pairs of clusters at each step, leading to a minimum increase in total within-cluster variance after merging. The agglomerative process can be pictured in a graph called a dendrogram, which is also helpful to identify the number of clusters. A partition with a few separated groups was not immediately recognisable in the dendrogram. We, therefore, calculated the Silhouette Index (Rousseeuw, 1986) to rank possible alternative solutions.[6]

The three clusters identified were described using the variables synthesised via MCA (Table 5.6) and were further characterised through additional variables (Table 5.7), mainly related to (i) the presence of a detailed framework for business continuity planning and management, (ii) country specificities, (iii) sector specificities, and (iv) the size of the organisations.

5.5 Results

This section shows the evidence obtained from our sample of respondents. A general inspection of the results in Table 5.6, presenting the percentage of the presence of each variable in each cluster, reveals the three different business reactions to the looming pandemic, which influenced the naming of the groups displayed at the top of the table. For example, cluster 2, with a quick anticipatory view of what was likely to happen, a stronger understanding of remote working, and agility in resorting to a variety of protective measures, was indeed able to secure that all the critical processes in the organisation were functioning correctly during the first wave of the COVID-19 pandemic. We labelled these organisations as "Alive & kicking".

Cluster 1, on the other hand, followed suit but at a slower pace. This explains the label "reactive in slow motion". Finally, cluster 3 was the least prepared for the pandemic and found it difficult to adjust to it quickly and effectively. It seems to comprise mainly "Followers" (or "Late risers"), which may have started to change their businesses following best practices on the market.

In addition, the results of cluster 2 ("Alive & kicking") show their better financial and contract management. Entities included in this cluster adapted more cash-protective measures and represented higher flexibility in external and internal adjustments (e.g., renegotiations of contracts, outsourcing). Against this backdrop, two other clusters represented a more passive approach, which was confirmed by indicating that no measures had been applied. Since public authorities in many countries approved state-aid packages for various industries, the role of state aid was similar in the distinguished clusters. The entities in cluster 3, although passive in other areas, seem to have used state aid extensively. Critical processes functioning properly were specific for clusters 2 and 1, while cluster 3 lagged behind. From a managerial point of view, assuring continuity of essential operations is most important for any organisation. Entities from cluster 3 faced a considerable challenge to ensure business continuity.

We further described the three-group partition using some variables not included in the clustering process. Differences detected, if any, would reinforce the results because they would highlight contrasts not produced via these features. We characterised the classification using the economic sector, country of origin, size of the company, and existence and peculiarities of the BCP/BCM. Table 5.7 presents the percentage of the presence of each variable in each cluster. The last column of the

Table 5.6 Clusters description using MCA variables

Question	*% in each cluster*		
	Cluster 1: reactive in slow motion	*Cluster 2: alive & kicking*	*Cluster 3: followers*
Was remote work used in the organisation before the outbreak of the pandemic? Yes, to a large extent	0.22	0.27	0.14
Was remote work used in the organisation before the outbreak of the pandemic? Yes, to a limited extent	0.62	0.66	0.40
Was remote work used in the organisation before the outbreak of the pandemic? No	0.17	0.07	0.46
To what extent is remote work currently used in the organisation? Large extent (over 75% of employees)	0.62	0.63	0.36
To what extent is remote work currently used in the organisation? Moderate extent (over 25–75% of employees)	0.21	0.21	0.14
To what extent is remote work currently used in the organisation? To a limited extent (up to 25% of employees)	0.17	0.16	0.21
To what extent is remote work currently used in the organisation? No	0.00	0.01	0.29
When did you first realise that the pandemic would impact your organisation? January 2020	0.00	0.58	0.03
When did you first realise that the pandemic would impact your organisation? February 2020	0.42	0.16	0.28
When did you first realise that the pandemic would impact your organisation? March 2020	0.57	0.27	0.50
When did you first realise that the pandemic would impact your organisation? April 2020	0.00	0.00	0.09
When did you first realize that the pandemic would impact your organisation? Did not impact the organisation	0.00	0.00	0.10
Did your organisation, by applying its existing or ad hoc business continuity solutions, manage to efficiently and quickly (in about 1 week) switch to the pandemic mode of work? Yes	1.00	0.93	0.37
Did your organisation, by applying its existing or ad hoc business continuity solutions, manage to efficiently and quickly (in about 1 week) switch to the pandemic mode of work? No	0.00	0.07	0.63

(*Continued*)

Table 5.6 (Continued)

Question	*% in each cluster*		
	Cluster 1: reactive in slow motion	*Cluster 2: alive & kicking*	*Cluster 3: followers*
Do you think that all the critical processes in your organisation are functioning properly? Yes	0.58	0.61	0.29
Do you think that all the critical processes in your organisation are functioning properly? Most of them are functioning properly	0.42	0.38	0.36
Do you think that all the critical processes in your organisation are functioning properly? Only a minority of them are functioning properly	0.00	0.02	0.34
Which of the following cash protection measures have been implemented in your organisation (you can select more than one item)? Revisiting variable costs	0.50	0.66	0.48
Which of the following cash protection measures have been implemented in your organisation (you can select more than one item)? Conversion cycle renegotiation (Account Payable and Receivable Management)	0.23	0.45	0.30
Which of the following cash protection measures have been implemented in your organisation (you can select more than one item)? Revisiting capital investment plan	0.36	0.55	0.30
Which of the following cash protection measures have been implemented in your organisation (you can select more than one item)? Inventory management to avoid supply chain disruption	0.15	0.41	0.18
Which of the following cash protection measures have been implemented in your organisation (you can select more than one item)? New financing source from alternative financing players	0.10	0.23	0.13
Which of the following cash protection measures have been implemented in your organisation (you can select more than one item)? Support from state or state agencies	0.26	0.33	0.33
Which of the following cash protection measures have been implemented in your organisation (you can select more than one item)? Other	0.26	0.20	0.21

(Continued)

Table 5.6 (Continued)

Question	*% in each cluster*		
	Cluster 1: reactive in slow motion	*Cluster 2: alive & kicking*	*Cluster 3: followers*
Which of the following cash protection measures have been implemented in your organisation (you can select more than one item)? None	0.20	0.09	0.20
Which of the following actions have you implemented to guarantee the business continuity (you can select more than one item)? Renegotiation of terms with suppliers	0.30	0.48	0.32
Which of the following actions have you implemented to guarantee the business continuity (you can select more than one item)? Production Redundancy (internal)	0.13	0.30	0.24
Which of the following actions have you implemented to guarantee business continuity (you can select more than one item)? Production Outsourcing (external)	0.00	0.36	0.01
Which of the following actions have you implemented to guarantee the business continuity (you can select more than one item)? Distribution channels reengineering	0.18	0.31	0.11
Which of the following actions have you implemented to guarantee the business continuity (you can select more than one item)? Post-sales outsourcing	0.00	0.20	0.00
Which of the following actions have you implemented to guarantee the business continuity (you can select more than one item)? Other	0.44	0.30	0.36
Which of the following actions have you implemented to guarantee the business continuity (you can select more than one item)? None	0.20	0.07	0.23

Source: Authors' calculations based on survey.

table shows the *p-value* of the ANOVA test that checked if the differences observed were statistically significant.[7] *Prima facie*, cluster 2 seems to be better equipped at business continuity planning (e.g., a higher percentage of regularly updated plans, with hardly any necessity to change the plan due to the recent pandemic). Cluster 3, on the other hand, appears to be the least equipped, though it is not the cluster in which all small and medium organisations are concentrated.

Most entities in cluster 3 had no BCP in place. While most of them answered that it would be necessary to develop a BCP/BCM, some concluded that a BCP/

Table 5.7 Cluster characterisation using further variables

Question	*% in each cluster*			
	Cluster 1: reactive in slow motion	*Cluster 2: alive & kicking*	*Cluster 3: followers*	*P-value**
Had a business continuity plan prior to the outbreak of the pandemic and it was regularly updated	0.41	0.48	0.25	0.000
Did not have a business continuity plan prior to the outbreak of the pandemic	0.44	0.32	0.62	0.000
It will be necessary to develop a business continuity plan	0.22	0.19	0.36	0.000
It will be necessary to change the BCP/ BCM in the organisation after the pandemic (yes, to a limited extent)	0.38	0.51	0.16	0.000
It will be not necessary to develop a business continuity plan	0.22	0.14	0.31	0.002
Does a Crisis Management Committee operate in your organisation? Yes	0.54	0.59	0.38	0.000
Does a Crisis Management Committee operate in your organisation? No	0.46	0.41	0.62	0.000
When was the Crisis Management Committee set up? Just recently	0.50	0.43	0.64	0.032
When was the Crisis Management Committee set up? A couple of years ago *Ward Method	0.45	0.49	0.29	0.025
Does the CMC include independent members appointed at purpose for the COVID-19? Yes	0.15	0.26	0.14	0.039
Does the CMC include independent members appointed at purpose for the COVID-19? No	0.85	0.74	0.86	0.039
Which of the following profile participates to the CMC: Chief Executive Officer	0.37	0.49	0.23	0.000
Which of the following profile participates to the CMC: Chief Financial Officer	0.30	0.43	0.22	0.000
Which of the following profile participates to the CMC: Chief Risk Officer	0.21	0.29	0.09	0.000
Which of the following profile participates to the CMC: Chief Operating Officer	0.32	0.42	0.24	0.004
Which of the following profile participates to the CMC: Chief Information Officer	0.20	0.19	0.07	0.000
Which of the following profile participates to the CMC: Chief Marketing Officer	0.13	0.22	0.09	0.003
Which of the following profile participates to the CMC: Investor Relations, Communication Officer	0.14	0.24	0.10	0.002
Which of the following profile participates in the CMC: Epidemiologist	0.04	0.06	0.01	0.058

(*Continued*)

Table 5.7 (Continued)

Question	*% in each cluster*			
	Cluster 1: reactive in slow motion	*Cluster 2: alive & kicking*	*Cluster 3: followers*	*P-value**
Which of the following profile participate to the CMC: Other	0.22	0.17	0.13	0.017
Finance	0.27	0.27	0.13	0.000
Education	0.13	0.08	0.17	0.051
IT	0.09	0.10	0.04	0.056
Industry	0.08	0.16	0.11	0.019
State/public administration	0.06	0.01	0.03	0.033
Size: Up to 9 people	0.15	0.16	0.24	0.014

*All the comparisons are statistically significant with respect to the significance level of 0.1.

BCM was not required. As micro firms are most concentrated in this cluster, it seems that very small firms did not see any advantage of having a BCP/BCM, since it is possible to manage small teams flexibly. The larger the organisation, the lower the inherent flexibility, and, therefore, the greater the need for a BCP/BCM.

The role of the crisis management committee (CMC) is the most visible in the case of cluster 2, with high-level solid management participation. Again, the "followers" cluster lagged behind the other two groups. With regard to the sectors, one can observe that financial entities are mostly present in clusters 1 and 2, with education in cluster 3. This partially explains the differences between the identified groups.

5.6 Conclusions

Aware of the limitations of our survey results due to the limited size of the global sample, we claim that BCPs were not a widespread feature of our global sample before the pandemic (47% of the sample did not have one) nor was the pandemic likely to be included in the BCPs that were in place. As expected, BCPs were more common in the financial sector (77% of the sample) given the regulatory requirements that characterise this industry. Having a BCP in place before the pandemic was helpful for swiftly reacting to the extreme event of COVID-19 and operating through the storm smoothly. Remote work was not a widespread feature before the pandemic; however, most organisations (with or without a BCP) were able to quickly shift to this new mode of working. This made it possible to continue business (not as usual) but with the majority of critical processes being managed for more than 92% of the sample.

Entities covered by our survey represented different features in a BCP/BCM – from leaders ("Alive and kicking", cluster 2) to the ones lagging behind ("Followers", or "Late risers", cluster 3). Leaders managed to adjust smoothly to operating in a pandemic environment and keeping their critical processes alive to the largest extent. High-level management was involved in crisis management with a crisis management committee in place, which shows that BCP/BCM had the highest priority in their case. Referring to the title of this chapter, entities from cluster 2 had both a proper life jacket and a captain. Entities from cluster 1 may be described as having a reasonable life jacket, but they were worse prepared for tail events with lower involvement of top management. Organisations from cluster 3 either had a faulty life jacket or none at all and, therefore, had to follow the practice of other organisations to continue their operations. Some of them learnt the lesson that a BCP/BCM is necessary, so they may be better prepared for the next tail event. In all cases, however, life jackets should be frequently checked with regard to their usefulness.

Notes

1 We extend a special thanks to Oliviero Roggi and Viktor Elliot, who joined us on the survey and took the lead on the Brazilian and Swedish markets. They did not, however, participate in the preparation of this work. We would also like to thank our social network for supporting the distribution of the survey, especially Gustavo Barboza and Viktor Trynchuk. A special thanks goes to Francesco Ricciutelli for his invaluable work of data processing and presentation, and Gianluca Baglini for data cleaning and database creation.
2 See Chartered Global Management Accountant website (https://www.cgma.org/).
3 ISO 22301–2019 Social Security – Business continuity management systems – requirements specify "*requirements to plan, establish, implement, operate, monitor, review, maintain and continually improve a documented management system to protect against, reduce the likelihood of occurrence, prepare for, respond to, and recover from disruptive incidents when they arise*".
4 Most of the questionnaire items were coded in ordinal or nominal scale.
5 In our case, we used a "bottom-up" approach – each observation starts in its cluster, and pairs of groups are merged as one moves up the hierarchy.
6 The Silhouette Index (SI) contrasts cohesion within clusters and separation between clusters by comparing the similarity of each instance to its own cluster and to other clusters. The synthetic measure is generally used to rank different partitions of clusters.
7 The one-way analysis of variance (ANOVA) is used to determine whether there are any statistically significant differences between the means of three or more independent (unrelated) groups. The null hypothesis tested suggested that mean values from different groups are equal. The F-test was used for the analysis.

References

Airmic A. I. (2002). *A Risk Management Standard*. Institute of Risk Management, Association of Insurance and Risk Managers, Brussels.

Benzècri J. (1973). *Analyse des Donnèes*, Dunod, Paris.

Burtles J., Noakes-Fry K. (2016). *Principles and Practice of Business Continuity: Tools and Techniques*, Second Edition. Rothstein Publishing, Brookfield, CT.

Cerullo V., Cerullo M.J. (2006). Business Continuity Planning: A Comprehensive Approach. *Information Systems Management* 21(3), 70–78.

Clark R. A. (2016). *Business Continuity and the Pandemic Threat. Potentially the Biggest Survival Challenge Facing Organisations*. IT Governance Publishing, Cambridgeshire.

Clayton M. (2019). "What Is a Business Continuity Plan? PM in Under 5". https://www.youtube.com/watch?v=G9JANBmTdqA.

Greenacre M. (1984). *Theory and Applications of Correspondence Analysis*, Academic Press, New York.

Herbane B. (2010). "The Evolution of Business Continuity Management: A Historical Review of Practices and Drivers". *Business History Journal*, 52, 978–1002.

Hiles A. (ed.). (2007). *The definitive handbook of business continuity management* (2nd ed.), Wiley, London.

Ketchen D. J., Shook C. L. (1996). "The Application of Cluster Analysis in Strategic Management Research: An Analysis and Critique". *Strategy Management Journal* 17, 441–458.

Lebart L., Morineau A., Wardwick K. M. (1984). *Multivariate Descriptive Statistical Analysis*. Wiley, New York.

Nocco B. W., Stulz R.M. (2006). "Enterprise Risk Management: Theory and Practice". *Journal of Applied Corporate Finance* 18, 8–20. doi:10.1111/j.1745-6622.2006.00106.x

Rezaei S. H., Torabi S.A., Sahebjamnia N. (2019). Developing a novel quantitative framework for business continuity planning, International Journal of Production Research, vol. 57, issue 3, p. 779–800.

Roggi O. (2015). *Risk, Value and Default.* World Scientific Press Singapore 2015 ISBN: 9789814641715, doi:10.1142/9430

Rousseeuw P. J. (1986). "A visual display for hierarchical classification". In *Data Analysis and Informatics*, Diday E., Escoufier Y., Lebart L., Pages J., Schektman Y., Tomassone R., Eds.; North-Holland: Amsterdam, Vol. 4, 743–748.

Shimpi P. (2002). "Integrating Risk Management and Capital Management". *Journal of Applied Corporate Finance* 14, 27–40. doi:10.1111/j.1745-6622.2002.tb00446.x

Smith M., Sherwoord J. (1995). "Business Continuity Planning". *Computers and Security* 14(1), 14–23.

Tenenhaus M., Young F. W. (1985). "An Analysis and Synthesis of Multiple Correspondence Analysis, Optimal Scaling, Dual Scaling, Homogeneity Analysis and Others Methods for Quantifying Categorical Multivariate Data". *Psychometrikas* 50, 91–119.

Ward J. H., Jr. (1963). "Hierarchical Grouping to Optimize an Objective Function". *Journal of the American Statistical Association* 58, 236–244.

Williams T. A., Gruber D. A., Sutcliffe K. M., Shepherd D. A., Zhao E. Y. (2017). "Organisational Response to Adversity: Fusing Crisis Management and Resilience Research Streams". *Academy of Management Annals* 11(2), 733–769.

Annex

Table A.5.1 Geographical distribution of the sample organisations

Geographical location of responding organisations	*All*	*Italy*	*Poland*	*Brazil*	*Sweden*	*HI countries*	*MI countries*	*LI countries*
EU countries	667	125	244		177	659	8	
Other European countries	64					23	41	
African countries	3					1	1	1
Asian countries	22					7	15	
North/Central American countries	48					40	8	
South American countries	120			107		1	119	
Australia and Oceania	0							
Total	924	125	244	107	177	731	192	1

Table A.5.2 Sectoral distribution of the sample organisations

Sector field	*All*	*Italy*	*Poland*	*Brazil*	*Sweden*	*HI countries*	*MI countries*	*LI countries*
Finance	222	40	79	14	19	184	37	1
Healthcare	33	6	11	5	5	28	5	
Education	124	15	42	12	7	93	31	
IT	74	10	16	8	15	64	10	
Commerce	70	5	13	13	21	49	21	
Other services	176	17	37	35	50	129	47	
Industry	92	10	16	15	21	66	26	
State/public admin	42	5	14	0	7	40	2	
Other	91	17	16	5	32	78	13	
Total	924	125	244	107	177	731	192	1

Table A.5.3 Size of the sample organisations

Size (no. employees)	*All*	*Italy*	*Poland*	*Brazil*	*Sweden*	*HI countries*	*MI countries*	*LI countries*
Up to 9 people	159	19	30	17	43	129	30	
10 to 49 people	189	22	45	21	53	146	43	
50 to 249 people	180	17	45	38	42	132	48	
250 people and more	396	67	124	31	39	324	72	1
Total	924	125	244	107	177	731	193	1

Table A.5.4 International network of the sample organisations

International scope	*All*	*Italy*	*Poland*	*Brazil*	*Sweden*	*HI countries*	*MI countries*	*LI countries*
Yes_parent of international group	131	27	25	4	43	117	14	
Yes_subsidiary/ branch of intl group	166	20	58	2	53	154	12	
No	627	78	161	101	42	460	166	1
Total	924	125	244	107	138	731	192	1

6 The COVID-19 loan moratorium and SMEs' liquidity shortfall[1]

Paola Brighi and Sabrina Severini

6.1 Introduction

Since the spring of 2020, policies aimed at restricting the spread of COVID-19 have required many small- and medium-sized enterprises (SMEs) throughout entire sectors of the economy to stop their activities while lockdowns and travel-related restrictions have severely limited global economies. As a result, many SMEs are sustaining losses that may threaten their survival. Such SMEs are particularly important to the Italian economy, accounting for over 13 million employees and 78% of all employment (ISTAT 2019).

Governments introduced multiple relief measures to support SMEs during the most severe moments of the health crisis. Among other measures, these efforts included a moratorium on loan repayments which worked to mitigate liquidity shortfalls among SMEs and households. Italian Decree-Law 18/2020 of 17 March 2020 (hereafter referred to as DL/18), specifically stated that micro-, small- and medium-sized enterprises[2] suffering temporary liquidity shortfalls due to the COVID-19 epidemic could defer interest and principal payments on loans. The Decree also suspended the revoking of credit lines, even if unused.

Unlike past negative events, such as the 2008 Global Financial Crisis or 2010 Sovereign Debt Crisis, the economic impacts of the COVID-19 pandemic were driven by factors external to the financial system itself. Thus, rather than being a cause, the banking system might be seen as offering solutions to the pandemic situation in terms of sustaining the economy and SMEs in particular. To this end, the Italian government has supported credit channels with public and private guarantee schemes. At the same time, monetary authorities like the European Central Bank (ECB) have bolstered the economy by continuing an accommodative monetary policy. With this in mind, the study aims to investigate whether the moratorium measures introduced by the Italian government have helped mitigate the financial liquidity needs which SMEs have experienced due to the coronavirus pandemic.

Our results suggest that the moratorium has reduced temporary financial stress among firms due to the pandemic emergency. The evidence also indicates that loan characteristics (such as maturity or the existence of guarantees) and bank-firm relationship conditions (such as duration, intensity and exclusivity) affect the link between moratoriums and liquidity needs. Our study reveals that financial stress

DOI: 10.4324/9781003310754-6

has been significantly alleviated for SMEs which are larger and at lower risk and have a well-established relationship with a bank (e.g., SMEs that have a high-debt concentration with one bank and a low number of overall bank relationships) and personal guarantees in place. The rest of this chapter is organised as follows: Section 6.2 reviews the national measures taken to alleviate SME liquidity shortfalls during the COVID-19 crisis. Section 6.3 then reviews the relevant literature. Section 6.4 presents the data and methodology used in the analysis. Section 6.5 considers the main findings and Section 6.6 presents the conclusions.

6.2 Government policy measures in response to COVID-19

Italian SMEs mainly resort to bank loans in terms of financing resources, and bank debt comprised 66.2% of financial liabilities among businesses in the country in 2020 (Annual Report of the Bank of Italy 2021). Given this situation, national policymakers introduced numerous measures to ensure that firms had sustainable debt burdens and less restrictive liquidity pressures in the wake of the COVID-19 crisis. A summary of the main policy measures which have targeted Italian SMEs are discussed below.

First, DL/18 introduced a loan moratorium for SMEs which employ fewer than 250 persons or have an annual turnover not exceeding €50 million and/or an annual balance sheet of under €43 million. To be eligible for the moratorium, companies had to be performing, i.e., without any impaired debt positions.[3] Given this, government public-guarantee approval is automatic. However, companies are required to submit a self-declaration stating that they have had temporary liquidity shortfalls as a result of COVID-19 impacts. Banks, and all other entities authorised to grant credit in Italy, must accept moratorium requests if the requirements laid down in DL/18 are met. Furthermore, additional voluntary moratorium schemes have been established by the Italian Banking Association (IBA) alongside the targeted ones offered by individual banks.

DL 18/2020 (known also as *DL Cura Italia*) specifically established the following measures in relation to loans granted by banks, financial intermediaries and other entities authorised to provide credit in Italy: (a) partly or entirely unused lines of credit (*aperture di credito*) and loans granted against advances on receivables (*i prestiti accordati a fronte di anticipi su crediti esistenti*) in existence as of 29 February 2020 or the decree date (if later) could not be partially or entirely revoked until 30 September 2020; (b) non-instalment loans expiring before 30 September 2020 were extended under the same conditions without any formalities, along with their related additional elements, until 30 September 2020; (c) mortgages and other instalment-based loan payments, including those linked to agricultural bills, or payments and leasing fees due before 30 September 2020, were suspended until 30 September 2020. Concurrently, instalments or fee payments and their related additional elements subject to suspension were also extended under existing conditions. This was done in a way that did not create greater burdens for either party while businesses had the option of requesting suspension of principal repayments only. The above measures were not applicable to businesses carrying existing debt classified as impaired credit (*credito deteriorato*) according to the relevant regulations for financial intermediaries.

Second, Italian Decree-Law 23/2020 (also known as the 'Liquidity Law Decree' and hereafter referred to as DL/23) aimed to strengthen the Central Guarantee Fund (hereafter referred to as CGF) with the aim of promoting access to credit for a broad range of SMEs. The maximum guaranteed amount for this access was, in fact, increased to €5 million and companies with up to 499 employees were able to access the Fund. The percentage of direct coverage was increased to at least 90% of all loans of up to six years, with the possibility of reaching 100% of all loans if certain conditions were met. Access to the Fund was also granted to beneficiaries who have exposures which the bank may have classified as 'unlikely to pay' or 'past due or impaired/overdue' on the request date, provided that this rating was given after 31 January 2020 or some conditions were met for performing loans.

DL/23 introduced three main loan thresholds: (a) 100% guaranteed loans of up to €30,000 were made available to SMEs; (b) the Fund guaranteed 90% of loans over €30,000 for companies with up to 499 employees cost-free (with a limit of €5 million per company remaining in place); (c) if companies with revenues of up to €3.2 million submitted to the bank a self-certification of negative business impacts due to COVID-19, they could obtain a 100% guarantee. Ninety percent of this would be issued by the state and the remaining 10% by a third party (e.g., *Confidi*). For loans that did not meet the Decree's requirements in terms of time (the six-year limit) or amount, firms could still get an 80% guarantee combinable with the guarantees issued by Confidi. Guarantees for larger firms were granted by the Italian Special Section for Export Credit Insurance (SACE) and involved coverage of 70–90% (with the amount adjusted to firm size).

6.3 Literature review

Recent literature on bank-borrower relationships emphasises the importance of small, more tightly structured ones with fewer managerial layers and how a relationship-banking model reduces information problems in small-firm finance (Agostino and Trivieri 2018, Dwenger et al. 2020, McNamara 2020). Since SMEs are financially more opaque than larger firms, they may be more financially constrained (Berger and Udell 1995, 2002). From a theoretical point of view, this lack of transparency implies that banks have more difficulties verifying the quality of SME project investments (an adverse-selection effect) as well as their willingness to repay loans or divert resources to riskier, alternative projects (a moral hazard effect). These features may undermine lending by financial institutions that engage in impersonal or arms-length financing processes based mainly on hard, objective and transparent information. In contrast, the SME business model may be better suited to dynamics involving small banks engaging in relationship-based lending processes.

Cooperative banks are highly representative of small banks in Italy. They are non-profit, cooperative, financial institutions governed by their membership on a one-member-one-vote basis with eligibility for membership being determined on the basis of a common bond with the bank. Cooperative banks are characterised by their small size, self-governance and principles of mutuality. That is, their activity favours members and the moral, cultural and economic development of the local community. They are not profit-seeking institutions and mainly aim to maximise member welfare via a cost-minimizing policy and a relationship-based business model (Bernini and Brighi 2018, Coccorese and Shaffer 2021).

Relationship lending is often based on soft data that is difficult to quantify, verify and communicate through the normal transmission channels of a banking organisation. It is also associated with a fundamentally different lending process compared to transaction-based lending technologies, which may be highly relevant to SMEs and strongly affect their financing choices (Iturralde et al. 2010, Dwenger et al. 2020). On one hand, relationship lending relies on soft information gathered on the customer's business behaviour. The main empirical literature (see, among others, Degryse and Van Cayseele 2000, Elsas 2005 and Banerjee et al. 2021) suggests the most common variables used to capture the bank-firm relationship derived from the bank's accumulated borrower history information (see, for example, Petersen and Rajan 1994 and Berger and Udell 1995). The relationship is facilitated if it is renewed and continuous over time. Empirical studies have measured the strength of relationship banking across three dimensions of the bank-firm link: (i) duration or how long the bank and the firm have been working together; (ii) breadth of relationship measured in terms of the different services the firm purchases from the bank; and (iii) concentration or the number of bank relationships that exist. Based on these variables, a stronger relationship is linked to longer duration and if a firm uses a large number of services from the same bank. Alternatively, the relationship is weaker if the firm interacts with more banks.

6.4 Data and methodology

6.4.1 Sampling and data set

In order to analyse the impact of moratorium measures on financial stress and liquidity flows in SMEs, we draw on a proprietary database from banks on lending positions. The study sample consists of unbalanced panel data for 1,958 SMEs, tracked over eight quarters from 31 March 2018 to 31 December 2020. In addition to internal bank data, other data were obtained from the Bank of Italy's Central Credit Register and the Bureau Van Dijk AIDA database.

Table 6.1 shows the final sample organised by size into three subgroups according to the European Commission thresholds (Commission Recommendation 2003/361/EC). Within the SME category, the EC defines micro-enterprises as having an annual turnover under €2 million, small enterprises under €10 million and medium-sized enterprises under €50 million. Our sample consists primarily of micro firms.

Table 6.1 SME sample distribution by size according to criteria set out in recommendation 2003/361/EC

	Percentage	*Median turnover*
Micro [Turnover ≤ 2 m]	66.72	523,000
Small [2 < Turnover < 10 m]	23.90	3,948,000
Medium & Large [Turnover ≥ 10 m]	9.38	16,455,000
Total	100	

6.4.2 Variables and research model

We employ a financial stress indicator in formulating a dependent variable for capturing firm liquidity needs and identifying potential liquidity shortfalls. From an operational point of view, this is a widely used indicator within the Italian banking system. It is also included in the Central Credit Register of the Bank of Italy and is a useful measure for assessing creditworthiness. A particularly high value for this indicator may affect access to credit as well as the conditions under which credit will be granted. We define this variable as follows:

$$\text{Financial}_{\text{stress}} = \frac{\text{Credit used} - \text{Credit granted}}{\text{Credit granted}} \tag{6.1}$$

Equation (6.1)[4] identifies the share of credit provided by the bank on the basis of the total credit lines for each firm in the sample at the end of each quarter. It is further defined as the ratio between the overdue credit (*sconfinato*) in relation to the credit granted by the bank (*accordato*), or rather the maximum amount available to meet the firm's financial needs (Busetta and Sacco 2001, Russo and Rossi 2001, Beretta and Del Prete 2013; Ongena et al. 2021).[5]

Turning to the independent variables used in the model, the main variable of interest is *Moratorium*. To account for this supportive measure, we define a dummy variable equal to 1 if the loan is subject to a moratorium and 0 if not. Since a moratorium *leads* to the suspension of loan payments to banks, firms find themselves with greater available liquidity. As a result, we expect that liquidity shortfalls (captured by the financial stress variable) will diminish with payment deferral. We also control for the firm's creditworthiness by adding a dummy variable (*Rating*) equal to 1 if the firm's risk class is greater than 4 (out of a range of 1–13 for low- to high-risk firms, respectively). The need to mitigate credit risks in a context of uncertainty and meet capital requirements has led to an increase in guaranteed loans, potentially undermining firm performance (Mayordomo et al. 2021). This is controlled for by introducing three specific variables. The *Personal_g* variable controls for whether the owner takes personal responsibility in the event of a company default. *Real_g* (*Special_g*) identifies the relationship between credit granted and the degree of collateral (special guarantee) coverage with respect to the credit amount granted (Brighi et al. 2019). The literature suggests mixed results with reference to these kinds of variables. On one hand, the bank can exploit the guarantee in the event of default. In this sense, the larger the guarantee, the better the firm's evaluation. On the other hand, a moral hazard effect may emerge since a riskier borrower may put up more personal and real goods as a loan guarantee since financed projects are riskier. We also consider loan characteristics by adding a *Maturity* variable and its square root (*Maturity_sqrt*) to control for the potential nonlinear effects of this factor.

As our sample consists mainly of SMEs, we borrowed a series of control variables from the relationship-based lending literature (see, for example, Degryse and Van Cayseele 2000). In particular, we add the number of banks a firm interacts with (*M_lending*) in order to investigate how the strength of the bank-firm relationship may affect the firm's liquidity needs. The literature is not uniform here. Multiple lending relationships may exacerbate the risk of liquidity shortfalls. However, exclusive relationships may give the bank an information advantage implying the risk of hold-ups on the borrower side. On the other hand, it may provide an opportunity for a sort of liquidity guarantee during crisis periods (e.g., as noted, among others, by Bhattacharya and Chiesa 1995 and Boot and Thakor 2000). To assess if this relationship persists over time, or is only transactional, we introduce a *Duration* variable defined as the number of days between opening a line of credit and the reference period. This variable is useful for testing the effects of the length of the relationship between the bank and firm and the probability of making the right decision during the loan evaluation process.

In this sense, in-depth knowledge of the customer resulting from a long-standing relationship could facilitate correct decision making by the bank (Ongena and Smith 2001, López-Espinosa et al. 2017). Conversely, if a bank uses an ongoing relationship with the borrower to accumulate private information, it could also translate into an informational advantage for the bank. They might then use this data to charge the borrower higher interest rates (see among others, Hale and Santos 2009 and Ioannidou and Ongena 2010). Moreover, to capture the idea that the accumulated information processes can follow a variable path over time (Diamond 1991, Berger and Udell 1995), the model also includes the square root of the duration of the bank-firm relationship or *Duration_sqr* (Berger and Udell 1995, Diamond 1991).

Another measure used in the literature to assess the intensity of bank-borrower relationships is the number of interactions that occur with the same customer around different products (Boot 2000). In this respect, we consider the overall number of links that the customer has with the loan institution (*Intensity*). We also consider the relevance of single-bank financing within the banking system through an *Exclusivity* variable or the ratio of credit granted by one bank versus by the overall banking system. As the degree of concentrated activity in banks increases, they may pay more attention to making the right decisions. However, as outlined in the literature, these decisions are also affected by bank exposure with respect to the client. Greater bank exposure can lead a bank to soft-budget constraints risk, that is, banks may provide liquidity insurance to firms when there is an unexpected deterioration in a borrower's rating (Elsas and Krahnen, 1998; Boot 2000, Avramidis et al. 2022).

In this respect, the expected sign or nature of impact is difficult to predict. In terms of the number of bank relationships, the *M_lending* variable tests whether the number of banking relationships may affect the probability of being more resilient both financially and liquidity-wise. The literature is not uniform in this regard. Multiple lending relationships can exacerbate the risk of liquidity shortfalls. At the same time, exclusive relationships give the bank an information advantage implying the risk of potential hold-ups on the borrower side. However, it also creates an opportunity for receiving a kind of liquidity guarantee during crisis periods (e.g., see, among others, Bhattacharya and Chiesa 1995 and Boot and Thakor 2000).

An additional measure used in the literature to assess the intensity of the relationship between banks and borrowers is one that captures 'multiple interactions with the same customer over time and/or across products' (Boot 2000). In this respect, an *Intensity* variable is logarithmically formulated to measure the number of operations associated with every customer. On one hand, this variable can be considered a proxy for a repeated relationship with the same customers and thus, can serve as a tool for reducing information asymmetry. On the other hand, the variable can also be considered a proxy for the dynamic commercial attitudes of SMEs which may want to shop for different types of lending products. Alternatively, it may also capture the cross-selling pressure exerted by banks on customers. All in all, the *Intensity* variable may be expected to negatively affect financial and liquidity pressure.

In order to analyse the relationship between the proximity of a firm's headquarters to a main bank branch, a geographical, categorical, distance variable was introduced (*Geo_proximity*). The Zone 1 category indicates a distance of under 20 km between the firm headquarters and the area covered by a main bank, the Zone 2 category a distance of 50 km and the Zone 3 category a distance over 50 km away. The literature suggests that the greater the physical (Degryse and Ongena 2005), functional (Alessandrini et al. 2009) and hierarchical distance (Stein 2002) between a firm's headquarters and bank branch, the greater the difficulty in getting access to bank financing. This is particularly the case with small local banks. Here, distance also exacerbates bank cost efficiencies which appear to increase with firm-bank distance (Bernini and Brighi 2018). Finally, we control for firm *Size* using the total turnover in the prior accounting period as a proxy for size (Cowling and Westhead 1996, Cenni *et al.* 2015, Brighi et al. 2019).

Our empirical investigation relies on panel regression using a Random-effect (RE) model. According to Nwakuya and Ijomah (2017), a key 'advantage of random effects is that you can include time-invariant variables'. Given their nature, fixed-effect models appear less suitable in this context since they do not estimate the effects of such variables (Bell et al. 2019, Nwakuya and Ijomah 2017, Mohammad et al. 2020). In this chapter, the use of RE is specifically motivated by the time-invariant variables used in the modelling, namely Size and Geo-proximity. The panel-data regression model was precisely specified as:

$$y_{it} = \mu + x'_{it}\beta + z'_{i}\gamma + \varepsilon_{it} + \alpha_{i} \tag{6.2}$$

Table 6.2 Variables definition

Variable	*Definition*	*Measure*	*Expected sign*
Dependent variables			
Financial_stress	Degree of credit overdue with respect to the amount of credit granted	$\frac{\text{Credit used} - \text{Credit granted}}{\text{Credit granted}}$	
Independent variables			
Moratorium	Variable that accounts for having a credit moratorium granted	Dummy variable = 1 if the credit is subject to a moratorium, 0 if not.	Negative
Rating	Risk class of the firm	Dummy variable = 1 if greater than risk class 4	Positive
Personal_g	Amount covered by personal guarantees on the credit granted	$\frac{\text{Peronal guarantees}}{\text{Credit granted}}$	Positive/Negative
Real_g	Amount covered by collateral on the credit granted	$\frac{\text{Collateral}}{\text{Credit granted}}$	Positive/Negative
Special_g	Amount covered by special guarantees on the credit granted	$\frac{\text{Special guarantees}}{\text{Credit granted}}$	Positive/Negative
Maturity	Credit residual period	Number of days between the period of reference and the credit maturity date.	Positive
Maturity_sqrt	Square root of Maturity	Controls for the potential nonlinear effects of Maturity.	Positive/Negative
M_lending	Number of banks with which the company operates	Number of banks with which the company operates.	Positive/Negative
Duration	Duration of the bank-borrower relationship	Number of days between the opening a line of credit and the period of reference.	Positive/Negative
Duration_sqr	Square root of Duration	Controls for the potential nonlinear effects of duration on relationship lending.	Positive/Negative
Intensity	Proxy for the intensity of the bank-firm relationship	Number of bank relationships that the borrower has with the institution.	Positive/Negative
Exclusivity	Degree of bank-firm relationship	Continuous variable calculated as the ratio between the credit agreed with the bank and the amount of credit agreed by the total banking system.	Positive/Negative

(*Continued*)

Table 6.2 (Continued)

Variable	*Definition*	*Measure*	*Expected sign*
Geo_proximity	Geographical area of operations of borrower and bank branch geo-localisation	A categorical variable with the value of zone 1 if bank is in a municipality within 20 km of firm headquarters, zone 2 within a distance of 50 km (Geo_proximity_2), zone 3 at a distance greater than 50 km (Geo_proximity_3).	Positive
Size	Proxy to account for the firm size	Logarithm of the Turnover.	Negative

where y_{it} is the dependent variable; μ is the intercept; x'_{it} is a K-dimensional row vector of time-varying explanatory variables; β is a K-dimensional column vector of parameters; z'_i is a M-dimensional row vector of time-invariant explanatory variables excluding the constant; γ is a M-dimensional column vector of parameters; ε_{it} is the error term; α_i is the *RE* $N\left(0;\sigma_{\alpha}^{2}\right)$.

6.5 Results

6.5.1 Descriptive data analysis

Table 6.3 presents the descriptive statistics for the overall sample. Less than 20% of the sample on average shows a value for the Moratorium variable and approximately 60% reflect a moderate or high level of risk. In relation to credit granted, loans are mostly backed by personal guarantees. This evidence is in line with Mayordomo et al. (2021), who find that personal guarantees are more often used than collateral. On average, the residual maturity of the loan is greater than 5 years with a maximum of 24 years. For the relationship lending variables, descriptive statistics appear to be in line with the literature (see, among others, Agostino and Trivieri 2018, Dwenger et al. 2020, Mc Namara 2020, Hussain et al. 2021). Each firm in our sample was borrowing from three banks on average via different relationships (M_lending). The overall Duration of the relationship shows a mean value of slightly over eight years, which implies that the sample is characterised by a long banking relationship duration. The number of relationships a firm undertakes with a bank (Intensity) is three on average while the median percentage of debt held by the main bank is 38.3% (Exclusivity). The credit relationships considered were mainly in Zone 1 or between firms and bank branches which were geographically closer. The Size variable shows that the average turnover of firms is less than €7 million, confirming the sample is made up of small enterprises.

Table 6.3 Summary statistics

	mean	*p50*	*sd*	*min*	*max*
Rating	0.588	1.000	0.492	0.000	1.000
Personal_g (%)	1.347	0.434	3.074	0.000	50.400
Real_g (%)	1.362	0.000	6.928	0.000	272.000
Special_g (%)	0.026	0.000	0.160	0.000	2.568
Maturity	2,076.914	1,507	1,731.259	0.000	8,952
Maturity_sqrt	41.603	38.852	18.725	0.000	94.615
M_lending	3.542	2.000	4.171	1.000	69.000
Duration	3,095.423	1,978	2,956.444	2.000	16439
Duration_sqrt	49.898	44.475	24.611	1.414	128.215
Intensity	3.593	3.000	2.507	1.000	23.000
Exclusivity (%)	0.393	0.383	0.354	0.000	1.000
Geo_proximity_1	0.585	1.000	0.492	0.000	1.000
Geo_proximity_2	0.224	0.000	0.417	0.000	1.000
Geo_proximity_3	0.190	0.000	0.392	0.000	1.000
Size (M)	6.889	6.901	1.798	0.000	13.356

Note: Moratorium is a dummy variable that equals 1 if credit is subject to a moratorium, 0 if not.; Rating is a dummy variable equal to 1 if risk class is greater than 4; Personal_g is the percentage of credit covered by personal guarantees in relation to the credit granted; Real_g is the percentage of credit covered by collateral in relation to the credit granted; Special_g is the percentage of credit covered by special guarantees in relation to the credit granted; Maturity represents the credit residual period; Maturity_sqrt is the square root of Maturity; M_lending is the number of banks with which the company operates; Duration captures the duration of the bank-borrower relationship; Duration_sqrt is the square root of the Duration variable; Intensity is the number of bank relationships that the borrower has with the institution; Exclusivity is a continuous variable calculated as the ratio between the credit granted with the bank and the amount of credit granted by the total banking system; Geo_proximity is a categorical variable equal to 1, 2 and 3 depending on the distance from the municipality of company operations to the bank headquarters (city). Zone 1 identifies the headquarter city and neighbouring municipalities; Size is the logarithm of turnover.

6.5.2 *Empirical findings*

This section presents the empirical results of the panel regression data with a RE model. This model is used to investigate how the financial measures introduced under DL/18 and the interest moratorium may have effectively reduced liquidity shortfalls among SMEs. Table 6.4 presents the resulting estimates according to different models. Model (1) is the baseline model showing how the *Moratorium* variable and SME risk level could impact potential liquidity shortfalls. Model (2) adds another set of variables to Model (1) to control for loan characteristics, i.e., if there are any guarantees and loan maturity. Model (3) adds a set of relationship-based lending variables to Model (1). Finally, Model (4) combines Models (2) and (3).

The results of Model (1) suggest that COVID-19-related government financing measures play an important role in supporting SME liquidity needs. In particular, we find that the introduction of the *Moratorium* variable reduces financial stress by about 2%. Moreover, the higher the client risk level, the greater the liquidity needs. The regression results for Model (2) show that personal guarantees have a negative effect on the dependent variable while collateral has a positive one. This mixed evidence supports the lively debate in the literature concerning the role of guarantees.

Table 6.4 Empirical results

	Dependent variable: financial_stress			
	(1)	*(2)*	*(3)*	*(4)*
	Baseline	*Guarantees*	*Relationship lending*	*Overall*
Moratorium	−0.0226***	−0.0312***	−0.0235***	−0.0183*
	(−4.67)	(−4.16)	(−3.74)	(−1.90)
Rating	0.0391***	0.0246**	0.0364***	0.0102
	(5.91)	(2.08)	(4.48)	(0.70)
Personal_g		−0.0177***		−0.0201***
		(−5.40)		(−5.15)
Real_g		0.00578***		0.00333
		(2.98)		(1.46)
Special_g		−0.0723		−0.143**
		(−1.24)		(−2.01)
Maturity		0.000119***		0.000108***
		(5.72)		(4.34)
Maturity_sqrt		−0.0123***		−0.0135***
		(−7.98)		(−7.42)
M_lending			0.00914***	0.0161***
			(4.74)	(2.80)
Duration			−0.0000245***	0.0000798
			(−2.87)	(1.23)
Duration_sqrt			0.00172*	−0.00692
			(1.85)	(−1.25)
Intensity			−0.0000453	−0.00462
			(−0.03)	(−0.94)
Exclusivity			−0.275***	−0.329***
			(−8.97)	(−4.26)
Geo_proximity_2			−0.0197	0.0352
			(−0.82)	(0.66)
Geo_proximity_3			−0.0340	−0.111
			(−1.31)	(−1.61)
Size			−0.0284***	−0.0663***
			(−4.14)	
_cons	0.669***	1.040***	0.979***	1.835***
	(75.11)	(28.87)	(18.12)	(10.46)
N	9111	1726	6907	1241
r2	0.0560	0.0539	0.0690	0.120

Notes: *significant at 10% level; **significant at 5% level; ***significant at 1% level; *t* statistics in parentheses.

Moratorium is a dummy variable that equals 1 if credit is subject to a moratorium, 0 if not.; Rating is a dummy variable equal to 1 if risk class is greater than 4; Personal_g is the percentage of credit covered by personal guarantees in relation to the credit granted; Real_g is the percentage of credit covered by collateral in relation to the credit granted; Special_g is the percentage of credit covered by special guarantees in relation to the credit granted; Maturity represents the credit residual period; Maturity_sqrt is the square root of Maturity; M_lending is the number of banks with which the company operates; Duration captures the duration of the bank-borrower relationship; Duration_sqrt is the square root of the Duration variable; Intensity is the number of bank relationships that the borrower has with the institution; Exclusivity is a continuous variable calculated as the ratio between the credit granted with the bank and the amount of credit granted by the total banking system; Geo_proximity is a categorical variable equal to 1, 2 and 3 depending on the distance from the municipality of company operations to the bank headquarters (city). Zone 1 identifies the headquarter city and neighbouring municipalities; Size is the logarithm of turnover.

In general, if the loan is backed by personal guarantees, the liability of the firm may become limitless. As a result, if transparent information is lacking, personal guarantees could serve to reduce risk-taking since they imply substantial exposure on the part of the firm owners or managers (Mayordomo et al. 2021). With respect to *Maturity*, it is quite evident that longer maturity is riskier for the bank since as time increases, the probability that a borrower's risk profile may worsen also increases, potentially giving rise to opportunistic behaviour. However, the statistical significance of the *Maturity_sqrt* variable suggests this type of path is not straight forward.

In Model (3), the positive effect of *M_lending* and *Intensity*, and the negative effect of *Duration*, show that in the event of liquidity shortfalls, it pays to be an exclusive and long-term customer. Moreover, this analysis suggests that public measures supporting liquidity shortfalls work better for larger firms. The results of Model (4) only confirm the previous findings. As such, the outcomes remain almost unchanged after jointly controlling for loan characteristic and relationship lending variables. In this context, it should be noted that the relationship lending variables become largely insignificant implying that other variables drive the results. While it is true that moratoriums were granted to customers classified as performing, there was some migration in the last quarter of 2020 from Stage 1 to Stage 2 (EBA 2021), making it difficult to assess the real extent of losses until the moratoriums are resolved. However, as our evidence shows, the policy response has been effective in achieving its short-term objectives.

6.6 Conclusions

This chapter investigates the vulnerability of Italian SMEs in terms of their liquidity needs during the COVID-19 crisis. The large decline in activity associated with quarantine measures generated widespread liquidity shortfalls, potentially leading to a wave of defaults among otherwise viable businesses. In an attempt to avert such economic disaster, policymakers have taken a wide range of actions to mitigate the risk of a liquidity crisis, including policies aimed at delaying financial obligations. These measures have included loan moratoriums which defer interest and principal payments or suspending the revocation of undrawn credit lines. Results suggest that these public interventions have been successful in easing the liquidity needs of SMEs. This is particularly true in the case of firms which have a higher standing (i.e., lower risk), larger size, personal guarantees in play, a strong relationship-based lending history (or a long-term bank-firm relationship), high-debt concentration with one bank and a low number of overall bank relationships.

Notes

1 We would like to thank Prof. Jan Szambelańczyk and the meeting participants at the 2021 Wolpertinger Conference on Banking and Finance for their helpful comments. We especially thank Prof. Paul Wachtel for his suggestions. The usual disclaimers apply. The authors contributed equally to this study.

2 DL/18 applies also to households with mortgages of < €400 k on their primary residence, individuals who are laid off for 30 days or more or self-employed persons who

have experienced a 33% or more fall in turnover. Since December 2020, the coverage threshold was reduced to mortgages < €250,000 and having an Equivalent Economic Situation Indicator (*indicatore della situazione economica equivalente*/ISEE) of under €30,000.

3 According to IFRS 9 nomenclature, this means that companies must belong to the Stage 1 bucket. IFRS 9 defines three stages of impairment: Stage 1 means credit risk has not increased significantly since initial recognition; Stage 2 means credit risk has increased significantly since initial recognition. Stage 3 means a financial asset is credit impaired. This is effectively the point when an incurred loss event occurs under the IAS 39 model.

4 To account for the potential liquidity shortfalls faced by businesses, we also defined an alternative Equation (6.1) or the ratio between the credit actually used by the firm (*utilizzato*) and the maximum amount of available financing (*accordato*). However, the results remained unchanged using this alternative specification.

5 Ongena et al. (2021, p. 8), for example, define "*the ratio between credit used and credit granted, a measure commonly used as a proxy for credit constraints.*"

References

Agostino, M., and F. Trivieri (2018). "Who Benefits from Longer Lending Relationships? An Analysis on European SMEs." *Journal of Small Business Management* 56(2), 274–293.

Alessandrini, P., A. F. Presbitero, and A. Zazzaro (2009). "Banks, Distances and Firms' Financing Constraints." *Review of Finance* 13, 261–307.

Avramidis, P., I. Asimakopoulos, and D. Malliaropulos (2022). "Disrupted Lending Relationship and Borrower's Strategic Default." *Journal of Financial Services Research* (1/4), 1–26.

Banerjee, R. N., L. Gambacorta, and E. Sette (2021). "The Real Effects of Relationship Lending." *Journal of Financial Intermediation*, 48, 100923.

Bell, A., M. Fairbrother, and K. Jones (2019). "Fixed and Random Effects Models: Making An Informed Choice." *Qual. Quant.* 53, 1051–1074.

Beretta, E., and S. Del Prete (2013). "Banking Consolidation and Bank-firm Credit Relationships: The Role of Geographical Features and Relationship Characteristics." *Bank of Italy, Temi di Discussione (Working Paper) No, 901.*

Berger, A. N., and G. F. Udell (1995). "Relationship Lending and Lines of Credit in Small Firm Finance." *Journal of Business* 68, 351–381.

Berger, A. N., and G. F. Udell (2002). "Small Business Credit Availability and Relationship Lending: The Importance of Bank Organisational Structure." *The Economic Journal* 112, 32–53.

Bernini, C., and P. Brighi (2018). "Bank Branches Expansion, Efficiency and Local Economic Growth." *Regional Studies* (52/10), 1332–1345.

Bhattacharya, S., and G. Chiesa (1995). "Proprietary Information, Financial Intermediation and Research Incentives." *Journal of Financial Intermediation* 4, 328–357.

Boot, A. (2000). "Relationship Banking: What Do We Know?" *Journal of Financial Intermediation* 9, 7–25.

Boot, A. W., and A. V. Thakor (2000). "Can Relationship Banking Survive Competition?" *The Journal of Finance* 55(2), 679–713.

Brighi, P., C. Lucarelli, and V. Venturelli (2019). "Predictive Strength of Lending Technologies in Funding SMEs." *Journal of Small Business Management* 57(4), 1350–1377.

Cenni, S., S. Monferrà, V. Salotti, M. Sangiorgi, and G. Torluccio (2015). "Credit Rationing and Relationship Lending. Does Firm Size Matter?" *Journal of Banking and Finance* 53, 249–265.

Commission Recommendation 2003/361/EC of 6 May (2003). "Concerning the Definition of Micro, Small and Medium-Sized Enterprises". EUR-Lex, document 32003H0361, https://eur-lex.europa.eu /LexUriServ/ LexUriServ.do?uri=OJ:L:2003:124:0036:0041:en:PDF

Coccorese, P., and S. Shaffer (2021). "Cooperative Banks and Local Economic Growth." *Regional Studies* 55(2), 307–321, DOI: 10.1080/00343404.2020.1802003.

Cowling, M., and P. Westhead (1996). "Bank Lending Decisions and Small Firms: Does Size Matter?" *International Journal of Entrepreneurial Behaviour & Research* 2(2), 52–68.

Degryse, H., and P. Van Cayseele (2000). "Relationship Lending within a Bank-based System: Evidence from European Small Business Data." *Journal of Financial Intermediation* 9(1), 90–109.

Degryse, H., and S. Ongena (2005). "Distance, Lending Relationships, and Competition." *Journal of Finance* 60, 231–266.

Diamond, D. W. (1991). "Monitoring and Reputation: The Choice between Bank Loans and Directly Placed Debt." *Journal of Political Economy 99*(4), 689–721.

Dwenger, N., F. M. Fossen, and M. Simmler (2020). "Firms' Financial and Real Responses to Credit Supply Shocks: Evidence from Firm-bank Relationships in Germany." *Journal of Financial Intermediation* 41, 100773, ISSN 1042–9573, https://doi.org/10.1016/j.jfi.2018.01.003.

Elsas, R., and J. P. Krahnen (1998). "Is Relationship Lending Special? Evidence from Credit-file Data in Germany." *Journal of Banking & Finance* 22, 1283–1316.

Elsas, R. (2005). "Empirical Determinants of Relationship Lending." *Journal of Financial Intermediation* 14(1), 32–57.

European Banking Authority (EBA) (2021). *Risk Dashboard Data as of Q4 2020*, https://www.eba.europa.eu/risk-analysis-and-data/risk-dashboard.

Hale, G., and J. A. Santos (2009). "Do Banks Price their Informational Monopoly?" *Journal of Financial Economics* 93(2), 185–206.

Ioannidou, V., and S. Ongena (2010). "Time for a Change: Loan Conditions and Bank Behaviour When Firms Switch Banks." *The Journal of Finance* 65(5), 1847–1877.

Iturralde, T., A. Maseda, and L. San-Jose (2010). "Empirical Evidence of Banking Relationships for Spanish SMEs." *International Small Business Journal* 28(3), 274–295.

López-Espinosa, G., S. Mayordomo, and A. Moreno (2017). "When does Relationship Lending Start to Pay?" *Journal of Financial Intermediation* 31, 16–29.

Mayordomo, S., A. Moreno, S. Ongena, and M. Rodriguez-Moreno (2021). "Bank Capital Requirements, Loan Guarantees and Firm Performance." *Journal of Financial Intermediation*, 45, 100825.

Mc Namara, A., S. Donohoe, and P. Murro (2020). "Lending Infrastructure and Credit Rationing of European SMEs." *The European Journal of Finance* 26(7–8), 728–745, DOI: 10.1080/1351847X.2019.1637357.

Mohammad, S., M. Asutay, R. Dixon, and E. Platonova (2020). "Liquidity Risk Exposure and Its Determinants in the Banking Sector: A Comparative Analysis between Islamic, Conventional and Hybrid Banks." *Journal of International Financial Markets, Institutions and Money* 66, 101196.

Nwakuya, M. T., and M. A. Ijomah (2017). "Fixed Effect Versus Random Effects Modelling in a Panel Data Analysis; A Consideration of Economic and Political Indicators in Six African Countries." *International Journal of Statistics and Applications* 7(6), 275–279.

Ongena, S., and D. C Smith (2001). "The Duration of Bank Relationships." *Journal of Financial Economics*, 61(3), 449–475, ISSN 0304–405X, https://doi.org/10.1016/S0304-405X(01)00069-1.

Ongena, S., S. Pinoli, P. Rossi, and A. Scopelliti (2021). "Bank Credit and Market-based Finance for Corporations: The Effects of Minibond Issuances." Bank of Italy Temi di Discussione (Working Paper) No. 1315, *Swiss Finance Institute Research Paper* No. 21–55.

Petersen, M. A., and R. G. Rajan (1994). "The Benefits of Lending Relationships: Evidence from Small Business Data." *Journal of Finance* 49, 3–37.

Stein, J. C. (2002). "Information Production and Capital Allocation: Decentralized versus Hierarchical Firms." *Journal of Finance* 57, 1891–1921.

7 The influence of the COVID-19 pandemic on bank lending

Evidence from European countries

Renata Karkowska

7.1 Introduction

Since the global financial crisis of 2008–2009, European banks have significantly improved asset quality, built larger capital buffers, and strengthened their liquidity, making them better prepared for the economic downturn triggered by the COVID-19 pandemic, declared on 11 March 2020 by the World Health Organization (WHO). The good times of the past few years, supervisory and policy actions, and banks' commitment have taken effective action to a significant decline in non-performing loans (NPLs). The difficult experience of the 2007–2008 crisis has led banks to establish a system for managing NPLs and to develop best practices for doing so, and to deal with the accumulation of non-performing exposures. Since then, we have seen a downward trend in the volume of NPLs. On the other hand, COVID-19 has had a significant impact on businesses, jobs, and incomes around the world. Together with the severe economic downturn triggered by the pandemic, high debt levels are likely to increase NPLs, especially once the soft regulatory and monetary policies to address the impact of the crisis are lifted. Higher unemployment and lower corporate income compound the debt service for households and businesses. As a consequence, changes in credit standards and a reduction in loan demand were observed, and more customers may have repayment problems. Therefore, it is important to verify whether additional bank loans helped firms avoid closure and maintain employment and whether these loans helped healthy firms compared to zombie firms (Ahearne and Shinada, 2005; San-Jose et al., 2021). This work investigates whether banks change their lending behaviour in response to increased uncertainty.

The outcomes of this trial will have serious implications because of: first, the literature answering the question how European banks responded to the COVID-19 pandemic is limited, second, an ongoing public debate about zombie lending to European firms.

The scientific problem to be solved is to verify how COVID-19 influences the lending activities of commercial banks in Europe. The research will calculate the reaction of banking loan growth: (i) at the level of individual banks in 36 selected countries in Europe, taking into account the average cases of COVID-19 cases per 1,000 people in European countries and population density per square kilometer.

DOI: 10.4324/9781003310754-7

Using this measure, the aim of this chapter is to study whether countries with greater exposure to the COVID-19 outbreak responded differently. This chapter focuses on the European banking sector, taking into account developed and developing countries. In the entire next step, the study sample is divided into two groups: high- and low-capitalized banks.

This chapter is organized as follows. Section 7.1 outlines the theoretical framework. Section 7.2 presents a review of the literature and hypotheses. The data and methodology are shown in Section 7.3. Next, Section 7.4 contains the main results. Section 7.6 concludes.

7.2 Literature review and hypotheses

The COVID-19 pandemic resulted in an increase in liquidity in the banking sector from aid programmes and a relatively high level of bank capital after the recent 2007–2008 crisis. This situation enabled banks to pursue an expansionary lending policy. This is different from the situation that accompanied the global financial crisis, when the number of new loans granted to borrowers dropped significantly. However, surveys among commercial banks confirm that banks around the world are tightening credit standards, driven by an uncertain economic outlook, worsening industry problems, and reduced risk tolerance. The Federal Reserve System survey on bank lending practice results indicated a deterioration in the bank's current or expected capital position. Respondents also highlighted increased concerns about the effects of legislative changes, supervisory actions, or changes in accounting standards. On the other hand, there was less competition between banks and non-bank lenders and reduced liquidity in the secondary market for mortgage loans (Federal Reserve, 2020).

Considering that banking risk may be a consequence of wrong decisions made by managers about the level of accepted risk and may result from market factors, it seems reasonable to assume that the level of this risk in individual countries is affected by the same categories of factors, yet with different intensity and with a different response of individual banks or the entire banking sector.

The literature on lending in the COVID-19 pandemic is also expanding rapidly (Al-Awadhi et al., 2020; Ari et al., 2021; Ashraf, 2020; Eichengreen et al., 2021; Elnahass et al., 2021; Rizwan et al., 2020; Salisu et al., 2020; Szczygielski et al., 2021; Zhang et al., 2020). Most COVID-19 banking papers focus on the US and do not examine how Europe was affected. Remy Beauregard and Jose A. Lopez, (2021) emphasize that the growing threat of the COVID-19 pandemic resulted in a sharp increase in bank borrowing by US businesses. In particular, corporate borrowing from banks rose $532 million overall, representing a 5.1% increase in the first half of the year. Jarque (2021) found that large domestic banks and foreign-related banks increased their lending to businesses during the last months of COVID-19. However, small domestic banks play an active role in providing paycheck protection loans.

On the other hand, Çolak and Öztekin (2021) used an international sample of banks from 125 countries and found that bank lending is weaker in countries that are more affected by the health crisis. This effect depends on the bank's financial conditions, market structure, regulatory and institutional environment, financial intermediary and debt market development, ease of access of corporate firms to debt capital, and the response of the public health sector to the crisis. Jarque (2021) found a strong negative impact of local pandemic severity on credit use, which decreases with time, consistent with pandemic fatigue. Restrictive public health interventions also negatively affect credit use, but the pandemic itself is the main driver. Park and Shin (2021) examined the impact of higher NPL ratios on bank lending accessibility between multi-national lenders and developing market debtors. They argue that the rise in NPL ratios is positively related to higher banking outflows from developing economies. First, given the high exposure to borrowers in the same region, lenders are more responsive to increases in NPL ratios at the local level. Second, lenders are less responsive to increases in NPL ratios in emerging economies if their liabilities are denominated in US dollars. Temesvary and Wei (2021) analyzed detailed bank regulatory datasets on lending activity and found strong evidence that US banks with higher foreign exposures were significantly more affected than other banks by credit contraction during the COVID-19 pandemic. Therefore, the main hypothesis of the investigation is as follows:

- H1: The COVID-19 pandemic leads to a lower bank lending activity in Europe. The study was inspired by the COVID-19 pandemic. The crisis has affected the countries of Central and Eastern Europe at a time of relatively strong financial integration with highly developed economies. However, given the different models and the development of financial markets, their vulnerability to external shocks was also different. Therefore, research aimed at discovering the market mechanisms that cause banking risk will identify new crisis transmission channels and allow early warning indicators to be developed. Additionally, a significantly stronger relationship between COVID-19 cases and bank lending activity in developed countries is expected. Feyen et al. (2021) investigate the financial sector policy response to COVID-19 in emerging markets and developing economies and find that policy makers in richer and more populous countries have been significantly more responsive and have taken more policy measures. Countries with higher levels of private debt levels tend to respond earlier to the banking sector and liquidity and funding measures. Thus, the next Hypothesis 2 is as follows:
- H2: The negative effect of COVID-19 on bank lending activity is stronger in developed European countries.

  Recent decades and financial crises have encouraged the European Central Bank (ECB) and other European central banks to provide expansionary monetary policies, including negative interest rates, refinancing operations, and asset purchase programmes. It was intended to support bank lending activities. Such forbearance towards institutions typically consists of government guarantees to depositors, allowing delayed recognition of non-performing or NPLs on banks' balance sheets, and various forms of liquidity support from the central bank. However, the literature suggests that such policies conducted too aggressively

> lead to "zombie lending", i.e., increasing the pool of new loans or extending existing loans to low-productivity businesses. Although it is assumed that such policies can stabilize the economy in the short term, in the long term they risk transforming temporary shocks into phases of delayed recovery and permanent loss of productivity and output. Action against the COVID-19 pandemic has renewed the debate on the effectiveness of interventions to stabilize the economy in response to economic shocks. In the face of loose monetary policy and supportive regulatory policies, the threat of a "zombification" phenomenon has arisen.[1] A zombification of the economy is of great concern because it can lead to a drop in productivity through credit misallocation. The situation is worrying because banks with low capitalization make new loans or roll over existing loans to low-productivity customers. Banks with high leverage and low capital lend to less productive companies. But if they allowed these companies to fail and replaced them with more productive entities, their aggregate output would increase. The spin of this mechanism is that subsidies from government guarantees go to banks with higher leverage and riskier assets (Acharya et al., 2020; Banerjee and Hofmann, 2020).

The impact of the size of the bank capital on its lending policies can be ambiguous. On the one hand, empirical studies acknowledge that some countries are dealing with the NPLs created by the European sovereign debt crisis (Ari et al., 2021), and show that banks with lower capital ratios lent to their troubled corporate borrowers so that these firms could continue to repay their outstanding loans. Additionally, during the COVID pandemic crisis, research findings suggest that banks with weaker capital ratios are likely to experience credit growth (Özlem Dursun-de Neef and Schandlbauer, 2021). In the literature there is a definition of a zombie firm, which has an economic net worth below zero but continues to operate and remains able to repay its debt because of banks' concerns about capital sufficiency and the government's desire to avoid massive firm failures. Dai et al. (2021) conducted an empirical study on a set of firms in China for the period 1998–2007. The authors define an insolvent firm that receives a loan subsidy as a "zombie firm". The authors tested whether injecting liquidity into firms could protect supplier firms from spreading business failures. The authors proved that bailing out customer firms cannot protect supplier firms from the spread of business failures. Furthermore, the misallocation of credit significantly distorts firms' ability to survive in the market. This is in line with Schumpeter's (2017) theory of creative destruction, which emphasized that the destruction of the old generates greater opportunities to create the new. This process is necessary to revolutionize the economic structure and has important implications for aggregate economic growth.

Dursun-de et al. (2021) showed that a higher exposure to COVID-19 led to a relative increase in loans from low-capitalized banks' loans, while their high-capitalized peers decreased their lending more. At the same time, only better-capitalized banks experienced a significantly larger increase in their delinquent and restructured loans. On the other hand, some studies highlight that banks with weaker capital ratios are perceived as riskier compared to better-capitalized banks, making it difficult for them to find adequate sources of funding during a pandemic. Kishan and Opiela (2000) and Meh and Moran (2010) emphasize that poorly capitalized banks would reduce their loans more during the COVID-19 pandemic. Therefore, the next Hypothesis 3 is as follows:

H3: Low-capitalized banks decrease their loan activity relatively more than high-capitalized banks during crises.

7.3 Data and methodology

Following the research undertaken by Dursun-de et al. (2021), this study verifies the research question: how the COVID-19 pandemic affects bank lending activity.

To test the hypotheses, the following form of the regression model is used:

$$Y_{n,\,i,\,t} = \alpha + \beta_1 COVID_{i,\,t} + \beta_2 DENSITY_{i,\,t} + \beta_3 GDP_{i,\,t} + \beta_4 BANK_{n,\,i,\,t} + \beta_5 RISK_{n,\,i,\,t} + \beta_6 INCOME_{n,\,i,\,t} + \delta_i + \delta_t + \varepsilon_{i,\,t} \quad \text{(Eq. 1)}$$

where:

Y – bank loan activity ratio calculated as loans to total assets in individual bank, as dependent variable. Independent variables: GDP as GDP growth rate, COVID – total confirmed deaths due to COVID-19 per million people, density – population density in the country (people per sq. km. of land area), BANK: [asset – logarithm of total assets, equity_asset – capital ratio, cash_asset – bank cash to total assets], RISK: [depo_asset – bank deposits to total assets, liquid_ratio – liquidity ratio calculated as bank loans to deposits, loans_loss_res – bank loans loss reserves to total loans], INCOME: [interest_income – bank interest income to total assets, income_asset – bank's net income to total assets]. The calculations were based on quarterly data. To additionally control for unobserved country-level heterogeneity, country fixed-effects, δ_i, as well as quarter-year fixed-effects, δ_t, are included. The choice of a fixed-effects model was based on the Hausman test.

Through a dataset that covers 652 commercial banks from the Orbis – Bureau van Dijk database during the 2018 Q3–2021 Q1 period and the panel regression methodology, the empirical findings document the effect of the COVID-19 effect on banking lending activity. The full range of banks from 36 developed and developing European countries (Albania, Austria, Belarus, Bosnia and Hercegovina, Bulgaria, Croatia, Cyprus, Czech Republic, Denmark, Estonia, Finland, France, Germany, Greece, Denmark, Iceland, Ireland, Kosovo, Latvia, Lithuania, North Macedonia, Norway, Poland, Portugal, Moldavia, Romania, Russia, Serbia, Slovakia, Slovenia, Spain, Sweden, Switzerland, Turkey, Ukraine, United Kingdom).[2]

Table 7.1 indicates the summary statistics for the changes in the nominal value of bank loans in different countries (panel A) and the summary statistics for the changes in the nominal value of bank loans in different capitalized banks (panel B), in European countries, in the period 2018 Q3–2021 Q1. And in developed countries, there is a higher value of the loan total asset ratio (0.07 versus 0.01), respectively. Although this statistic is different for banks with different capitalizations, 0.07 for low-capitalized banks and 0.01 for high-capitalized banks.

Table 7.1 Summary statistics for changes in the nominal value of bank loans in different countries (panel A) and summary statistics changes in the nominal value of bank loans in different capitalized banks (panel B), in European countries, 2018 Q3–2021 Q1

	Panel (A)						
	Count	*mean*	*p50*	*sd*	*Min*	*max*	*skewness*
Panel (A)							
Developing	2,764	0.01	0.00	0.10	−0.71	2.00	3.27
Developed	3,238	0.07	0.01	3.29	−0.94	187.25	56.71
Total	6,002	0.04	0.01	2.42	−0.94	187.25	77.14
Panel (B)							
Low-capitalized	2,998	0.07	0.01	3.42	−0.94	187.25	54.59
High-capitalized	3,004	0.01	0.00	0.11	−0.89	1.07	0.41
Total	6,002	0.04	0.01	2.42	−0.94	187.25	77.14

Table 7.2 Summary statistics for the full sample in European banks, 2018 Q3–2021 Q1

	Count	*mean*	*p50*	*sd*	*min*	*Max*	*skewness*
Loans	397	0.02	0.03	0.13	−0.60	1.07	−0.79
GDP	397	0.36	0.07	1.53	−4.28	2.84	−1.20
Density	397	3.50	3.21	1.00	1.23	5.61	0.37
COVID	397	5.03	4.39	1.18	2.98	7.25	0.57
Asset	397	14.99	14.40	2.32	11.23	21.37	0.81
Equity_asset	397	0.11	0.11	0.04	0.03	0.57	3.26
Cash_asset	397	0.06	0.01	0.08	0.00	0.49	2.02
Depo_asset	397	0.66	0.69	0.16	0.05	0.93	−1.07
Liquid_ratio	397	1.16	1.04	1.18	0.10	16.92	10.43
Loans loss res	397	0.03	0.01	0.05	0.00	0.38	3.28
Interest income	397	0.02	0.02	0.01	0.00	0.10	2.84
Income_asset	397	0.01	0.01	0.01	−0.09	0.05	−5.30

Source: Author's calculations based on Orbis and World Bank database loans – loans to total assets in individual bank as dependent variable. Independent variables: GDP as GDP growth rate, density – population density in the country (people per sq. km of land area), COVID – total confirmed deaths due to COVID-19 per million people, asset – logarithm of total assets, equity_asset – capital ratio, cash_asset – bank cash to total assets, depo_asset – bank deposits to total assets, liquid_ratio – liquidity ratio calculated as bank loans to deposits, loans loss res – bank loan loss reserves to total loans, interest_income – bank interest income to total assets, income_asset – bank net income to total assets.

Table 7.2 reports the descriptive statistics for the entire sample of 652 commercial banks from Europe. The average value for the loan ratio activity is 0.02, with the standard deviation 0.03%. This means that the diversification of lending activity varied across the entire sample of commercial banks. And the asset variable is 14.99%, with a standard deviation of 2.32%. The mean value of equity_asset is 0.11 with a standard deviation of 0.04%. The average liquid_ratio is 1.16%. Regarding interest, the average value of income ratio is 0.02%. The median value of loan loss reserve (loans_loss_res) is 0.03, with the standard deviation 0.05.

Table 7.3 Correlation matrix

	Loans	*GDP*	*Density*	*COVID*	*Asset*	*Equity_ asset*	*Cash_ asset*	*Depo_ asset*	*Liquid_ ratio*	*Loans loss res*	*Interest income*	*Income_ asset*
Loans	1.00											
GDP	−0.00	1.00										
	(0.98)											
Density	0.08***	0.01	1.00									
	(0.00)	(0.75)										
COVID	0.04	−0.27***	0.34***	1.00								
	(0.10)	(0.00)	(0.00)									
Asset	0.05***	−0.02	0.11***	0.19***	1.00							
	(0.00)	(0.27)	(0.00)	(0.00)								
Equity_asset	−0.01	0.02	−0.03	−0.08***	−0.49***	1.00						
	(0.47)	(0.26)	(0.14)	(0.00)	(0.00)							
Cash_asset	−0.01	−0.01	0.20***	0.08***	−0.23***	0.25***	1.00					
	(0.37)	(0.68)	(0.00)	(0.00)	(0.00)	(0.00)						
Depo_asset	0.00	0.02	0.15***	−0.01	−0.08***	−0.45***	−0.02	1.00				
	(0.96)	(0.30)	(0.00)	(0.74)	(0.00)	(0.00)	(0.17)					
Liquid_ratio	−0.00	−0.02	0.02	0.03	−0.01	0.03**	−0.01	−0.06***	1.00			
	(0.99)	(0.38)	(0.35)	(0.16)	(0.66)	(0.01)	(0.39)	(0.00)				
Loans loss res	−0.04**	0.04	0.15***	−0.07*	−0.14***	0.16***	0.10***	−0.11***	−0.00	1.00		
	(0.01)	(0.09)	(0.00)	(0.01)	(0.00)	(0.00)	(0.00)	(0.00)	(0.74)			
Interest income	−0.05***	0.05**	−0.00	0.01	−0.24***	0.20***	0.12***	−0.07***	0.05***	0.15***	1.00	
	(0.00)	(0.01)	(0.84)	(0.72)	(0.00)	(0.00)	(0.00)	(0.00)	(0.00)	(0.00)		
Income_asset	0.03*	−0.01	−0.05*	0.02	0.01	0.13***	0.01	−0.04**	0.02	−0.08***	0.15***	1.00
	(0.02)	(0.76)	(0.03)	(0.37)	(0.33)	(0.00)	(0.49)	(0.00)	(0.06)	(0.00)	(0.00)	

Table 7.4 presents the average scores for the effect of COVID-19 on lending activity in European banks. In particular models/columns, there are added three groups of control variables. In Model 1, there is included COVID reaction only. COVID is the average measure of COVID-19 death cases per 1,000 people. The next regressions include the control variables of the bank's asset variables (Model 2), risk taking (Model 3), and income (Model 4). In all models, both the COVID-19 coefficients and the density ratio are negative and statistically significant (COVID −0.018 in Model 1). It means that more COVID-19 death cases decreased lending activity in commercial banks in Europe. Furthermore, increasing population density in the country significantly reduces bank loans (density −0.023). A factor that improves bank lending activity is an increase in bank equity and taken deposits. The relationship is positive and statistically significant (equity_asset +0.763, depo_asset +0.763). This indicates that bank capital and deposits increased lending activity in banks.

Among the risk factors of the bank, the changes in the liquidity ratio exhibited a positive result, which means that a balanced relationship between loans and deposits is conducive to the development of credit activity (liquid_ratio +0.018). On the other hand, an increase in reserve for loan losses also appeared to have a positive impact on lending (loan_loss_res +0.364). In other words, banks are building up reserves and not limiting the size of loans.

The study also showed a strong positive relationship between the COVID-19 outbreak and lending volume (interest_income +1.902 versus income_asset +2.740).

In summary, the results so far support the importance of the COVID-19 pandemic in bank lending activity. The relationship is consistent with hypothesis H1, which stated that the COVID-19 pandemic leads to a lower bank lending activity in Europe.

To further explore the study, the entire sample is divided into developed and developing country groups. Table 7.5 presents the average lending scores in developing countries and Table 7.6 in developed countries. The results show that the COVID effect disaggregated by a group of countries also influences negatively on bank lending; however, the results in developed countries are stronger. The comparison of Tables 7.5 and 7.6 indicates that the inclusion of the pandemic situation in the output results in mean lending scores depends on the level of development. Thus, hypothesis H2 was confirmed, and the effect of COVID-19 on bank lending activity was higher in developed European countries.

As a last step, the changes in the bank capitalization are examined (Table 5.7). The loosening of bank regulatory requirements to resign from some buffers might have differential effects on banks with low and high capital ratios. The findings imply that there is a significant difference in the lending responses of low-capitalized versus high-capitalized banks. High (low) capitalized banks have a total equity ratio in the last quarter of 2019 above (below) the median. High-capitalized banks decrease their lending more than low-capitalized banks.

These findings are consistent with the literature. The zombie lending literature emphasizes that banks with low capital ratios engage in excessive lending during crises in an attempt to write off less NPLs on their capital since they would like to avoid a decrease in their capital (Acharya and Steffen, 2020; Dursun-de et al., 2021). Finally, Hypothesis H3, that low-capitalized banks decrease their loan activity relatively more than high-capitalized banks during crises, can be rejected, as the relationship is negative and stronger in high-capitalized banks.

Table 7.4 COVID-19 and bank lending activity in commercial banks in European countries (full sample), over the period 2018 Q3–2021 Q1

	Full sample (model 1)	*Bank_asset (model 2)*	*Bank_risk (model 3)*	*Income (model 4)*
GDP	0.011***	0.013***	−0.009***	−0.004
	(0.002)	(0.003)	(0.003)	(0.003)
Density	−0.023***	−0.025***	−0.089***	−0.078***
	(0.005)	(0.006)	(0.011)	(0.011)
COVID	−0.018***	−0.020***	−0.020***	−0.013**
	(0.004)	(0.005)	(0.006)	(0.006)
Asset		0.005**	0.041***	0.036***
		(0.003)	(0.006)	(0.005)
Equity_asset		0.004	0.763***	0.523***
		(0.070)	(0.199)	(0.196)
Cash_asset		0.068*	0.084	0.118
		(0.040)	(0.096)	(0.092)
Depo_asset		−0.009	0.189**	0.114
		(0.029)	(0.079)	(0.078)
Liquid_ratio			0.018*	0.015*
			(0.009)	(0.009)
Loans loss res			0.364*	0.360*
			(0.192)	(0.186)
Interest income				1.902***
				(0.614)
Income_asset				2.740***
				(0.622)
Cons	0.197***	0.134**	−0.430***	−0.408***
	(0.020)	(0.055)	(0.125)	(0.120)
Country FE	YES	YES	YES	YES
Time FE	YES	YES	YES	YES
#Observations	6002	6909	4936	6449

Loans to total assets in an individual bank as a dependent variable. Independent variables: GDP as GDP growth rate, density – population density in the country (people per sq km of land area), COVID – total confirmed deaths due to COVID-19 per million people, asset – logarithm of total assets, equity_asset – capital ratio, cash_asset – bank cash to total assets, depo_asset – bank deposits to total assets, liquid_ratio – liquidity ratio calculated as bank loans to deposits, loans loss res – bank loans loss reserves to total loans, interest_income – bank's interest income to total assets, income_asset – bank's net income to total assets. The models have been estimated using panel regression. Statistics t are given in parentheses. # – means the number of banks. The *p*-value denotes the significance levels at $^{*}p < 0.1$, $^{**}p < 0.05$, $^{***}p < 0.01$, respectively.

Table 7.5 COVID-19 and bank lending activity in commercial banks in developing countries, over the period 2018 Q3–2021 Q1

	Full sample (1)	*Bank_asset (2)*	*Bank_risk (3)*	*Income (4)*
GDP	0.003	0.020***	0.037***	0.033**
	(0.009)	(0.007)	(0.012)	(0.013)
Density	−0.003	−0.036**	−0.002	0.007
	(0.013)	(0.016)	(0.028)	(0.029)
COVID	−0.011***	−0.003	0.010	0.008
	(0.004)	(0.004)	(0.007)	(0.007)
Asset		0.004	−0.012	−0.011
		(0.004)	(0.008)	(0.009)
Equity_asset		0.257*	−0.002	−0.040
		(0.152)	(0.226)	(0.230)
Cash_asset		−0.109**	0.085	0.103
		(0.051)	(0.092)	(0.094)
Depo_asset		0.223	0.031	−0.033
		(0.149)	(0.205)	(0.215)
Liquid_ratio			0.199***	0.177***
			(0.054)	(0.056)
Loans loss res			−0.256*	−0.246
			(0.151)	(0.152)
Interest income				0.489
				(0.505)
Income_asset				0.159
				(0.554)
Cons	0.088*	−0.095	−0.040	−0.018
	(0.052)	(0.152)	(0.210)	(0.215)
Country FE	YES	YES	YES	YES
Time FE	YES	YES	YES	YES
#Observations	2,764	3,085	2,515	3,090

Loans to total assets in an individual bank as a dependent variable. Independent variables: GDP as GDP growth rate, density – population density in the country (people per sq km of land area), COVID – total confirmed deaths due to COVID-19 per million people, asset – logarithm of total assets, equity_asset – capital ratio, cash_asset – bank cash to total assets, depo_asset – bank deposits to total assets, liquid_ratio – liquidity ratio calculated as bank loans to deposits, loans loss res – bank loans loss reserves to total loans, interest_income – bank's interest income to total assets, income_asset – bank's net income to total assets. The models have been estimated using panel regression. Statistics t are given in parentheses. # – means the number of banks. The p-value denotes the significance levels at $^{*}p < 0.1$, $^{**}p < 0.05$, $^{***}p < 0.01$, respectively.

Table 7.6 COVID-19 and bank lending activity in commercial banks in developed countries in Europe, during the period 2018 Q3–2021 Q1

	Full sample (1)	*Bank_asset (2)*	*Bank_risk (3)*	*Income (4)*
GDP	0.010***	0.011***	−0.010***	−0.003
	(0.003)	(0.003)	(0.004)	(0.004)
Density	−0.019***	−0.020***	−0.097***	−0.084***
	(0.006)	(0.007)	(0.014)	(0.014)
COVID	−0.024***	−0.034***	−0.020**	−0.012
	(0.006)	(0.007)	(0.009)	(0.009)

(*Continued*)

Table 7.6 (Continued)

	Full sample (1)	*Bank_asset (2)*	*Bank_risk (3)*	*Income (4)*
Asset		0.007**	0.043***	0.039***
		(0.003)	(0.007)	(0.007)
Equity_asset		−0.030	0.935***	0.438
		(0.080)	(0.301)	(0.300)
Cash_asset		0.163***	0.135	0.122
		(0.052)	(0.140)	(0.134)
Depo_asset		0.018	0.200**	0.147
		(0.033)	(0.099)	(0.095)
Liquid_ratio			0.020*	0.017*
			(0.011)	(0.010)
Loans_loss_res			0.634**	0.573**
			(0.263)	(0.254)
Interest income				2.227***
				(0.804)
Income_asset				3.727***
				(0.736)
Cons	0.215***	0.152**	−0.481***	−0.471***
	(0.023)	(0.063)	(0.164)	(0.157)
Country FE	YES	YES	YES	YES
Time FE	YES	YES	YES	YES
#Observations	3,238	3,824	2,421	3,364

Loans to total assets in an individual bank as a dependent variable. Independent variables: GDP as GDP growth rate, density – population density in the country (people per sq km of land area), COVID – total confirmed deaths due to COVID-19 per million people, asset – logarithm of total assets, equity_asset – capital ratio, cash_asset – bank cash to total assets, depo_asset – bank deposits to total assets, liquid_ratio – liquidity ratio calculated as bank loans to deposits, loans loss res – bank loans loss reserves to total loans, interest_income – bank's interest income to total assets, income_asset – bank's net income to total assets. The models have been estimated using panel regression. Statistics t are given in parentheses. # – means the number of banks. The p-value denotes the significance levels at $^{*}p < 0.1$, $^{**}p < 0.05$, $^{***}p < 0.01$, respectively.

Table 7.7 The effect of COVID-19 on high versus low-capitalized banks, over the period 2018 Q3–2021 Q1

	(1)	*(2)*	*(3)*	*(4)*	*(5)*	*(6)*	*(7)*	*(8)*
	Low capital	*High capital*	*Low capital*	*High capital*	*Low capital*	*High capital*	*Low capital*	*High capital*
GDP	0.012***	0.007	0.013***	0.011*	−0.002	−0.039***	0.004	−0.025***
	(0.003)	(0.005)	(0.003)	(0.006)	(0.003)	(0.010)	(0.003)	(0.009)
Density	−0.023***	−0.023**	−0.020***	−0.028***	−0.074***	−0.082***	−0.068***	−0.093***
	(0.006)	(0.009)	(0.007)	(0.010)	(0.014)	(0.025)	(0.013)	(0.023)
COVID	−0.013***	−0.030***	−0.019***	−0.028***	−0.012**	−0.045**	−0.001	−0.038**
	(0.005)	(0.009)	(0.006)	(0.010)	(0.006)	(0.018)	(0.006)	(0.015)
Asset			0.004	0.004	0.037***	0.045***	0.033***	0.023*
			(0.003)	(0.006)	(0.006)	(0.015)	(0.006)	(0.013)
Equity_asset			0.079	0.149	1.855***	0.945**	1.458***	0.924***
			(0.218)	(0.122)	(0.461)	(0.388)	(0.440)	(0.339)

(*Continued*)

Table 7.7 (Continued)

	(1)	*(2)*	*(3)*	*(4)*	*(5)*	*(6)*	*(7)*	*(8)*
	Low capital	*High capital*	*Low capital*	*High capital*	*Low capital*	*High capital*	*Low capital*	*High capital*
Cash_asset			0.092*	0.003	0.161*	−0.087	0.139	0.163
			(0.048)	(0.079)	(0.091)	(0.216)	(0.086)	(0.191)
Depo_asset			−0.035	0.036	0.065	0.604***	−0.022	0.412**
			(0.034)	(0.064)	(0.092)	(0.211)	(0.087)	(0.184)
Liquid_ratio					0.013	0.152**	0.009	0.086
					(0.008)	(0.072)	(0.008)	(0.063)
Loans_loss_res					−0.067	1.395***	0.019	1.446***
					(0.178)	(0.486)	(0.168)	(0.434)
Interest income							3.720***	−1.690*
							(0.629)	(1.003)
Income_asset							−0.044	9.239***
							(0.547)	(1.241)
Cons	0.173***	0.252***	0.133**	0.153	−0.466***	−0.857***	−0.469***	−0.386
	(0.025)	(0.036)	(0.066)	(0.122)	(0.132)	(0.326)	(0.124)	(0.290)
Country FE	YES	YES	YES	YES	YES	YES	YES	YES
Time FE	YES	YES	YES	YES	YES	YES	YES	YES
#Observations	2,998	3,004	3,494	3,415	2,277	2,659	3,106	3,348

Loans to total assets in an individual bank as a dependent variable. Independent variables: GDP as GDP growth rate, density – population density in the country (people per sq km of land area), COVID – total confirmed deaths due to COVID-19 per million people, asset – logarithm of total assets, equity_asset – capital ratio, cash_asset – bank cash to total assets, depo_asset – bank deposits to total assets, liquid_ratio – liquidity ratio calculated as bank loans to deposits, loans loss res – bank loans loss reserves to total loans, interest_income – bank's interest income to total assets, income_asset – bank's net income to total assets. The models have been estimated using panel regression. Statistics t are given in parentheses. # – means the number of banks. The *p*-value denotes the significance levels at $^{*}p < 0.1$, $^{**}p < 0.05$, $^{***}p < 0.01$, respectively.

7.4 Conclusions

This chapter verifies how European banks responded to the COVID-19 pandemic by focusing on: (1) differences in the level of development of countries, (2) low-capitalized and high-capitalized banks. The study used a sample of 652 commercial banks from 36 developed and developing European countries during the 2018 Q3–2021 Q1 period and the impact of the COVID-19 outbreak on bank lending volumes.

The study confirmed that European banks have significantly reduced their lending in countries with greater exposure to the COVID-19 outbreak. A closer investigation shows a negative relationship between the bank loan volume and two proxies: death cases of COVID-19 per 1,000 people and population density. In all cases, lending is mainly negatively correlated with the share of loans in bank assets. Furthermore, by dividing a sample into low- and high-capitalized banks, findings imply that low-capitalized banks decrease their lending less than high-capitalized banks as a result of zombie lending. These findings are in line with the zombie lending hypothesis that low-capitalized banks might have an incentive to issue more loans during a crisis to help their weaker borrowers so that they can avoid write-offs on their capital and losses (Acharya and Steffen, 2020; Dursun-de et al., 2021).

The proposed study should provide interesting conclusions: (a) for commercial banks stakeholders: a crisis outbreak may bring negative effects on bank lending and, as a consequence, on the banks' results; (b) for supervisors: the COVID-19-induced economic slowdown and the risk of decreasing lending activity are significant threats to business in developed and developing economies alike. Loan guarantees, which were introduced quickly during the outbreak of the pandemic, need to be refined to ensure that money goes to profitable companies with liquidity problems. On the other hand, supervisors need to ensure that banks maintain a stable capital position, as poorly capitalized banks are vulnerable to lending to zombie customers. After a pandemic, many banks may show significantly reduced capital buffers. The problem is that there are no effective techniques for distributing government support that reaches companies that are illiquid despite not being insolvent. In times of crisis turmoil, it is difficult to distinguish between illiquid and insolvent companies. Consequently, government intervention involves a consensus on maintaining liquidity versus the risk of financing insolvent businesses. The conclusions of the study show how important it is to improve the regulation of insolvency and bankruptcy law in the banking sector in Europe and that it is probably not possible to apply them uniformly to all countries. Developed countries are more vulnerable to disruptions in lending activities. However, given the large expansion of their cross-border banking activities through global banking networks, an adverse shock to the developed banking system could easily spread to emerging markets.

Finally, the study has two broad implications for the research on commercial banks in Europe. First, the loosening of capital requirements, due to the COVID-19 pandemic, caused a significant reduction in bank lending. However, the findings show differences in the response: low-capitalized banks decreased their lending significantly less than their high-capitalized peers. Second, the COVID-19 outbreak tends to express bank lending stronger in developed countries than in developing countries in Europe.

Notes

1 https://voxeu.org/article/zombification-europe-times-pandemic, date of access 4 January 2022.

2 According to the World Bank classification (according to GDP per capita). A similar study on 1999–2006 was carried out by Lozano-Vivas and Pasiouras (2010).

References

Acharya, V.V., Crosignani, M., Eisert, T., Eufinger, C., 2020. Zombie Credit and (Dis) Inflation: Evidence from Europe. NBER Working Paper Series. https://doi.org/10.3386/W27158

Acharya, V.V., Steffen, S., 2020. The risk of being a fallen angel and the corporate dash for cash in the midst of COVID. *Review of Corporate Finance Studies* 9, 430–471. https://doi.org/10.1093/rcfs/cfaa013

Ahearne, A.G., Shinada, N., 2005. Zombie firms and economic stagnation in Japan. *International Economics and Economic Policy* 2, 363–381. https://doi.org/10.1007/S10368-005-0041-1

Al-Awadhi, A.M., Alsaifi, K., Al-Awadhi, A., Alhammadi, S., 2020. Death and contagious infectious diseases: Impact of the COVID-19 virus on stock market returns. *Journal of Behavioral and Experimental Finance* 27. https://doi.org/10.1016/j.jbef.2020.100326

Ari, A., Chen, S., Ratnovski, L., 2021. The dynamics of non-performing loans during banking crises: A new database with post-COVID-19 implications. *Journal of Banking and Finance* 106140. https://doi.org/10.1016/j.jbankfin.2021.106140

Ashraf, B.N., 2020. Stock markets' reaction to COVID-19: Cases or fatalities? *Research in International Business and Finance* 54, 101249. https://doi.org/10.1016/j.ribaf.2020.101249

Banerjee, R., Hofmann, B., 2020. Corporate zombies: Anatomy and life cycle. BIS Working Paper.

Çolak, G., Öztekin, Ö., 2021. The impact of COVID-19 pandemic on bank lending around the world. *Journal of Banking & Finance* 106207. https://doi.org/10.1016/j.jbankfin.2021.106207

Dai, Y., Li, X., Liu, D., Lu, J., 2021. Throwing good money after bad: Zombie lending and the supply chain contagion of firm exit. *Journal of Economic Behavior and Organization* 189, 379–402. https://doi.org/10.1016/j.jebo.2021.06.042

Dursun-de, Schandlbauer, A., Neef, D., Schandlbauer, A., 2021. COVID-19 and lending responses of European banks. *FRBSF Economic Letter*. https://doi.org/10.1016/j.jbankfin.2021.106236

Eichengreen, B., Park, D., Shin, K., 2021. The shape of recovery: Implications of past experience for the duration of the COVID-19 recession. *Journal of Macroeconomics* 69, 103330. https://doi.org/10.1016/j.jmacro.2021.103330

Elnahass, M., Trinh, V.Q., Li, T., 2021. Global banking stability in the shadow of COVID-19 outbreak. *Journal of International Financial Markets, Institutions and Money* 72, 101322. https://doi.org/10.1016/j.intfin.2021.101322

Federal Reserve, 2020. Senior loan officer opinion survey on bank lending practices. Federal Reserve Report of July 2020.

Feyen, E., Alonso Gispert, T., Kliatskova, T., Mare, D.S., 2021. Financial sector policy response to COVID-19 in emerging markets and developing economies. *Journal of Banking & Finance* 106184. https://doi.org/10.1016/j.jbankfin.2021.106184

Jarque A., H. Ennis, (2021), Bank Lending in the Time of COVID, Richmond Fed Economic Brief, 21, (05).

Kishan, R.P., Opiela, T.P., 2000. Bank size, bank capital, and the bank lending channel. *Journal of Money, Credit and Banking* 32, 121. https://doi.org/10.2307/2601095

Meh, C.A., Moran, K., 2010. The role of bank capital in the propagation of shocks. *Journal of Economic Dynamics and Control* 34, 555–576. https://doi.org/10.1016/J.JEDC.2009.10.009

Özlem Dursun-de Neef, H., Schandlbauer, A., 2021. COVID-19 and lending responses of European banks. *Journal of Banking and Finance* 133. https://doi.org/10.1016/j.jbankfin.2021.106236

Park, C.Y., Shin, K., 2021. COVID-19, nonperforming loans, and cross-border bank lending. *Journal of Banking and Finance* 133, 106233. https://doi.org/10.1016/j.jbankfin.2021.106233

Remy Beauregard, Jose A. Lopez, Mark M. Spiegel, (2020). Small Business Lending during COVID-19, FRBSF Economic Letter, Federal Reserve Bank of San Francisco, vol. 2020(35), pages 01–05, November

Rizwan, M.S., Ahmad, G., Ashraf, D., 2020. Systemic risk: The impact of COVID-19. *Finance Research Letters* 36. https://doi.org/10.1016/j.frl.2020.101682

Salisu, A.A., Ebuh, G.U., Usman, N., 2020. Revisiting oil-stock nexus during COVID-19 pandemic: Some preliminary results. *International Review of Economics & Finance* 69, 280–294. https://doi.org/10.1016/j.iref.2020.06.023

San-Jose, L., Urionabarrenetxea, S., García-Merino, J.D., 2021. Zombie firms and corporate governance: What room for maneuver do companies have to avoid becoming zombies? *Review of Managerial Science*. https://doi.org/10.1007/S11846-021-00462-Z

Schumpeter, J.A., 2017. The theory of economic development: An inquiry into profits, Capita I, credit, interest, and the business cycle. *The Theory of Economic Development*. https://doi.org/10.4324/9781315135564

Szczygielski, J.J., Charteris, A., Bwanya, P.R., Brzeszczyński, J., 2021. The impact and role of COVID-19 uncertainty: A global industry analysis. *International Review of Financial Analysis* 101837. https://doi.org/10.1016/j.irfa.2021.101837

Temesvary, J., Wei, A., 2021. Domestic lending and the pandemic: How does banks' exposure to COVID-19 abroad affect their lending in the United States? *SSRN Electronic Journal*. https://doi.org/10.2139/ssrn.3886989

Zhang, D., Hu, M., Ji, Q., 2020. Financial markets under the global pandemic of COVID-19. *Finance Research Letters* 101528. https://doi.org/10.1016/j.frl.2020.101528

8 The impact of the COVID-19 pandemic on bank stability and performance in the CEE region[1]

Ewa Miklaszewska and Krzysztof Kil

8.1 Introduction

Banks are for-profit companies with a direct responsibility towards their shareholders (Fiordelisi 2007), but simultaneously, as public institutions, have a broad responsibility for supporting economic growth and efficient credit distribution (De Haas et al. 2010; Beck et al. 2000). The financial crisis of 2008 made it clear how important is bank stability and systemic risk avoidance (Allen and Carletti 2013). The crisis has changed the approach to bank assessment by stressing the importance of bank stability and risk control (Allen et al. 2009) and proper capitalization (Demirgüç-Kunt and Huizinga 2010). Post-2008 crisis restructuring was aimed at building a stable and resilient banking sector, with new measures for problem-solving, such as the resolution regulations (Philippon and Salord 2017).

The COVID-19 pandemic, however, has disrupted the restructuring and recovery, as this time the vulnerabilities came from outside the financial sector. In addition to the existing challenges created by the technological revolution, new problems emerged, which were largely related to the overwhelming uncertainty (Ahir, Bloom and Furceri 2022). In addition to the very large GDP plunge in 2020, trends became very unpredictable, which affected bank risk taking, the performance of firms and customer behavior. In banking, business models were threatened by low interest rates (Carletti et al. 2020), lower demand for credit, tight regulatory and compliance requirements (IMF 2021) and low bank profitability (Giese and Haldane 2020; Bongini et al. 2019). These shocks could have been more devastating, where it not for the substantial fiscal and monetary stimuli in all major countries, which stabilized the economies at the cost of rapidly expanding public debt (European Parliament 2021). The extend and speed in distribution of public funding to the real sector have a long-term negative impact on the banking industry, both directly by phasing-out banking loans and indirectly by creating a moral hazard behavior (de Guindos 2021).

The COVID-19 pandemic has strongly affected the economic and financial trends, both globally and in Central and Eastern Europe (Danielsson at al. 2022) and created a number of vulnerabilities for the banking sector, such as pushing out bank loans by public grants and subsidies and endangering the portfolio of corporate loans. It has also triggered or strengthened structural changes, particularly

DOI: 10.4324/9781003310754-8

Table 8.1 Comparison of the policy response to the financial crisis of 2008 and economic crisis of 2020

Characteristics	*2008 crisis*	*2020 crisis*
Direct source	Bank excessive risk taking, assets bubble, low interest rates	Lockdowns, low demand for loans
Most affected sector	Banking and financial markets	Real sector, services
Direction of public aid	Banks	Enterprises
Main stabilization tool	Monetary policy	Fiscal policy

Source: Own presentation.

in respect to product delivery channels. The governments were reacting to this external shock by employing fiscal stabilization measures at a massive scale, which were successful in reduction of shocks and stimulation of the recovery of GDP growth. However, they in many cases brought a negative side effects on the banking and financial sectors, which were only indirectly supported (Table 8.1).

During the global financial crisis the Central and East European (CEE) region proved to be very resilient, because of the sound capitalization, tight regulation and high profitability achieved before the crisis (Horobet et al. 2021). The outbreak of the pandemic has challenged this assessment. Consequently, the aim of this research is to analyze the impact of the pandemic on bank performance, represented by bank stability, bank profitability and credit accessibility, in the CEE region. The main research hypothesis is that although challenges were universal, bank resilience and sustainability was not, depending on the country-specific factors and strategies. The methodology employed is the dynamic panel data model – generalized method of moment (GMM-SYS version), using an adjusted dataset from the BankFocus database for unconsolidated bank data for the 2016–2022(2q) period.

8.2 Economic environment, market structure and bank profitability in the CEE region: An overview

The Central and Eastern Europe is a broad term, and the number of included countries and the division into subgroups varies. For the purposes of this research, ten countries that were members of the European Union at the end of 2021 were selected and categorized as Central and Eastern European Countries (CEE). They were further divided into three subgroups:

- CE – Central Europe: Poland, Czech Republic, Slovakia, Hungary;
- SEE – South-Eastern Europe: Bulgaria, Croatia, Romania; and
- BC – the Baltic Countries: Estonia, Lithuania, Latvia.

Despite their geographical proximity and many shared historical experiences, the countries of the CEE region are characterized by many significant differences in the level of economic development (Figure 8.1), GDP growth (Figure 8.2) and

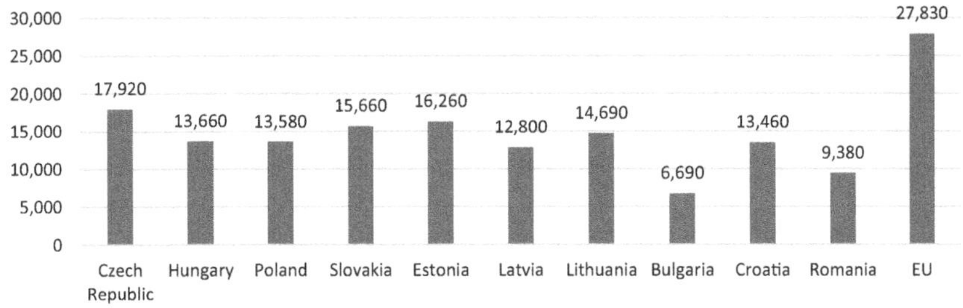

Figure 8.1 Real GDP per capita in CEE in 2021 (euro) Note: EU27 (fixed composition) as of 31 January 2020 (Brexit)

Source: Own study based on EUROSTAT database: https://ec.europa.eu/eurostat/databrowser/view/sdg_08_10/default/tablese

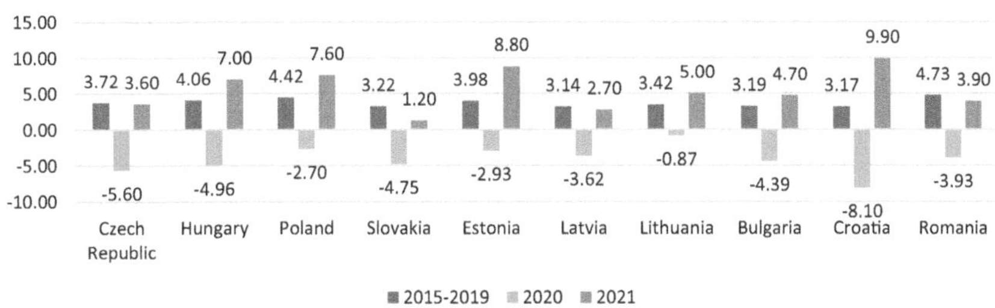

Figure 8.2 GDP growth in 2015–2019 period and in 2020 and 2021 in CEE (%)

Source: Own study based on World Bank and EUROSTAT databases: https://data.worldbank.org/indicator/NY.GDP.MKTP.KD.ZG, https://ec.europa.eu/eurostat/databrowser/

banking sector development (Table 8.2). At the end of 2021, the CE group had on average the highest average value of real GDP per capita at €15,205, followed by the BC (€14,583) and the SEE region (€9,843). The highest value of GDP per capita was recorded by the Czech Republic, Estonia and Slovakia, while the lowest by Bulgaria and Romania, the latter representing, respectively, 24% and 33.7% of the average EU level (Figure 8.4).

Between 2015 and 2019, all countries in the region grew at similar rate and the average annual GDP growth exceeded 3% (Figure 8.2). The entire group experienced a recession in 2020, but the magnitude was varying: the smallest decline in GDP growth rate was observed in Lithuania, the largest in Croatia, which was largely determined by the fact that the Croatian economy was heavily dependent on the tourism industry. In 2021, the economic growth returned to the pre-COVID rate, with exception of Slovakia, and for some countries (Hungary, Poland, Estonia, Croatia) has even exceed it considerably.

The analyzed countries are also characterized by a different level of banking sector development. Using credit availability as a yardstick (*domestic credit to private sector as % of GDP*), the highest credit availability in 2015–2020 period was characteristic for Estonia, Slovakia and Croatia, followed by Poland, Czech Republic and Bulgaria, while the lowest for Romania and Hungary (Table 8.2).

As illustrated in Figure 8.3, till 2019 in all CEE countries, the average TL/TA ratio exceeded 50% and had an upward trend between 2017 and 2019. In 2020, there was a significant reduction of total loans in banks' assets for all groups, particularly for BCs.

The CEE region was also characterized by a strong variation in terms of banking market concentration, as measured by Herfindahl-Hirschman Index (Figure 8.4). The highest concentration level was in the BC group (HHI in 2020 of 0.23), significantly higher than in the SEE (0.124) and CE countries (0.113). In 2020, the concentration level increased slightly in all analyzed countries.

Table 8.2 Domestic credit to private sector by banks (% of GDP) in CEEC in 2015–2020

Period	*CEC*				*BC*			*SEEC*		
	Czech Republic	*Hungary*	*Poland*	*Slovakia*	*Estonia*	*Latvia*	*Lithuania*	*Bulgaria*	*Croatia*	*Romania*
2015	49.54	35.11	53.56	52.72	68.21	48.33	41.55	54.70	63.60	29.93
2016	51.06	33.41	54.42	57.06	68.89	46.72	42.69	51.92	59.40	28.13
2017	50.90	32.43	52.46	60.20	63.77	42.16	40.98	49.71	56.33	26.47
2018	51.33	32.37	52.53	62.07	61.92	36.62	40.39	50.28	54.63	25.73
2019	50.64	33.36	50.80	62.87	58.96	34.62	38.88	49.48	53.11	24.74
2020	53.60	38.16	50.24	67.59	64.04	34.56	37.87	51.68	59.76	26.05
Av. 15-20	51.18	34.14	52.34	60.42	64.30	40.50	40.39	51.30	57.80	26.84

Source: Own study based on World Bank database: https://data.worldbank.org/indicator/FS.AST.PRVT.GD.ZS.

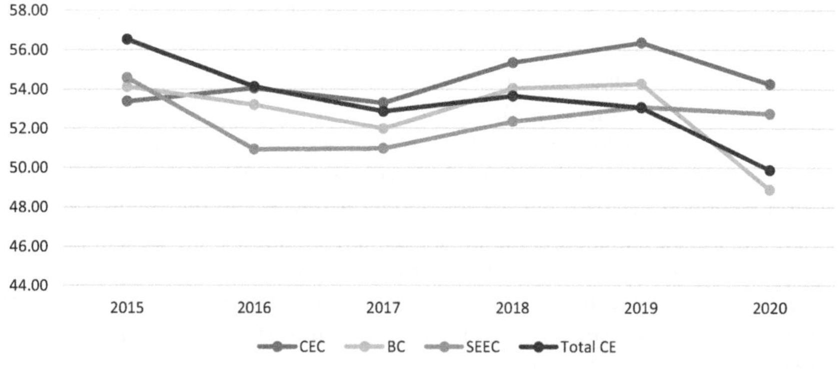

Figure 8.3 Average level of Total Loans/Total Asset ratio for CEE banks, 2015–2020 (arithmetic mean of the analyzed sample)

Source: Own study – calculation based on data from BankFocus database

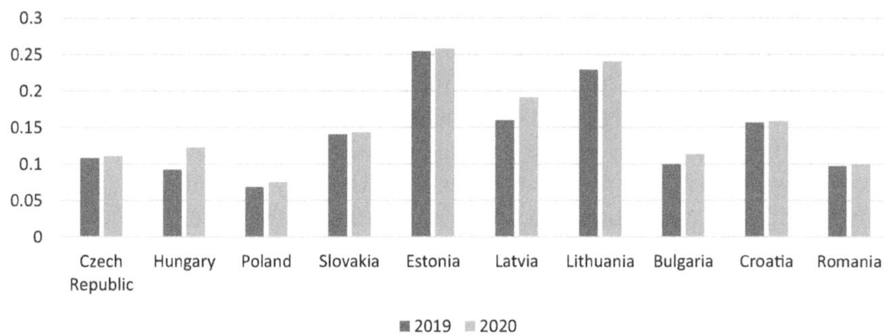

Figure 8.4 Herfindahl-Hirschman Index (total assets) in CEEC in 2019–2020

Source: Own study based on ECB database – Banking Structural Financial Indicators: https://sdw.ecb.europa.eu/browse.do?node=9691570

Table 8.3 Ownership structure of bank total assets (%) in 2020

Structure	*CE*				*BC*			*SEE*		
	Czech Republic	*Hungary*	*Poland*	*Slovakia*	*Estonia*	*Latvia*	*Lithuania*	*Bulgaria*	*Croatia*	*Romania*
Public sector ownership	0.9	4.4	44.1	0.6	0	0	0	3.2	5.9	10.6
Domestic ownership	8.1	21.9	56.3	0.8	9.4	13.4	9.8	22.4	9.3	29.5
Foreign ownership	91.9	78.1	43.7	99.2	90.6	86.6	90.2	77.6	90.7	70.5

Source: Polish Financial Supervision Authority (PFSA), *BSCEE Review 2020*, Warsaw 2021: https://www.bscee.org/knf/pl/komponenty/img/Raport_Roczny_2020_76908.pdf.

At the end of 2020, foreign capital dominated in almost all banking sectors of the analyzed countries (Table 8.3). In most CEE countries, it exceeded 90% (Czech Republic, Slovakia, Estonia, Lithuania, Croatia); in Hungary, Latvia, Bulgaria and Romania it exceeded 70%, only in Poland foreign capital controlled less than half of the banking sector's assets (43.7%). For Poland, there is also a significantly higher (in comparison to the other countries) level of public control in the banking sector (44%).

Between 2016 and 2021, in all analyzed CEE groups, the level of banking sector profitability (both in terms of return on assets and return on equity) was higher than the average for the European Union and the Euro Area (Figure 8.5). A significant deterioration in profitability ratios – a reduction of nearly 50% on average, relative to 2019, was observed for all groups in 2020. In 2021q3, a slight improvement was observed for the SEE and CE. During the COVID-19-affected period (2020–2021q3), the highest level of ROA was observed in Romania and the lowest in Poland, where strong deterioration in bank profitability was also due to one-off event – the creation of provisions for legal risk related to litigations concerning the use of abusive clauses in Swiss franc indexed and denominated residential mortgages. However, Poland had also the worst bank profitability as measured by ROA for the whole 2015–2021 period, while Bulgaria the highest (Table 8.4). Also in the case of ROE, a strong polarization across banking sectors is evident throughout the period under study (Table 8.4). In 2015–2021, ROE exceeding 10% was achieved by banks in Romania, Czech Republic, Hungary and Lithuania, while the Croatian (5.28%,) and Polish banks (6.23%) had the lowest score.

The COVID-19 pandemic had a very significant impact on the increase of public debt in all CEE countries (Figure 8.6). After a period of its reduction (2015–2019), as measured by Gross Public Sector Debt to GDP ratio, the trend reversed in 2020, due to the implementation of expansionary fiscal measures and to the negative rate

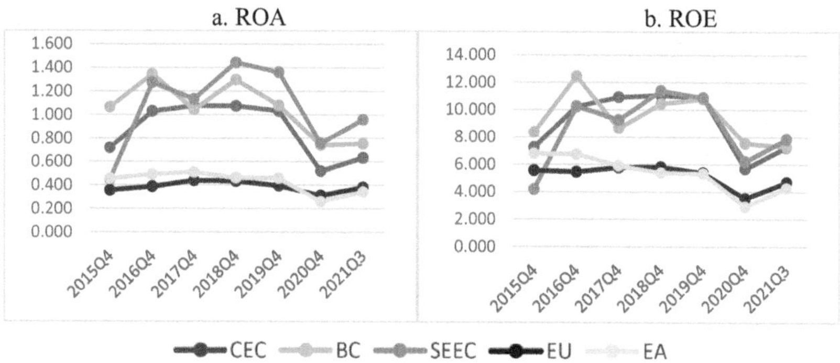

Figure 8.5 Profitability of banks in CE, BC, SEE, EU and EA Countries in 2015–2021 (in %)

Source: Own study based on ECB Consolidated Banking Data: https://sdw.ecb.europa.eu/browse.do?node=9691533.

Table 8.4 CEE banks profitability in 2015–2021 period (in %)

a. ROA

Period	*CEC*				*BC*			*SEEC*		
	Czech Republic	*Hungary*	*Poland*	*Slovakia*	*Estonia*	*Latvia*	*Lithuania*	*Bulgaria*	*Croatia*	*Romania*
2015Q4	1.172	−0.094	0.863	0.930	1.077	1.195	0.919	1.026	−0.854	1.169
2016Q4	1.150	1.267	0.819	0.884	1.546	1.508	0.978	1.480	1.225	1.112
2017Q4	1.091	1.548	0.801	0.862	1.361	0.884	0.877	1.314	0.798	1.283
2018Q4	1.102	1.597	0.761	0.838	1.421	1.221	1.243	1.614	1.179	1.532
2019Q4	1.191	1.471	0.709	0.755	1.120	1.024	1.091	1.409	1.213	1.458
2020Q4	0.576	0.701	0.007	0.490	0.848	0.630	0.741	0.639	0.616	1.011
2021Q3	0.601	1.001	0.365	0.565	0.770	0.884	0.597	0.876	0.836	1.162
Av. 15-21	0.983	1.070	0.661	0.760	1.163	1.049	0.921	1.194	0.716	1.247

(*Continued*)

Table 8.4 (Continued)

b. ROE

Period	CEC				BC			SEEC		
	Czech Republic	*Hungary*	*Poland*	*Slovakia*	*Estonia*	*Latvia*	*Lithuania*	*Bulgaria*	*Croatia*	*Romania*
2015Q4	11.275	0.268	7.743	9.689	6.790	10.746	7.480	8.011	−6.797	11.298
2016Q4	11.857	11.718	7.494	9.886	11.100	14.345	11.895	11.316	8.892	10.601
2017Q4	13.019	14.529	6.882	9.266	9.189	7.607	9.117	10.158	5.870	11.742
2018Q4	13.270	14.685	7.006	9.300	9.801	9.209	12.313	11.778	8.844	13.576
2019Q4	13.944	14.342	6.897	8.268	8.278	9.613	14.454	11.231	9.091	12.327
2020Q4	6.709	7.582	0.124	5.311	7.363	5.206	10.020	4.923	4.695	8.989
2021Q3	7.479	10.606	4.430	6.489	6.705	7.323	7.832	6.832	6.354	10.340
Av. 15-21	11.079	10.533	6.225	8.316	8.461	9.150	10.445	9.179	5.279	11.268

Source: Own study based on ECB Consolidated Banking Data: https://sdw.ecb.europa.eu/browse.do?node=9691533.

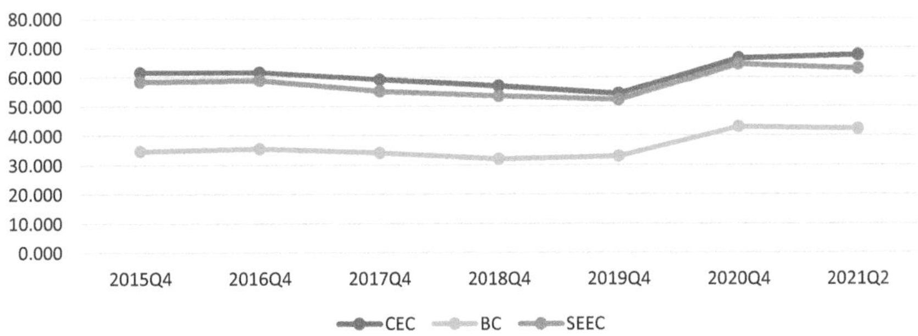

Figure 8.6 Gross public sector debt (general gov., all maturities, all instruments, nominal value), % of GDP, in CE, BC, SEE, 2015–2021q2

Source: Own study based on World Bank database: https://databank.worldbank.org/source/quarterly-public-sector-debt

of change of GDP, resulting in a reduction of the denominator. In 2021, the highest public debt level was observed in Croatia (103.7%), Hungary (77.2%) and Poland (73.8%), and the lowest in all BCs, particularly in Estonia (25.2%) (Table 8.5).

The increase in the size of public debt in 2020 was mainly due to a very significant increase in the scale of the public sector deficit in all CEE groups (Figure 8.7), ranging from 5.8% (BC) to 6.9% (SEE) of GDP, similarly to the EU (6.9%) and EA (7.2%) average levels. Although between 2015 and 2019, almost all CEE countries complied with the deficit limit restriction of 3%, and the Czech Republic, Lithuania, Bulgaria and Croatia had predominantly budget surplus, in 2020 the trend reversed (Table 8.6). The highest levels of public sector deficit in 2020 had Romania, followed by Hungary, Croatia, Lithuania and Poland (all above 7%), and the lowest Bulgaria (4%) and Latvia (4.5%).

Table 8.5 Gross public sector debt (General Gov., all maturities, all instruments, nominal value), % of GDP, in CEE in 2015–2021q2

Period	*CE*				*BC*			*SEE*		
	Czech Republic	*Hungary*	*Poland*	*Slovakia*	*Estonia*	*Latvia*	*Lithuania*	*Bulgaria*	*Croatia*	*Romania*
2015Q4	46.622	74.948	67.146	57.591	12.713	44.525	46.693	30.992	100.178	43.685
2016Q4	43.056	74.286	70.771	58.538	13.605	48.587	44.288	34.863	97.097	44.482
2017Q4	40.949	72.015	66.606	56.871	13.023	46.057	43.123	30.993	92.226	41.915
2018Q4	38.349	69.029	64.795	55.183	12.873	45.325	37.663	28.361	90.140	41.753
2019Q4	35.924	65.812	61.510	53.643	13.401	44.934	40.219	26.392	88.729	41.294
2020Q4	44.475	80.075	74.657	66.165	25.040	51.599	52.030	32.131	108.082	52.833
2021Q2	50.192	77.175	73.806	68.680	25.241	50.828	50.549	31.280	103.70	53.469
Av. 15–21	42.795	73.334	68.470	59.524	16.557	47.408	44.938	30.716	96.075	45.633

Source: Own study, World Bank database: https://databank.worldbank.org/source/quarterly-public-sector-debt.

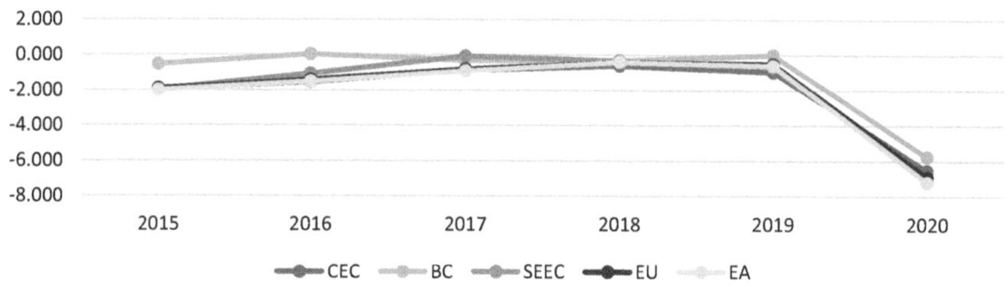

Figure 8.7 General government deficit/surplus (% of GDP) in CE, BC, SEE, EU and EA countries in 2015–2020

https://ec.europa.eu/eurostat/databrowser/view/GOV_10DD_EDPT1__custom_1834442/default/table

Table 8.6 General government deficit/surplus (% of GDP) in CEEC in 2015–2020

Period	*CE*				*BC*			*SEE*		
	Czech Republic	*Hungary*	*Poland*	*Slovakia*	*Estonia*	*Latvia*	*Lithuania*	*Bulgaria*	*Croatia*	*Romania*
2015	−0.6	−2.0	−2.6	−2.7	0.1	−1.4	−0.3	−1.9	−3.4	−0.6
2016	0.7	−1.8	−2.4	−2.6	−0.4	0.2	0.3	0.3	−0.9	−2.6
2017	1.5	−2.5	−1.5	−1.0	−0.5	−0.8	0.4	1.6	0.8	−2.6
2018	0.9	−2.1	−0.2	−1.0	−0.6	−0.8	0.5	1.7	0.2	−2.9
2019	0.3	−2.1	−0.7	−1.3	0.1	−0.6	0.5	2.1	0.3	−4.4
2020	−5.6	−8.0	−7.1	−5.5	−5.6	−4.5	−7.2	−4.0	−7.4	−9.4
Av. 15–20	−0.5	−3.1	−2.4	−2.4	−1.2	−1.3	−1.0	0.0	−1.7	−3.8

https://ec.europa.eu/eurostat/databrowser/view/GOV_10DD_EDPT1__custom_1834442/default/table

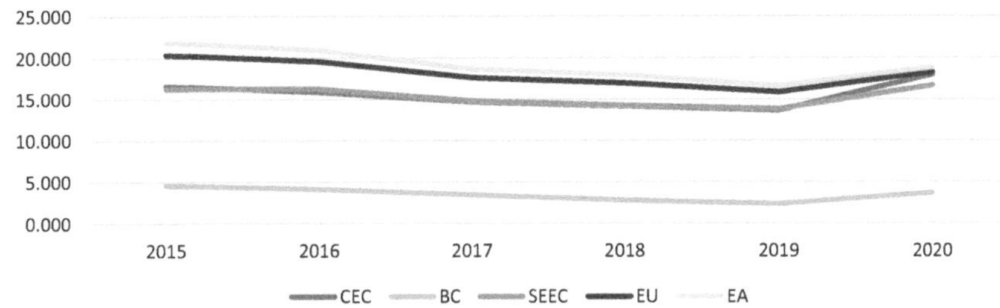

Figure 8.8 Government debt held by banks (as % of government debt) in CEC, BC, SEEC in 2015–2020

Data Source in SDW: https://sdw.ecb.europa.eu/browse.do?node=9693774

The rapidly growing public debt created a heavy burden for the economy and financial units, such as banks, the more that banks in the CEE (except the Baltic countries) have been purchasing a large share of the government debt securities (Figure 8.8).

8.3 An assessment of the CEE banks' financial stability

The overall assessment of CEE banks' financial stability, from the regulatory point of view, is positive. In Q3 2021, the average value of the total capital ratio TCR ranged from 19.6% for CE to 24.6% in the BC group (Figure 8.9), while the average capitalization level in the EU and the EA was in between. In all groups, there was a trend of a significant increase in the TCR level in 2020, mainly due to a reduction in the denominator – risk-weighted assets and off-balance sheet liabilities – as a consequence of an increase in the share of domestic treasury securities in total banking assets; with the value of regulatory capital almost unchanged. In 2021, this indicator decreased slightly across all groups, but remaining significantly higher than the regulatory minima set by the CRR Regulation and the regulations of national macroprudential supervisors. Similar conclusions can be drawn when analyzing capital adequacy measured by Tier 1 ratio.

More stable trends for CE and SEE groups can be observed when analyzing E/TA ratio (Figure 8.10). The highest average leverage ratio in 2021 was obtained by SEE banks (above 12%) and in all regions this indicator was above the EU/EA level. However, most countries show a significant downward trend between 2015 and 2021. In the analyzed period, Lithuanian banking sector had the highest decline and the lowest level of E/TA ratio in 2021, and Estonian the highest.

In addition to capital regulatory measures, the Z-Score index, commonly used in the literature as a stability indicator, was also analyzed. It is based on the notion that bank risk has an adverse impact on profitability and leads to the solvency risk of being unable to absorb losses with the available capital. The score estimates the probability that a bank will run out of capital, on the basis of its capitalization, profitability and the volatility of its returns. It measures the number of

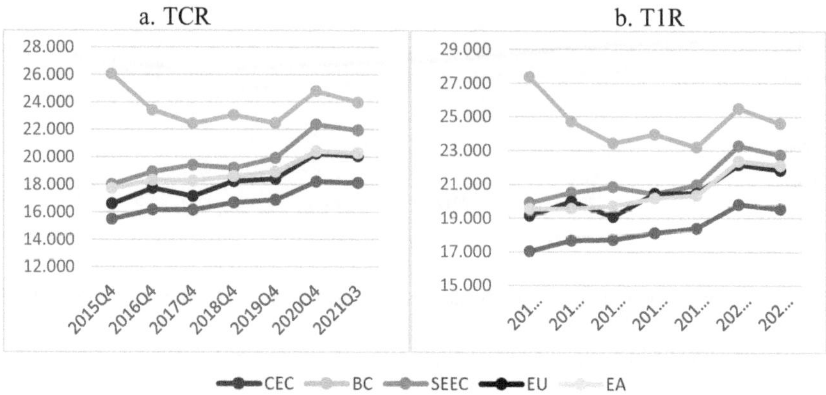

Figure 8.9 Level of TCR and T1R of banks in CEE, BC and EU/EA countries, 2015–2021, (in %)

Source: Own study based on ECB SDW data: https://sdw.ecb.europa.eu/browse.do?node=9691533 (8.05.2022)

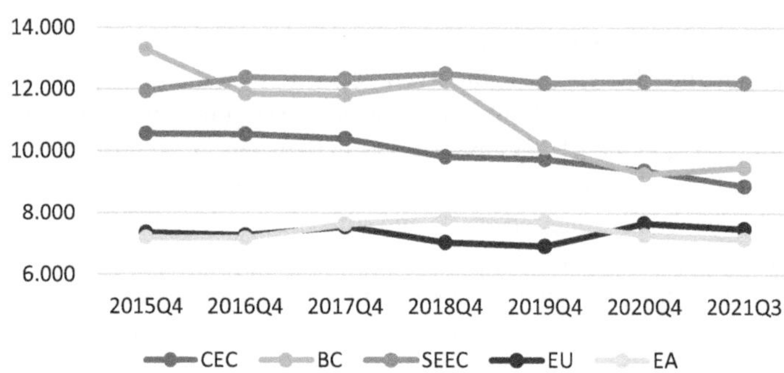

Figure 8.10 Level of Equity/Total Assets ratio in CE, BC, SEE, EU and EA, 2015–2021, (in %)

Source: Own study based on ECB SDW data: https://sdw.ecb.europa.eu/browse.do?node=9691533 (8.05.2022)

standard deviations the ROA must decrease by before the bank's equity is depleted. Consequently, a high Z-score level indicates a low default risk, and vice-versa.

The Z-score ratio is defined as:

$$Z-score=\frac{\frac{\sum_{t=1}^{n}\frac{2\pi_t}{A_t+A_{t-1}}}{n}+\frac{\sum_{t=1}^{n}\frac{E_t+E_{t-1}}{A_t+A_{t-1}}}{n}}{\sigma_{ROA}}=\frac{ROA+CAR}{\sigma_{ROA}}$$

where, A_t – assets in a period t; π_t – net profit in t; $2\pi_t/(A_t + A_{t-1})$ the average value of ROA in t; σROA – standard deviation of ROA; E_t – bank equity in t; $(E_t + E_{t-1})/(A_t + A_{t-1})$ denotes CAR in t; n – number of researched periods (years).

Among the analyzed CEE countries, a slight variation of the level of the Z-score index is observed (Figure 8.11). The highest average values were obtained by the CE group, while the lowest values by the SEE group. A downward trend is in all groups can be observed since 2018. For individual CEE countries (Table 8.7), the highest Z-score level had Poland and Slovakia, while the lowest Romania. In 2020, a significant increase in the score was recorded by the Czech Republic and Latvia, and decrease by Estonia.

To sum up, the capitalization level of all CEE banking sectors is high, although slightly declining in 2021 across all groups, but remaining significantly higher than

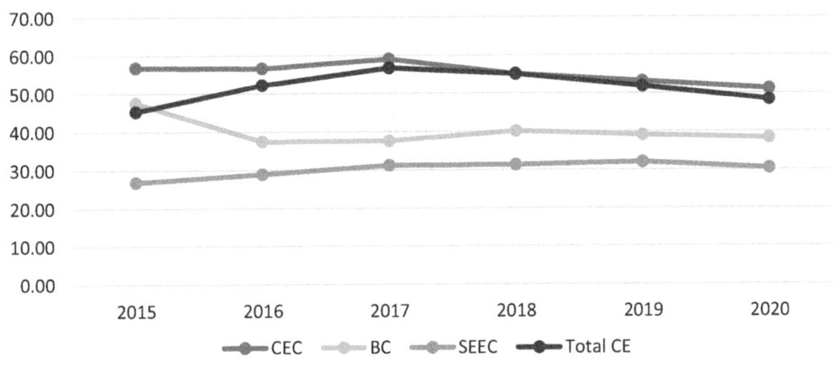

Figure 8.11 Average Z-score index level of banks in CE, BC, SEE in 2015–2020 (arithmetic mean of the survey sample)

Source: Own study – calculation based on data obtained from the BankFocus database

Table 8.7 Average Z-score of banks in CEECs in 2015–2020 (arithmetic mean of the survey sample)

Period	CE				BC			SEE		
	Czech Republic	*Hungary*	*Poland*	*Slovakia*	*Estonia*	*Latvia*	*Lithuania*	*Bulgaria*	*Croatia*	*Romania*
2015	44.01	52.84	59.65	70.89	49.93	28.63	64.06	32.17	28.77	19.48
2016	46.19	36.51	73.46	70.53	42.19	26.86	43.23	35.82	29.59	21.30
2017	45.15	37.21	80.75	73.10	42.21	26.93	43.54	32.75	34.31	26.46
2018	34.91	31.99	80.43	73.02	41.41	34.69	44.16	31.80	33.68	28.44
2019	36.58	30.94	73.67	71.41	46.43	26.61	43.89	31.11	35.66	29.12
2020	43.52	25.71	64.34	71.22	32.68	41.87	40.11	28.43	34.59	28.02
Av. 15–20	41.52	34.64	73.36	71.69	42.03	31.84	44.98	31.94	32.82	25.96

Source: Own study – calculation based on data obtained from the BankFocus database.

the regulatory minima. The CE group has the worst TCR/T1R results (below the UE average); however, the Z-score stability indicator gives a different picture – the highest score for the CE group, particularly for Poland and Slovakia; the lowest for the SEE region.

8.4 Bank efficiency in the CEE region

Bank efficiency is a complex concept, and in this section it will be assessed based on a comprehensive indicator: multi-level performance score (MLPS), as proposed by Miklaszewska and Kil (2016), and by analyzing credit accessibility in the CEE countries, which is a prime responsibility of banks (Calomiris and Haber 2014). The role of bank credit to the private sector for stimulating the economy can be clearly illustrated by the following comparison: in 2019, it constituted 116% of GDP in highly developed countries and 48% in developing countries (10% in Argentina) (BIS 2020). Credit availability depends also on the structure of the financial system and trends in the macroeconomy (Bhattacharya, Boot and Thakor 2004).

The MLPS is an index which assesses bank profit-generating capacity, cost efficiency, accessibility of credit to the non-financial sector and stability indicators. The score is computed as a sum of five areas vital to bank long-term stability and performance: three efficiency ratios: ROE, C/I, and Loans to Assets (L/A) ratio and two stability indicators: Z-score and NPLs. It is defined by the following formula:

$$\text{MLP Score} = \text{ROE} + \text{L/A} + \text{C/I} + \text{Z-Score} + \text{NPL}$$

Scores for the MLPS in all five areas are allocated by taking the results for each indicator for the whole group in a given year and dividing it into ten deciles. Each subsequent decile above the median for ROE, L/A, and the Z-Score has a score ranging from +1 to +5, while each subsequent decile below the median has a score ranging from −1 to −5. For C/I and NPL indicators, the signs are opposite. The median for the group has a value of 0. Due to this scoring methodology, the ratio has a simple interpretation – the higher the value of the MLPS, the better the assessment of the bank.

Analyzing the MLPS indicator for the CEE group, a large variation in results over the period under study (2015–2020) was observed (Table 8.8). The highest values were obtained by banks operating in Lithuania (11.91), Estonia (8.63), Slovakia (6.65) and the Czech Republic (5.88), while the lowest in Latvia (−5.24), Hungary (−5.10) and Croatia (−4.85). The COVID pandemic has a relatively strong negative impact for Croatian and Romanian banks and a positive one for Lithuanian banks.

To sum up, the comprehensive MLPS index complements the picture from previous observations. It stresses a strongly negative performance assessment for Hungary, Latvia and Croatia, and a positive assessment for Lithuania, Estonia, Slovakia and the Czech Republic. MLPS supports some conclusions from the profitability-based section: that the Baltic Countries (without Latvia) and the CE countries (without Poland and Hungary) have the best overall assessment of their

Table 8.8 Average MLPS level of CEE banks in 2015–2020 (arithmetic mean of the survey sample)

Period	*CE*				*BC*			*SEE*		
	Czech Republic	*Hungary*	*Poland*	*Slovakia*	*Estonia*	*Latvia*	*Lithuania*	*Bulgaria*	*Croatia*	*Romania*
2015	5.76	−3.11	−1.06	8.23	7.33	−8.29	12.50	0.29	−2.30	0.05
2016	6.60	−2.59	−0.41	6.23	7.78	−8.06	13.75	−2.81	−2.39	−2.30
2017	6.88	−4.80	0.14	6.38	9.56	−6.38	12.25	−2.14	−6.65	−1.68
2018	3.88	−6.15	1.24	4.69	11.00	−5.23	10.75	−4.65	−5.39	−2.47
2019	6.05	−8.08	0.88	6.46	8.63	0.75	9.50	−3.80	−4.65	−2.84
2020	6.24	−8.78	1.70	7.92	7.63	−0.90	13.00	−3.50	−7.82	−5.07
Av. 15–20	5.88	−5.10	0.27	6.65	8.63	−5.24	11.91	−2.73	−4.85	−2.24

Source: Own study – calculation based on data obtained from the BankFocus database.

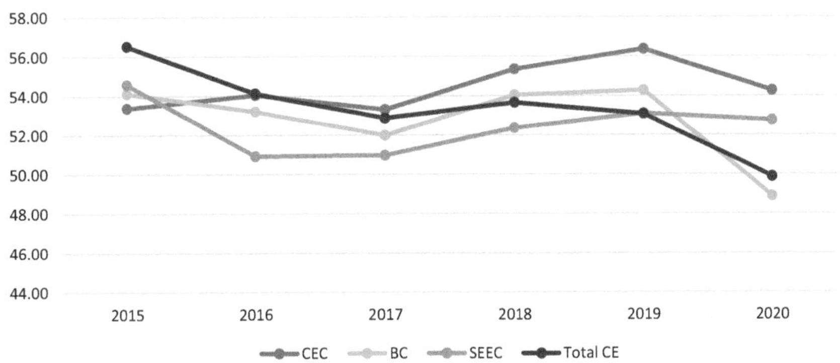

Figure 8.12 Average level of Total Loans/Total Asset ratio for CEE banks, 2015–2020 (arithmetic mean of the analyzed sample)

Source: Own study – calculation based on data from BankFocus database

banking sector performance. However, both MLPS and the Z-score indicate that the SEE group lags behind in the overall assessment of bank stability and performance.

Analyzing bank efficiency and performance, an important part is also played by banks' lending policies and credit availability, as measures by changes in the value of the loan portfolio and its structure. To analyze credit availability, the following key indicators were used: a share of loans to the non-financial sector in total assets (L/A), the rate of change in the value of loan portfolio to the non-financial sector (including corporate loans, consumer loans and housing loans. Due to a limited data availability, the analysis is based on the BankFocus database and presented as a sample average.

As illustrated in Figure 8.12, till 2019 in all CEE countries, the average TL/TA ratio exceeded 50% and had an upward trend between 2017 and 2019. In 2020,

Table 8.9 Average level of Total loans/Total asset ratio of banks in CEC, BC and SEEC in 2015–2020 (arithmetic average of survey sample)

Period	*CEC*				*BC*			*SEEC*		
	Czech Republic	*Hungary*	*Poland*	*Slovakia*	*Estonia*	*Latvia*	*Lithuania*	*Bulgaria*	*Croatia*	*Romania*
2015	56.91	32.25	61.39	62.94	63.44	36.86	62.03	50.28	58.16	55.28
2016	55.48	40.28	57.58	62.84	61.93	36.68	60.99	43.01	54.62	55.15
2017	50.65	42.54	56.21	63.81	60.63	32.87	62.45	44.38	53.41	55.12
2018	53.42	45.62	55.23	67.14	62.01	37.69	62.41	47.96	54.71	54.40
2019	52.74	50.77	53.04	68.93	63.98	35.48	63.35	48.52	55.91	54.85
2020	53.81	46.85	46.91	69.46	59.09	35.42	52.11	48.46	55.60	54.18
Av. 2015–2020	53.72	44.01	54.70	65.85	61.82	35.76	60.49	47.07	55.38	54.80

Source: Own study – calculation based on data obtained from the BankFocus database.

there was a significant reduction of total loans in banks' assets for all groups, particularly for BCs.

However, there is a significant variation of this ratio among countries (Table 8.9). For the whole analyzed period, the highest share of TL/TA had Slovakia, followed by Estonia and Lithuania (above 60%), while the lowest ratio had Latvia (35.8%) and Hungary (44%). Only two countries (the Czech Republic and Slovakia) saw an increase in the ratio in 2020, and the highest reduction in the value of the ratio was recorded in Lithuania and Poland (Table 8.9).

8.5 Bank financial stability in Central and Eastern European countries: The result of panel data regressions

To perform panel data regressions, the type and scope of the available data have to be taken in consideration. Thus, the dynamic panel model was employed – generalized method of moment – commonly referred to as GMM, in the GMM-SYS version (Blundell and Bond 1998), which is considered most adequate in financial research, particular in studies regarding banking. One of the advantages of this method is the deviation from the standard assumption of strict exogeneity of regressors. It also allows for employing the lagged values of the dependent variable. Method based on GMM are, therefore, particularly useful for models including endogenous or predetermined explanatory variables (Danska-Borsiak 2009). Moreover, the small sample, ranging from 471 to 761 observations, is also a factor that supports the use of the GMM-SYS model. Statistical inference for model parameters has been carried out based on the 1-step estimate; 2-step method could lead to erroneous conclusions, especially in the case of heteroscedasticity of the random component. For diagnostic purposes, the Sargan test for the 2-step method was used (Hansen test), as well as Arellano-Bond autocorrelation tests for first differences: AR (1) and AR (2).

The estimated dynamic models of regression is given by the equation:

$$FIN.\ STABIL_{it} = const + a_1 xFIN.\ STABIL_{it-1} + a_2 xMACRO.VAR_{it} + a_3 xMICRO.VAR_{it} + a_4 xPUB.DEBT_{it} + v_{it}$$

where, FIN.STABIL – measure of bank financial stability; MACRO.VAR – the vector of values of macroeconomic variables in period t; MICRO.VAR – a vector of control variables characterizing the specific operation of a particular bank in the period t; PUB.DEBT – vector of experimental variables on the size and composition of the country's public debt and deficit and on the bank's involvement in public debt financing; v_{it} – the random component, which is the sum of the individual, unchanged in time effect and the pure random error ε.

All control variables were applied in the model, because they can be endogenous, with only one lag of each endogenous variable in the GMM estimations. Time effects are included as exogenous instruments. A description of the explanatory and explanatory variables is presented in Table 8.10 and their descriptive statistics in the appendix (Tables A.8.1–A.8.4). The explanatory variables were also analyzed for possible significant correlation using correlation coefficients and the results are presented in the form of a correlation matrix in the appendix. The results of the analyses using panel data regression are presented in Table 8.11.

Table 8.10 Characteristics of variables used in panel model for bank stability in the CEE, 2015–2020

Variable	*Description*	*Data source*
Explained variables		
TCR	Total Capital Ratio – a measure of a bank solvency (broad approach)	BankFocus
T1R	Tier 1 Capital Ratio – a measure of a bank solvency (narrow approach)	BankFocus
E_A	Equity to total assets – a measure of bank financial leverage	BankFocus
Z-SC	Stability measure of bank distance from bankruptcy	Own calculations based on the data from BankFocus
MLPS	Multi-Level Performance Score – performance measure based on 5 profitability and safety indicators	Own calculations based on the data from BankFocus
Explanatory variables – macroeconomic characteristics		
GDP_GR	Annual average GDP rate of change – a measure of the economic growth	World Bank
INF	Inflation, consumer prices (annual %)	World Bank
DOMC_GDP	Domestic credit to private sector by banks (% of GDP) – a measure of the development of the banking market	World Bank
HHI	Herfindahl-Hirschman Index – a measure of concentration of banking sector	ECB – Banking Structural Financial Indicators

(*Continued*)

Table 8.10 (*Continued*)

Variable	*Description*	*Data source*
Explanatory variables – microeconomic characteristics		
TL_TA	Share of net loans in total assets – measure of bank credit exposure	BankFocus
LN_A	Total assets – a measure of bank size	BankFocus
ROA	Average rate of return on assets – a measure of profitability	BankFocus
NPL	Share of impaired loans in a bank loan portfolio – a measure bank credit risk materialization	BankFocus
NII_OR	Non-interest income to operating revenues (%) – measure of income diversification	BankFocus
LIQA_TA	Relation of liquid assets to total assets – a measure of a bank liquidity	BankFocus
S	Binary variable specifying the organizational and legal form: 1 – commercial bank, 0 – cooperative and savings bank	BankFocus
Experimental variables – public debt (country level)		
PD_GDP	Public sector debt as a share of GDP	World Bank
LTPD_TPD	Long-term public sector debt to total public sector debt – the term structure of public debt	World Bank
SEC_TPD	Debt securities to total gross PSD (%) – the instrumental structure of public debt	World Bank
CGD_TPD	Central government debt to total public debt (%) – the entity structure of public debt issuer	World Bank
DEF	General government deficit/surplus (% of GDP) – measure of government debt growth	Eurostat
COV*PD_GDP	Interaction variable – product of the binary variable COV (1 – for 2020, 0 – for 2015-2019 period, and the variable PD GDP	Own calculations based on the data from World Bank
Experimental variables – public debt (bank level)		
GOVS_TA	Government securities purchased by the bank as a proportion of total assets (%) – bank involvement in investing in the government debt	Own calculations based on the data from BankFocus
GOVS_GR	Annual change in the bank's claims on government securities (%) – the increase in the bank's exposure to the government debt securities	Own calculations based on the data from BankFocus

Table 8.11 Determinants of bank financial stability in CEE countries – panel data regression (GMM-SYS dynamic model)

Explained variable	*TCR*	*T1R*	*E_A*	*Z_SC*	*MLPS*
Lagged value of dependent variable (−1)	0.681***	0.786***	0.741***	0.921***	0.500***
	(0.129)	(0.113)	(0.197)	(0.117)	(0.084)
Const	−1.335	−7.41	−7.671*	−53.125**	5.392
	(8.280)	(8.312)	(4.393)	(21.503)	(5.528)

(*Continued*)

Table 8.11 (*Continued*)

Explained variable	*TCR*	*T1R*	*E_A*	*Z_SC*	*MLPS*
GDP_GR	−0.162	−0.120	0.086	0.552*	0.121
	(0.171)	(0.176)	(0.099)	(0.307)	(0.187)
INF	0.102	0.292*	0.057	0.029	−0.139
	(0.154)	(0.155)	(0.078)	(0.27)	(0.160)
DOMC_GDP	0.064	0.084	0.067*	0.199	0.084
	(0.062)	(0.069)	(0.035)	(0.143)	(0.053)
HHI	−4.428	−4.486	−10.124*	−27.081	−29.748**
	(9.067)	(10.499)	(5.727)	(16.733)	(12.360)
TL_TA	−0.051	−0.043	0.006	0.141	
	(0.038)	(0.035)	(0.019)	(0.12)	
LN_TA	0.018	−0.027	−0.202*	−0.228	0.908***
	(0.188)	(0.191)	(0.109)	(0.443)	(0.190)
ROA	1.13***	1.244***	0.818**		
	(0.338)	(0.358)	(0.392)		
NPL	0.035	0.027	0.033	0.144*	
	(0.032)	(0.026)	(0.037)	(0.084)	
NII_OR	−0.027	−0.017	−0.017	0.008	0.057***
	(0.018)	(0.017)	(0.016)	(0.029)	(0.022)
LIQA_TA	0.008	0.003	0.021	0.111	−0.152***
	(0.030)	(0.028)	(0.021)	(0.14)	(0.021)
S	1.19	1.321*	0.779	0.917	1.825***
	(0.724)	(0.723)	(0.59)	(1.454)	(0.691)
PD_GDP	0.015	0.012	0.014	−0.005	−0.076
	(0.025)	(0.025)	(0.02)	(0.052)	(0.05)
LTPD_TPD	−0.056	−0.075	−0.046	0.072	0.090
	(0.077)	(0.09)	(0.061)	(0.153)	(0.081)
SEC_TPD	0.005	0.038	0.028	0.048	−0.010
	(0.055)	(0.063)	(0.031)	(0.123)	(0.057)
GD_TPD	**0.117***	0.131	0.103**	0.288**	−0.186**
	(0.071)	(0.083)	(0.048)	(0.12)	(0.076)
DEF	−0.448**	−0.407**	0.288***	−0.493	−0.483**
	(0.183)	(0.206)	(0.106)	(0.326)	(0.242)
COV*PD_GDP	−0.022	−0.021	−0.016	0.002	−0.014
	(0.018)	(0.019)	(0.011)	(0.027)	(0.018)
GOVS_TA	0.031	0.040	0.014	0.193	−0.120***
	(0.028)	(0.031)	(0.019)	(0.134)	(0.026)
GOVS_GR	0.000	0.000*	0.000	0.000	0.001
	(0.000)	(0.000)	(0.000)	(0.001)	(0.000)
No. of observations	584	471	617	584	761
No. of banks	135	115	140	138	180
No. of instruments	36	36	36	35	33
AR (1)	−3.934	−4.247	−2.324	−2.456	−5.623
	[0.000]	[0.000]	[0.020]	[0.014]	[0.000]
AR (2)	−0.852	−1.429	1.149	0.374	0.508
	[0.394]	[0.153]	[0.250]	[0.708]	[0.612]
Sargan test	19.859	19.030	19.592	16.564	18.098
(two-step)	[0.099]	[0.122]	[0.106]	[0.220]	[0.154]

Note: AR (1) – 1st order autocorrelation test. AR (2) – 2nd order autocorrelation test. Robust standard errors in parentheses and *p*-values in brackets. Time effects are included but not reported. System GMM (1 lag used as instrument).

***significance at the level of 1%, **significance at the level of 5%, *significance at the level of 10%.

Source: Own calculations.

The regression results presented in Table 8.11 allows to form the following observations:

- TCR and T1R are negatively affected by the deficit of the public sector, i.e., banks operating in CEE countries tend to increase their capital adequacy ratios under higher public finance deficits, which, as shown in earlier analysis, is due primarily to reducing the value of risk-weighted assets (purchasing domestic zero-risk-weighted securities) rather than by increasing the value of regulatory capital.
- For the leverage ratio (E_TA), budget deficit (with minus sign) has a positive impact on the ratio, which means that in condition of deteriorating public finances, the ability to issue new shares and accumulate profits is reduced and, with a systematic increase in the balance sheet total, results in a reduction in the value of the E_TA ratio.
- for the MPLS index, the impact of the budget deficit, central government debt to total debt and the share of government securities in bank assets are negative and statistically significant. This means that countries with a higher relative level of public deficit and debt and banks investing their funds to a greater extent in government securities observe lower MLPS index values and, consequently, have worst assessment of overall performance,
- there is no evidence of the impact of the currency structure, the instrumental structure and the structure of debt buyers (PD_BANKS) on the financial stability and performance of individual CEE banks.

For other variables, in the case of the MLPS index, a positive effect of bank size (LN_TA), greater diversification of income sources (NII_OR) and commercial bank business model (S) was observed and a negative impact of banking concentration was also confirmed. It is also important to note the positive impact of banks' profitability (ROA) on financial stability.

To sum up, the regression results confirm a various negative effects of public debt (deficit) on bank stability. Banks tended to increase their capital adequacy ratios but mostly due to reducing the value of risk-weighted assets (purchasing government securities) rather than by increasing the value of regulatory capital, with a reduction also in the value of the E_TA ratio. Bank efficiency as measured by the MPLS index was also negatively affected by the impact of the budget deficit, central government debt to total debt and the share of government securities in bank assets.

8.6 Bank lending in Central and Eastern European countries: Panel data regressions results

The panel data regression method (dynamic models, GMM-SYS) was also used to analyze the impact of public debt on bank lending policies. The estimated dynamic model of regression is given by the equation:

$$CR.\,POL_{it} = const + a_1 xCR.POL_{it-1} + a_2 xMACRO.VAR_{it} + a_3 xMICRO.VAR_{it} + a_4 xPUB.DEBT_{it} + v_{it}$$

where, CR. POL – variable characterizing the bank's lending policy; MACRO. VAR – the vector of values of macroeconomic variables in period t; MICRO. VAR – a vector of control variables characterizing the specific operation of a particular bank in the period t; PUB.DEBT – vector of experimental variables on the size and composition of the country's public debt and deficit and on the bank's involvement in public debt financing; v_{it} – the random component, which is the sum of the individual, unchanged in time effect and the pure random error ε.

All control variables were applied in the model, because they can be endogenous. Only one lag of each endogenous variable was used. Time effects were included as exogenous instruments. A description of the variables is presented in Table 8.12; their descriptive statistics are included the evaluation of correlations was based on the correlation matrix provided as Appendix.

The results of the analyses using panel data regression are presented in Tables 8.13.

Table 8.12 Characteristics of variables used in panel studies of bank lending policies in selected CEE countries in 2015–2020

Variable	*Decription of variable*	*Data source*
Explained variables		
TL_TA	Total loans to the non-financial sector to total assets	BankFocus
TL_GR	Percentage annual change in net total loan portfolio (receivables from non-financial sector) – a measure of the change in the bank loan exposure – data in local currency	Own calculations based on the data from BankFocus
CONSL_TL	Consumer loans to total loans	Own calculations based on the data from BankFocus
CORL_TL	Corporate loans to total loans	Own calculations based on the data from BankFocus
MORL_TL	Mortgage loans to total loans	Own calculations based on the data from BankFocus
CONSL_GR	Percentage annual change in net worth of consumer loans portfolio – a measure of the change in the bank's exposure to household credit financing – data in local currency	Own calculations based on the data from BankFocus
CORL_GR	Percentage annual change in net worth of corporate loans portfolio – a measure of the change in the bank's exposure to corporate finance – data in local currency	Own calculations based on the data from BankFocus
MORL_GR	Percentage annual change in net portfolio value of mortgage loans – a measure relating to the change in the bank's exposure to financing the purchase of real estate – data in local currency	Own calculations based on the data from BankFocus
Explanatory variables – macroeconomic characteristics		
GDP	Annual average GDP rate of change – a measure of the economic growth rate (%)	World Bank
INF	Inflation, consumer prices (annual %)	World Bank

(*Continued*)

Table 8.12 (Continued)

Variable	*Decription of variable*	*Data source*
DOMC_GDP	Domestic credit to private sector by banks (% of GDP) – a measure of the development of the banking market	World Bank
HHI	Herfindahl-Hirschman Index – a measure of concentration of banking sector	ECB: Banking Structural Financial Indicators
Explanatory variables – microeconomic characteristics		
LN_A	Total assets – a measure of the size of the bank	BankFocus
ROA	Average rate of return on assets – a measure of profitability (%)	BankFocus
NPL	Share of impaired loans in a bank's loan portfolio – a measure of the scale of the bank's credit risk materialization (%)	BankFocus
TCR	Total Capital Ratio (%) – a measure of a bank's stability based on its solvency (broad approach)	BankFocus
NII_OR	Non-interest income to operating revenues (%) – measure of diversification of a bank's sources of income	BankFocus
LIQA_TA	Relation of liquid assets to total assets – a measure of a bank's liquidity	BankFocus
S	Binary variable specifying the organizational and legal form of banking activity: 1 – commercial banks, 0 – cooperative and savings banks	BankFocus
Experimental variables – public debt (country)		
PD_GDP	Public sector debt as a share of national GDP – a measure of the total debt of the public finance sector (%)	World Bank
LTPD_TPD	Long-term public sector debt to total public sector debt – variable characterizing the term structure of the country's public debt (%)	World Bank
SEC_TPD	Debt securities to total gross PSD (%) – variable characterizing the instrumental structure of the country's public debt	World Bank
CGD_TPD	Central government debt to total public debt (%) – variable characterizing the entity structure of public debt issuers	World Bank
DEF	General government deficit/surplus (% of GDP) – measure of government debt growth	Eurostat
PD_BANKS	Government debt held by other monetary financial institutions (as % of government debt) – a measure of the banking sector's exposure to the country's sovereign debt market	ECB: Government Finance Statistics
PD_WALU	Government debt denominated in currencies other than national currency – variable characterizing the entity structure of public debt issuers (%)	World Bank

(*Continued*)

Table 8.12 (Continued)

Variable	*Decription of variable*	*Data source*
COV*PD_GDP	Interaction variable – product of the binary variable COV (1 – year 2020, COVID-19 pandemic period; 0 – years 2015-2019, COVID-19 pre-pandemic period) and the variable PD_GDP	Own calculations based on the data from World Bank
Experimental variables – public debt (bank policy)		
GOVS_TA	Government securities purchased by the bank as a proportion of total assets (%) – variable characterizing the bank's policy on investing in the government debt market	Own calculations based on the data from BankFocus
GOVS_GR	Annual change in the bank's claims on government securities (%) – variable characterizing the increase in the bank's exposure to the government debt securities market	Own calculations based on the data from BankFocus

Źródło: Opracowanie własne.

Table 8.13 Determinants of access to credit in the CEE countries (structural approach): Panel data regression (GMM-SYS dynamic model)

Explained variable	*TL_TA*	*CONSL_TL*	*CORL_TL*	*MORL_TL*
Lagged value of dependent variable (−1)	0.308	0.962***	0.794***	0.509**
	(0.2)	(0.041)	(0.125)	(0.248)
Const	71.351***	2.46	19.53	5.453
	(24.202)	(10.677)	(13.534)	(20.696)
GDP_GR	0.323	0.574	−0.306	0.448
	(0.295)	(0.433)	(0.476)	(0.649)
INF	0.069	0.219	0.012	−0.468
	(0.154)	(0.282)	(0.319)	(0.291)
DOMC_GDP	0.149*	0.136	−0.122	0.084
	(0.081)	(0.123)	(0.098)	(0.158)
HHI	6.231	35.372	19.679	−35.719
	(19.106)	(23.433)	(21.97)	(25.169)
LN_TA	0.482	−0.161	−0.419	1.514
	(0.293)	(0.171)	(0.408)	(0.969)
ROA	0.261**	−0.138	0.773*	1.502**
	(0.112)	(0.281)	(0.449)	(0.638)
NPL	−0.141***	0.005	0.071	−0.069
	(0.046)	(0.042)	(0.066)	(0.075)
TCR	−0.059	0.08	0.068	−0.087
	(0.057)	(0.066)	(0.076)	(0.085)
NII_OR	−0.088**	−0.016	−0.006	−0.036
	(0.036)	(0.023)	(0.034)	(0.052)
LIQA_TA	−0.488***	−0.016	0.031	0.000
	(0.112)	(0.026)	(0.043)	(0.063)
S	−0.788	2.048*	1.072	3.333
	(1.056)	(1.159)	(1.31)	(2.466)

(Continued)

Table 8.13 (Continued)

Explained variable	*TL_TA*	*CONSL_TL*	*CORL_TL*	*MORL_TL*
PD_GDP	−0.013	−0.045	−0.055	0.060
	(0.058)	(0.065)	(0.064)	(0.081)
LTPD_TPD	−0.226**	−0.110	−0.248	0.037
	(0.104)	(0.155)	(0.179)	(0.228)
SEC_TPD	0.050	0.254*	0.149	−0.200
	(0.068)	(0.139)	(0.107)	(0.164)
GD_TPD	−0.056	−0.223*	0.074	0.08
	(0.139)	(0.134)	(0.165)	(0.204)
DEF	−0.533	−0.046	0.334	−1.212
	(0.419)	(0.371)	(0.514)	(0.977)
PD_BANKS	−0.183	−0.098	0.176	−0.390
	(0.167)	(0.167)	(0.194)	(0.392)
PD_WALU	0.098*	0.138**	−0.032	−0.052
	(0.059)	(0.065)	(0.064)	(0.087)
COV*PD_GDP	−0.025	0.049	−0.012	−0.032
	(0.018)	(0.03)	(0.029)	(0.028)
GOVS_TA	−0.262***	0.031	−0.006	−0.177
	(0.077)	(0.034)	(0.057)	(0.122)
GOVS_GR	−0.001***	−0.001***	−0.001**	0.003
	(0.000)	(0.000)	(0.000)	(0.003)
Number of observations	591	482	472	223
Number of banks	135	113	111	56
Number of instruments	36	36	36	36
AR (1)	−2.254	−2.721	−3.727	−2.929
	[0.024]	[0.007]	[0.000]	[0.003]
AR (2)	1.291	1.716	0.171	1.785
	[0.197]	[0.086]	[0.864]	[0.074]
Sargan test (two-step)	8.322	15.233	22.022	16.270
	[0.822]	[0.293]	[0.055]	[0.235]

Note: AR (1) – 1st order autocorrelation test. AR (2) – 2nd order autocorrelation test. Robust standard errors in parentheses and *p*-values in brackets. Time effects are included but not reported. System GMM (1 lag used as instrument).

***significance at the level of 1%, **significance at the level of 5%, *significance at the level of 10%.

Source: Own calculations.

Based on the results presented in Table 8.13, total loan volume in relation to total assets was significantly affected by the following:

- positively by domestic credit to private sector by banks (DOMC_GDP) and the currency structure of public debt,
- negatively by the share of government debt securities and changes in the value of treasury securities held by banks in their assets and the term structure of loans (LTPD_TPD).

Analyzing the types of loans, a negative influence of the GOVS_GR variable was also confirmed for corporate and consumer loans. The share of consumer loans in total loans was positively influenced by the instrumental structure of debt issuance (SEC_TPD) and the currency structure of debt issued (PD_WALU), while negatively by the institutional structure of issuers (GD_TPD) Mortgage loans were positively influenced only by bank profitability (ROA), similarly like corporate loans. For the CONSL_TL variable, a positive impact of the commercial (universal) bank business model was shown (S). For variables unrelated to public debt, banks' loans were positively influenced by profitability of individual banks (ROA) and negatively by NPLs, diversification of banks' sources of income (NII_OR) and banks' liquidity ratio (LIQA_TA).

8.7 Conclusions

This chapter assessed empirically the impact of the new bank environment, related largely to the pandemic, on bank stability and efficiency in the CEE region, at country and bank level. The empirical findings allow to formulate the following conclusions:

- the shock of the pandemic in 2020 created a strong disruption in macroeconomic trends and have resulted in largely expanding budget deficits in 2020 and in reversing the tendency to control public debt through the region;
- some countries, such as Croatia, were disproportionally affected in terms of GDP growth and bank profitability, because of the structural characteristics (strong dependence on the services sector);
- some banking sectors have exposed resilience to the external shocks (such as in the Czech Republic or Estonia), for some the shock strengthen already detrimental trends (Poland, Hungary);
- banks operating in CEE countries tended to increase their capital adequacy ratios primarily due to reducing the value of risk-weighted assets (purchasing domestic zero-risk-weighted securities), rather than by increasing the value of regulatory capital;
- particularly for the MLPS, the impact of the budget deficit, central government debt to total debt and the share of government securities in bank assets were negative and statistically significant. This means that countries with a higher relative level of public deficit and debt and banks investing their funds to a greater extent in government securities observe lower MLPS values and, consequently, have worst assessment of overall performance,
- for some banking sectors there were additional factors explaining poor banking performance, which were not analyzed in this chapter, such as reputational scandals in the banking sector in Latvia (Samson and Kusz 2019).

Overall, economic and statistical analysis support the initial hypothesis that although pandemic-related shocks were universal, bank resilience in the CEE region was not. The Baltic countries (without Latvia) and the CE countries (without Poland and Hungary) have the best overall assessment of their banking sector stability and performance. Both MLPS and the Z-score indicate that the SEE group, despite many positive economic characteristics, lags behind in the overall assessment of bank stability and performance. The analysis has also indicated that the level of concentration in the banking sector is irrelevant for the outcomes – in both highly concentrated region (BC) and a low concentrated(CE) one can observed well-performing and poorly performing banking sectors.

Finally, it is worth noticing that the Polish banks, once among the best performing sectors in the CEE, now are among the most problematic, particularly with respect to profitability (ROA) and efficiency (MLPS) indicators, which partially can be attributed to the way of financing public debt and a large proportion of government-owned banking assets. Poland has a high GDP growth, low banking concentration and an acceptable level of domestic credit accessibility, so the explanation for a steadily deteriorating profitability might be the highest proportion among CEE countries of public sector control of the banking assets, which may be a subject of a further studies. While publicly controlled banks may play an important role in mitigating some market failures and broadening access to finance, their ownership structure, mandate and other specific characteristics can create unique risks to financial stability and public finances and publicly controlled banks tend to underperform private banks in standard bank performance metrics (IMF 2022).

Note

1 Publication financed by the Cracow University of Economics within the framework of the Conference Activity Support Program – WAK 2022.

References

Ahir H., Bloom N., Furceri D. (2022), The World Uncertainty Index, NBER Working Paper, www.nber.org/papers/w29763.

Allen, F., Babus, A., Carletti, E. (2009), Financial Crises: Theory and Evidence, European University Institute, June, available at, http://apps.eui.eu/Personal/Carletti/ARFE-Crises-08June09-final.pdf, referred on 07/03/2016.

Berger A.N., Humphrey D. (1997), Efficiency of Financial Institutions: International Survey and Direction for Future Research, *Journal of Operational Research*, Vol. 98, No. 2, pp. 175–212.

Bhagat, S., Bolton, B., Lu, J. (2015), Size, Leverage, and Risk-taking of Financial Institutions, *Journal of Banking & Finance*, Vol. 59, No. 10, pp. 520–537.

Bhattacharya S., Boot A., Thakor A. (2004), *Credit, Intermediation and the Macroeconomy*, Oxford University Press, Oxford.

BIS (2018), Structural Changes in Banking After the Crisis, CGFS Papers No 60, Jan.

BIS (2020), Financial Market Development, Monetary Policy and Financial Stability in Emerging Market Economies, Paper No 113.

Blundell R.W., Bond S.R. (1988), Initial Conditions and Moment Restrictions in Dynamic Panel Model Data Models, *Journal of Econometrics*, Vol. 87, No. 1, August, pp. 115–143.

Bongini P., Cucinelli P., Di Battista M.L., Nieri L. (2019), Profitability Shocks and Recovery in Time of Crisis Evidence from European Banks, *Finance Research Letters*, nr 30.

Carletti E., Claessens S., Fatás A., Vives X. (2020), *The Bank Business Model in the Post-Covid-19 World*, CEPR, London.

Checherita Ch., Rother P. (2010), The Impact of High and Growing Government Debt on Economic Growth. An Empirical Investigation for the Euro Area, ECB Working Paper No. 1237/August.

Danielsson J., Valenzuela M., Zer I. (2022). How Global Risk Perceptions Affect Economic Growth, FEDS Notes, Washington: Board of Governors of the Federal Reserve System, February 03.

Deloitte (2020), CEE Banks Facing Challenging Times. Economic turbulence to boost consolidation, December, https://www2.deloitte.com/lt/en/pages/finance/articles/Deloitte-CEE-Banking-MA-Study-2020.html

Demirgüç-Kunt, A., Huizinga, H. (2010), Bank Activity and Funding Strategies: The Impact on Risk and Return, *Journal of Financial Economics*, Vol. 98, No 3, pp. 626–650.

European Parliament (2021), Impacts of the COVID-19 Pandemic on EU Industries, https://www.europarl.europa.eu/thinktank/en/document.html?reference=IPOL_STU(2021)662903.

Fiordelisi F. (2007), Shareholder Value Efficiency in European Banking, *Journal of Banking & Finance*, Vol. 31, No. 7, July, pp. 2151–2171.

Fiordelisi F., Marques-Ibanez D., Molyneux P. (2011), Efficiency and Risk in European Banking, *Journal of Banking & Finance*, Vol. 35, No. 5., pp. 1315–1326.

Giese J., Haldane A. (2020), COVID-19 and the Financial System: A Tale of Two Crises, *Oxford Review of Economic Policy*, nr 36/1, pp. 200–214.

de Guindos L. (2021), Sources of Risk and Vulnerabilities for Financial Stability, ECB, https://www.ecb.europa.eu/press/key/date/2021/html/ecb.sp210225_1~e613d9b2c3.en.pdf

Horobet A., Radulescu M., Belascu L., Dita S.M. (2021), Determinants of Bank Profitability in CEE Countries: Evidence from GMM Panel Data Estimates, *Journal of Risk and Financial Management*, Vol. 14, No. 7, 307.

IMF (2021), Policy Responses to COVID-19, https://www.imf.org/en/Topics/imf-and-covid19/Policy-Responses-to-COVID-19#P

IMF (2022), Regulating, Supervising, and Handling Distress in Public Banks, Departmental Paper No 2022/010, https://www.imf.org/en/Publications/Departmental-Papers-Policy-Papers/Issues/2022/04/28/Regulating-Supervising-and-Handling-Distress-in-Public-Banks-511609, pp. 1–44.

Larch M. (2022), Countercyclical Properties of Fiscal Rules: An EU perspective, European Fiscal Board, JVI Webinar Brussels, 18 February.

McKinsey (2020), Global Banking Annual Review 2020: A Test of Resilience.

Miklaszewska E., Kil K. (2016), The Impact of 2007–2009 Crisis on the Assessment of Bank Performance: The Evidence from CEE-11 Countries. *Transformations in Business & Economics*, 2A(38A), pp. 459–479.

OECD (2022), Sovereign Borrowing Outlook, www.oecd-ilibrary.org/governance/oecd-sovereign-borrowing-outlook-2022_b2d85ea7-en.

OECD (2022), www. stats.oecd.org/glossary/detail.asp?ID=303.

Philippon T., Salord A. (2017), Bail-ins and Bank Resolution in Europe: A Progress Report, International Center for Monetary and Banking Studies, Geneva Reports on the World Economy Special Report no. 4.

Raiffeisen Research (2022), Crisis & Recovery Mode At The Same Time, https://www.raiffeisenresearch.com/servlet.

Samson K., Kusz G. (2019), The Silver Lining of the Baltic Banking Crisis, Global Trade Magazine, December 31st.

Szybowski D. (2018), Causes of Public Debt and Budget Deficit, *International Journal of New Economics and Social Sciences*, Vol. 8, No. 2, pp. 57–67.

Appendix

Table A.8.1 Correlation matrix of variables used in the study of determinants of financial stability of CEE banks

	GOVS_GR	*GOVS_TA*	*COV*PD_GDP*	*PD_WALU*	*PD_BANKS*	*DEF*	*GD_TPD*	*SEC_TPD*	*LTPD_TPD*	*PD_GDP*	*S*	*LIQA_TA*	*NII_OR*	*NPL*	*ROA*	*TL_TA*	*LN_TA*	*HHI*	*DOMC_GDP*	*INF*	*GDP_GR*	*MLPS*	*Z_SC*	*CAR*	*T1R*	*TCR*
TCR	−0.04	0.09	0.05	−0.03	−0.12	−0.02	0.26	0.00	0.11	−0.12	0.21	0.18	0.08	0.04	0.00	−0.13	0.11	0.20	−0.08	0.06	−0.10	−0.01	0.10	0.54	0.97	1.00
T1R	−0.05	0.03	0.04	−0.04	−0.08	−0.02	0.19	−0.02	0.09	−0.11	0.16	0.07	−0.05	0.03	0.02	−0.06	0.05	0.14	0.03	0.03	−0.09	0.09	0.24	0.58	1.00	
CAR	−0.05	−0.07	−0.05	−0.02	−0.06	0.04	0.15	−0.03	0.07	−0.05	0.13	−0.01	−0.07	−0.03	0.27	0.09	0.00	0.15	0.10	−0.03	0.02	0.11	0.26	1.00		
Z_SC	−0.01	−0.02	−0.01	−0.10	0.09	0.00	−0.31	−0.01	−0.10	0.11	−0.18	−0.08	−0.10	0.02	0.05	0.04	−0.26	−0.17	0.18	−0.01	0.07	0.22	1.00			
MLPS	−0.03	−0.21	−0.02	−0.26	−0.17	0.03	−0.08	−0.04	0.13	−0.18	−0.08	−0.42	−0.23	−0.55	0.41	0.55	0.18	0.11	0.21	0.02	0.01	1.00				
GDP_GR	−0.02	−0.02	−0.90	−0.08	−0.20	0.64	−0.22	−0.11	−0.17	−0.16	−0.07	−0.02	0.01	0.03	0.10	0.07	−0.06	−0.23	−0.08	−0.15	1.00					
INF	0.01	0.00	0.26	−0.30	−0.07	−0.11	0.12	0.15	0.09	−0.20	0.02	0.05	0.01	−0.15	−0.01	−0.11	0.13	0.02	−0.24	1.00						
DOMC_GDP	0.02	−0.21	0.02	0.13	0.12	0.17	−0.25	−0.44	−0.10	0.15	−0.13	−0.16	−0.29	−0.04	0.07	0.22	−0.27	0.18	1.00							
HHI	−0.06	−0.15	0.09	−0.03	−0.39	0.05	0.68	−0.37	0.15	−0.28	0.31	0.06	0.13	−0.05	0.04	0.03	−0.02	1.00								
LN_TA	−0.01	0.20	0.03	0.04	0.15	−0.04	0.38	0.45	0.42	0.03	0.31	−0.02	0.05	−0.26	0.11	0.07	1.00									
TL_TA	−0.05	−0.29	−0.07	0.04	0.05	0.01	−0.09	−0.10	−0.04	0.05	−0.07	−0.79	−0.45	−0.25	0.16	1.00										
ROA	0.01	−0.04	−0.08	−0.06	−0.07	0.12	0.01	−0.07	0.00	−0.11	0.00	−0.08	−0.06	−0.34	1.00											
NPL	0.03	0.00	−0.06	0.15	0.04	0.10	0.01	−0.01	−0.06	0.10	0.09	0.16	0.19	1.00												
NII_OR	0.01	0.16	−0.04	−0.12	−0.20	0.04	0.24	0.11	0.07	−0.12	0.19	0.40	1.00													
LIQA_TA	0.03	0.01	−0.02	−0.01	−0.12	0.09	0.16	0.01	0.04	−0.13	0.06	1.00														
S	−0.01	0.10	−0.02	0.00	−0.18	0.07	0.43	0.06	0.24	−0.18	1.00															
PD_GDP	0.03	0.12	0.29	0.68	0.67	−0.34	−0.21	0.20	−0.17	1.00																
LTPD_TPD	−0.05	−0.04	0.02	−0.29	−0.22	0.08	0.45	0.70	1.00																	
SEC_TPD	−0.03	0.12	0.09	−0.13	0.18	−0.14	0.14	1.00																		
GD_TPD	−0.09	0.03	0.07	0.11	−0.16	0.00	1.00																			
DEF	−0.03	−0.15	−0.62	−0.08	−0.38	1.00																				
PD_BANKS	0.04	0.17	0.35	0.70	1.00																					
PD_WALU	0.00	0.11	0.08	1.00																						
COV*PD_GDP	0.03	0.08	1.00																							
GOVS_TA	0.09	1.00																								
GOVS_GR	1.00																									

Table A.8.2 Correlation matrix of variables used in the model of determinants of dynamics and structure of credit portfolio of CEE banks

	GOVS_GR	*GOVS_TA*	*COVPD_GDP*	*PD_WALU*	*PD_BANKS*	*DEF*	*GD_TPD*	*SEC_TPD*	*LTPD_TPD*	*PD_GDP*	*S*	*LIQA_TA*	*NII_OR*	*NPL*	*ROA*	*TCR*	*LN_TA*	*HHI*	*DOMC_GDP*	*INF*	*GDP_GR*	*ML_GR*	*CORL_GR*	*CONSL_GR*	*MORL_TL*	*CORL_TL*	*CONSL_TL*	*TL_GR*	*TL_TA*
TL_TA	−0.05	−0.30	−0.03	0.03	0.07	−0.02	−0.13	−0.11	−0.06	0.06	−0.11	−0.81	−0.47	−0.26	0.16	−0.09	0.05	0.03	0.23	−0.07	0.05	0.00	0.07	0.13	0.54	−0.41	0.26	−0.06	1.00
TL_GR	0.01	−0.05	−0.02	−0.03	0.00	0.00	0.08	0.00	−0.04	−0.03	0.03	0.08	0.11	−0.21	0.03	−0.06	0.04	0.03	−0.04	0.05	0.04	0.36	0.41	0.37	0.01	−0.01	−0.05	1.00	
CONSL_TL	−0.01	0.00	0.06	0.15	0.25	−0.02	−0.01	0.08	0.12	0.24	−0.09	−0.23	−0.33	−0.17	0.14	−0.11	0.16	−0.03	0.19	−0.03	−0.04	−0.10	−0.12	0.08	0.05	−0.64	1.00		
CORL_TL	−0.02	0.01	−0.03	0.02	−0.07	0.06	0.14	0.08	0.04	−0.09	0.07	0.36	0.27	0.23	−0.02	0.23	−0.15	−0.01	−0.14	0.03	−0.03	0.10	0.15	0.00	−0.66	1.00			
MORL_TL	0.02	−0.16	−0.02	−0.17	0.00	−0.08	−0.13	−0.02	0.01	−0.01	0.09	−0.40	−0.37	−0.31	0.06	0.07	0.38	−0.04	0.03	0.00	0.07	−0.01	0.07	0.01	1.00				
CONS_L_GR	0.01	−0.08	−0.03	−0.01	−0.01	0.01	0.01	−0.04	−0.03	−0.03	0.02	−0.09	−0.11	−0.13	0.10	−0.05	0.00	0.01	0.00	0.07	0.04	0.04	0.41	1.00					
COR_L_GR	−0.02	−0.03	−0.05	−0.09	−0.12	0.00	0.00	−0.03	−0.03	−0.10	0.00	−0.03	0.00	−0.15	0.13	−0.03	−0.01	0.04	−0.07	0.08	0.06	0.23	1.00						
ML_GR	0.08	−0.01	0.02	−0.06	−0.11	−0.01	0.07	−0.05	0.01	−0.12	0.01	0.02	0.00	−0.18	0.09	−0.04	−0.03	0.10	−0.03	0.03	−0.04	1.00							
GDP_GR	−0.01	0.01	−0.90	−0.09	−0.17	0.70	−0.17	−0.10	−0.15	−0.18	−0.03	−0.02	0.04	0.03	0.09	−0.08	−0.02	−0.21	−0.12	−0.10	1.00								
INF	0.01	−0.01	0.19	−0.31	−0.14	−0.08	0.11	0.16	0.11	−0.23	0.02	0.03	0.01	−0.15	−0.01	0.04	0.14	0.00	−0.24	1.00									
DOMC_GDP	0.02	−0.21	0.04	0.13	0.10	0.19	−0.19	−0.43	−0.05	0.12	−0.08	−0.16	−0.27	−0.03	0.07	−0.03	−0.24	0.28	1.00										
HHI	−0.06	−0.21	0.11	−0.05	−0.36	0.03	0.61	−0.46	0.02	−0.22	0.20	0.06	0.07	−0.06	0.04	0.14	−0.28	1.00											
LN_TA	0.00	0.19	0.05	0.02	0.30	−0.09	0.12	0.46	0.30	0.16	0.13	−0.01	−0.01	−0.29	0.12	0.07	1.00												
TCR	−0.04	0.05	0.04	−0.02	−0.08	−0.03	0.22	−0.02	0.06	−0.10	0.19	0.14	0.00	0.04	0.01	1.00													
ROA	0.01	−0.04	−0.08	−0.06	−0.07	0.12	0.01	−0.07	0.00	−0.11	0.00	−0.08	−0.06	−0.34	1.00														
NPL	0.03	−0.01	−0.06	0.15	0.05	0.10	−0.02	−0.01	−0.07	0.11	0.07	0.17	0.19	1.00															
NII_OR	0.01	0.14	−0.06	−0.12	−0.18	0.05	0.18	0.09	0.01	−0.09	0.15	0.40	1.00																
LIQA_TA	0.03	0.04	−0.03	0.00	−0.12	0.10	0.19	0.01	0.04	−0.13	0.13	1.00																	
S	0.01	0.04	−0.02	−0.02	−0.12	0.04	0.27	0.01	0.11	−0.11	1.00																		
PD_GDP	0.02	0.14	0.29	0.72	0.88	−0.32	−0.10	0.24	−0.11	1.00																			
LTPD_TPD	−0.05	−0.08	0.02	−0.32	−0.17	0.07	0.32	0.71	1.00																				
SEC_TPD	−0.02	0.11	0.09	−0.13	0.22	−0.16	0.08	1.00																					
GD_TPD	−0.09	−0.03	0.06	0.12	−0.08	−0.04	1.00																						
DEF	−0.02	−0.15	−0.81	−0.09	−0.34	1.00																							
PD_BANKS	0.03	0.19	0.30	0.74	1.00																								
PD_WALU	0.00	0.11	0.11	1.00																									
COVPD_GDP	0.02	0.06	1.00																										
GOVS_TA	0.10	1.00																											
GOVS_GR	1.00																												

Table A.8.3 Descriptive statistics of variables used as determinants of bank financial stability

Variable	*Mean*	*Median*	*St. dev.*	*Min.*	*Max.*
TCR	20.39	18.11	9.49	2.54	108.80
T1R	20.00	17.44	10.61	5.64	106.90
E_A	11.09	9.67	8.69	−87.85	82.94
Z_SC	51.99	40.32	50.62	−10.36	520.80
MLPS	0.08	0.00	9.24	−25.00	23.00
GDP_GR	2.64	3.53	3.19	−8.10	7.32
INF	1.40	1.81	1.55	−1.54	4.63
DOMC_GDP	49.27	51.68	9.55	24.74	68.89
HHI	0.10	0.09	0.04	0.06	0.27
TL_TA	53.20	54.16	16.66	0.00	99.71
LN_A	8.13	7.59	2.76	2.05	16.23
ROA	0.39	0.57	3.14	−72.67	7.11
NPL	10.38	6.67	11.36	0.00	95.51
NII_OR	33.89	31.55	16.97	−78.26	100.0
LIQA_TA	32.88	30.73	16.85	0.08	98.82
S	0.76	1.00	0.43	0.00	1.00
PD_GDP	59.11	64.80	19.30	12.71	108.10
LTPD_TPD	79.93	77.16	7.05	60.54	96.32
SEC_TPD	62.97	60.79	13.33	5.84	87.16
GD_TPD	90.67	92.94	7.86	79.99	104.20
DEF	−1.98	−1.50	2.51	−9.40	2.10
PD_BANKS	14.59	15.74	6.16	1.82	27.49
PD_WALU	16.85	16.03	14.86	0.00	66.34
COV*PD_GDP	10.98	0.00	25.97	0.00	108.10
GOVS_TA	13.63	11.57	11.22	0.00	71.58
GOVS_GR	56.00	5.95	397.10	−100.00	1056.30

Table A.8.4 Descriptive statistics of variables used as determinants of bank lending policies

Variable	*Mean*	*Median*	*St. dev.*	*Min.*	*Max.*
TL_TA	53.20	54.16	16.66	0.00	99.71
TL_GR	8.68	4.19	69.49	−100.00	2050.00
CONSL_TL	30.92	24.95	25.21	0.00	100.00
CORL_TL	52.36	50.28	24.17	0.04	100.00
MORL_TL	24.93	22.64	19.62	0.00	100.00
CONSL_GR	6.99	4.20	41.45	−100.00	565.20
CORL_GR	6.69	3.77	36.37	−97.14	581.90
MORL_GR	10.23	6.40	40.41	−92.53	389.00
LN_A	8.13	7.59	2.76	2.05	16.23
ROA	0.39	0.57	3.14	−72.67	7.11
NPL	10.38	6.67	11.36	0.00	95.51
TCR	20.39	18.11	9.49	2.54	108.80
NII_OR	33.89	31.55	16.97	−78.26	100.0
LIQA_TA	32.88	30.73	16.85	0.08	98.82

(*Continued*)

Table A.8.4 (Continued)

Variable	*Mean*	*Median*	*St. dev.*	*Min.*	*Max.*
S	0.76	1.00	0.43	0.00	1.00
GDP_GR	2.64	3.53	3.19	−8.10	7.32
INF	1.40	1.81	1.55	−1.54	4.63
DOMC_GDP	49.27	51.68	9.55	24.74	68.89
HHI	0.10	0.09	0.04	0.06	0.27
PD_GDP	59.11	64.80	19.30	12.71	108.10
LTPD_TPD	79.93	77.16	7.05	60.54	96.32
SEC_TPD	62.97	60.79	13.33	5.84	87.16
GD_TPD	90.67	92.94	7.86	79.99	104.20
DEF	−1.98	−1.50	2.51	−9.40	2.10
PD_BANKS	14.59	15.74	6.16	1.82	27.49
PD_WALU	16.85	16.03	14.86	0.00	66.34
COV*PD_GDP	10.98	0.00	25.97	0.00	108.10
GOVS_TA	13.63	11.57	11.22	0.00	71.58
GOVS_GR	56.00	5.95	397.10	−100.00	1056.3

9 Relationship between banks and FinTechs

Does the pandemic have an impact on it?

Małgorzata Pawłowska and Aleksandra Staniszewska

9.1 Introduction

After the 2008 financial crisis, FinTech credit platforms became a leading factor in the transformation of the global financial sector (Nicoletti 2017, Blakstad and Allen 2018, Sironi, 2022, Pawłowska and Staniszewska, 2021). Furthermore, they had a tremendous impact on the banking sector by early 2020. The outbreak of the COVID-19 pandemic in Europe, which has completely changed the functioning of the entire economy of the European Union, has further amplified the growth of digital technologies and the development of the FinTech sector. On the one hand, for the banking sector, FinTech may provide opportunities to increase efficiency and profit margins. On the other hand, FinTech companies deprive banks of clients who seek cheaper and faster solutions for borrowing and may take away profits from traditional banks.

After almost two years, the COVID-19 pandemic has caused the digital technology and FinTech sectors to grow even faster. Financial organizations have had to adapt to a new reality in order to survive. Individual and corporate clients responded differently to lockdown and reported different needs. Remote learning platforms, business communications and analytics programmes at financial institutions were improved to maximize their online functionality. Lockdown caused the textile, food service and travel industries to plummet. Only businesses that managed to adapt to remote sales and advertising survived. The FinTech sector was initially designed to streamline existing sales, communication and financial processes. It has now become a standard without which no industry, whether it be in logistics, communications or sales, could have survived the pandemic. Banks faced an even greater challenge. Not only did they have to deal with problems within their own institutions during the pandemic, but they also had to respond to the needs of their customers and the market. Banks closed traditional branches while encouraging customers to use mobile banking channels or online banking. While the COVID-19 pandemic caused an economic slowdown and a decline in banks' performance, it also resulted in the development of sales channels using new FinTech technologies (Pawłowska, 2022).

The aim of this chapter is to investigate the impact of innovative financial technology (FinTech) on EU banking performance. Furthermore, we take into account the impact of the COVID pandemic, which forced the banking sector to

DOI: 10.4324/9781003310754-9

implement innovations and catch up with emerging advanced IT solutions, on bank performance.

This research consists of a qualitative and quantitative analysis of FinTech impact on banking services. The main objective of the qualitative assessment is to determine scope and intensity of FinTech's impact on the financial sector. Furthermore, based on the reports from international financial institutions (e.g. European Commission, 2020a, 2020b), it has been shown that the COVID-19 pandemic caused a significant acceleration in the development of digital technologies, including the FinTech sector. The quantitative analysis, in this chapter, is based on an empirical model estimated of panel data for the national level of EU economies.

The empirical model concerns of the impact of digital technologies on bank profitability. The research hypothesis is that *the development of new technologies had an impact on bank performance in the European Union*. In order to verify the research hypothesis, we try to empirically measure the phenomenon of FinTech based on available data sets. Furthermore, we take into account the impact of the early stage of the pandemic of 2020. Finally, in the qualitative part, the impact of the COVID-19 pandemic on the financial and FinTech sectors is also presented (Pawłowska 2022).

This chapter consists of four parts and a conclusion. The first part is the introduction. The second part presents the definition of the FinTech sector and impact of the pandemic on the development of the FinTech sector and the banking sector. The third section presents the descriptive statistics impact of the pandemic on development of new technologies. The fourth section embraces a description of methodology, variables and data for the quantitative study concerning impact of digitalization on bank performance in the EU. The fifth section describes the model and the model results. Conclusions constitute the final part.

9.2 New technology in the financial sector: FinTech and banking sector

FinTech is a broad concept. There is no single, uniform definition of FinTech (Pawłowska, Staniszewska, 2021). As a sector, it is defined by the services and products it co-creates. However, broad expansion of FinTech functionality expands this definition. The Financial Stability Board (2019) defines FinTech as 'technologically enabled financial innovation that could result in new business models, applications, processes, or products with an associated material effect on financial markets and institutions, and the provision of financial services'.

It seems that FinTech companies (for example, for money transfers: PayPal, Transfer Wise, Revolut; for crypto-currencies platforms: Bitpanda; for funding: back office for crowd-funding platforms) may have a competitive advantage over traditional banks, especially in the retail banking segment. There is no uniform and single market-accepted definition of the FinTech sector. FinTech sector is defined by the services and products it co-creates. As the functionality of FinTech-enabled solutions increases, its definition expands. As a powerful market for financial services, the EU stands at the threshold of achieving huge economies of scale. Paradoxically, the pandemic caused many industries (e.g., tourism, entertainment and catering) to plunge while resulting in even faster growth of the FinTech sector and even greater interest in digital finance solutions. However, it should be noted that the term 'FinTech' can also refer to large technology companies known as BigTechs (technological giants such as Amazon, Apple and Google). Traditional banks collect information on customers' credit histories over a long period of time, while BigTech companies can use their customers data from non-financial activity, on the lending market (Frost, 2020).

Thanks to the use of digital technologies, FinTech companies can provide banking services at lower costs than traditional banks. The P2P lending mechanism attracts unsecured borrowers. In the long run, banks prefer secured loans, which results in pushing unsecured loans outside the banking market (Besanko and Thakor, 1987). In turn, a diverse borrower base increases the stability of the banking sector. An undiversified loan portfolio in terms of currency, borrower type, term or collateral type is susceptible to impairment in a crisis situation. Typically, more competition means lower margins, which in turn makes it more attractive to purchase higher risk assets (Besanko and Thakor, 1993). Another approach suggests that in a competitive market with low funding costs, borrowers have less reason to engage in riskier ventures, and as a result, the stability of the banking sector as a whole increases (Boyd and De Nicolo, 2005). Local markets have had varied responses to competition from the P2P sector and FinTech companies. Depending on their size, capital, regulation and timing of the economic cycle, banks may benefit or lose from the rise of the FinTech sector. Goetz (2018) presented a study confirming that lowering the barrier to entry in the credit market improves asset quality and increases competition and profitability, thus improving the stability of the sector. Competition forces efficiency and protects against excessive lending. Navaretti, Calzolari and Pazzolo (2017) showed that countries with relatively low banking regulations as measured by the World Bank (2018) index achieved higher FinTech investments. Claessens et al. (2018) indicated that FinTech credit achieved higher values in countries where specific regulations allowed innovative solutions to exist on the financial market. Based on their quantitative study, Pawłowska and Staniszewska (2021) found that despite ongoing consolidation, competition in the banking market is not decreasing as a result of FinTech factors. These findings are consistent with a study by Navaretti, Calzolari and Pazzolo (2017).

The pandemic has affected the digitization of the financial industry. Technological solutions have allowed bank customers to access remote financial products such as loans and credit. Supporting digitization has become a key element in housing post-pandemic economies. Noting their role, the European Commission (2020b) issued a communication on the EU digital finance strategy to make digital finance more mainstream for the benefit of consumers and businesses (European Commission 2020a). The EC has adopted as priorities: to eliminate the fragmentation of the Digital Single Market for financial services, enabling European consumers to access cross-border services and helping European financial firms to scale up their operations in the digital environment; to ensure that the EU regulatory framework facilitates digital innovation that is in the interest of consumers and promotes market efficiency; to create a European financial data space to promote data-driven innovation based on the European Data Strategy, including increasing access to data and sharing data within the financial sector (European Commission, 2020b); addressing the challenges and risks of digital transformation, with a focus on the "same business, same risks, same rules" principle to ensure a level playing field for both existing financial institutions and new entrants.

In the EU and all over the world as a result of the pandemic, the process of digitizing the public and private lives of citizens have been speeded up. A report by McKinsey & Company (2020) indicated that the pandemic affected global payment values by 7% in 2020 compared to 2019. Payments have moved from POS terminals to e-commerce. Health concerns have forced older adults to shop online. Cash payments have declined in favour of debit card payments and mobile payments made through phones. FinTech has revolutionized the functionality of web browsers, apps and social networking for mobile devices, changing consumer habits. More and more customers are shopping, exchanging currency, paying bills, ordering domestic and international money transfers, using online banking, making donations, organizing fundraisers, learning and communicating (non-telephone) via their smartphone. Moreover, the use of mobile devices has generated large amounts of additional information, such as geolocation, transaction time and place, types of applications used, device model and mobile carrier. The pandemic crisis will bring permanent changes to the financial sector's products, communications and sales channels. It seems that after the pandemic, the financial market is not expected to return to its pre-pandemic situation. Self-isolation and restrictions have forced new behaviours and needs in customers that they will now not give up.

9.3 Impact of the pandemic on the financial sector: Descriptive statistics

The pandemic has had a huge impact on cross-border transactions. Due to travel restrictions, profits made on international transactions have fallen sharply. It is estimated that the business and leisure travel market has shrunk by as much as 70%. Due to liquidity problems, companies were late making payroll payments. At the same time, however, the value of transactions made through FinTech tools offered by PayPal and UPS increased. This solidified the trend of phasing out cash payments, which had been prevailing even before the pandemic. Thus far, the need for social distancing and remote shopping has proven to be a catalyst for pushing out cash transactions in favour of cashless ones. ATM withdrawal transactions increased sharply at the start of the pandemic. This was to provide households with liquidity and savings protection. The general panic was conducive to pulling cash out of accounts. However, as households adapted to the new pandemic situation, they stopped accumulating cash in favour of electronic payments.

After the WHO issued a statement restricting the circulation of cash due to the virus being found on banknotes and coins, bank customers changed their existing payment habits overnight. In addition, merchants began accepting card payments even for very small amounts that were previously unprofitable. This happened because banks reduced indirect fees on non-cash transactions. Among the types of cards, the proximity card segment, which does not require the need for a pin code, is growing fastest. According to Visa (2020), 78% of consumers made changes to their payment preferences because of COVID-19. In addition, 70% of those surveyed used a new payment method for the first time due to fear of the virus.

Due to development of new IT technology, there have been changes in the habits of bank customers. The pandemic has accelerated these changes even more. According to Visa (2020), ordering goods is expected to increase to over 80% and selling to over 40% due to the pandemic. The FinTech Stock Index is up 30% in less than a year. An ongoing ten-year rising trend of e-commerce development has only intensified during the pandemic. Figure 9.1 indicates that over the past nine years (2008–2020), the share of people using the Internet for purchase and sale transactions has doubled for every age group (Eurostat, 2020d) while KFTX[1] index rose over six times since it was introduced (Nasdaq 2020).

As FinTech services and platforms are offered worldwide (by US companies to EU customers and other way round), and also continental European biggest stock markets (DAX) do not quote the FinTech index, we assumed that in a big picture, trends for US FinTech companies will be reflecting trends for European companies from this sector.

The development of the FinTech sector is related to the development of the use of the Internet and mobile devices by households. With the rise of smartphones and mobile apps, consumers have switched from making transactions on the computer to making transactions through mobile apps. Nowadays, all e-commerce solutions require adaptation to mobile device standards. It shall be noted that e-commerce is supported by FinTech payment solutions like PayPal or other online banking payments. Figure 9.2 takes into consideration not only e-commerce but also transaction

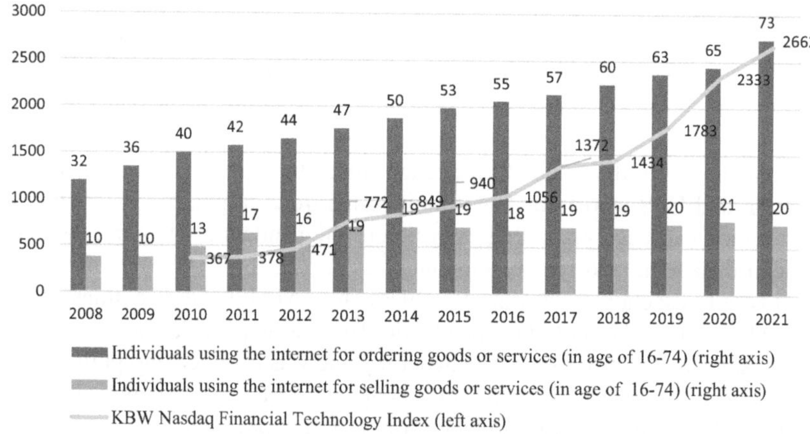

Figure 9.1 Share of people ordering and selling goods and services online and value of KBW Nasdaq Financial Technology Index from 2010 to 2021

Data source: Nasdaq open source data and Eurostat (2021) open source data. For 2010–2015, the value of the KFTX index was calculated based on Nasdaq stock market back-tests. For 2021, the KFTX level is from December 31, 2021

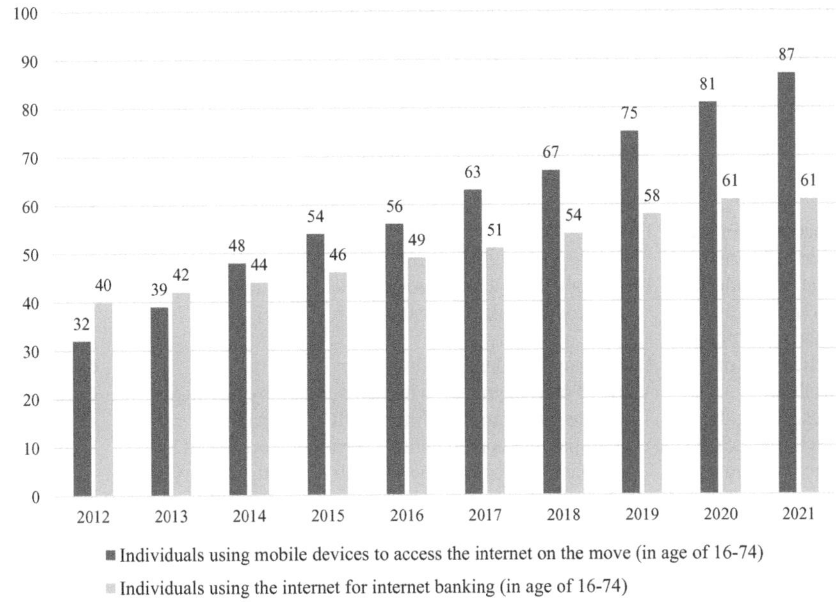

Figure 9.2 Share of people using the Internet on mobile devices versus share of people using the Internet for banking transactions

Data source: E-commerce statistics for individuals, Eurostat (2021) open source data

carried out from mobile devices. Before smart-phone era, the whole Internet usage was perceived as accessed from computers.

It seems that the development of online banking (i.e., the introduction of transactional interface functionality on websites) has moved to the next phase, mobile transactional banking. In the light of competitive pressures from FinTech solutions (e.g., Revolut, Blik and Transfer Wise), banks had to introduce apps to keep up with their competitors.

9.4 Methodology, variables and data for the quantitative study concerning impact of digitalization on bank performance in the EU

In order to analyse the impact of FinTech financial innovation on bank performance in the banking sectors of EU countries, we constructed an econometric model based on panel data. First, on the basis of the available literature channels of FinTech impact on banks' have been identified and then the channels through which new technologies influence the performance of the banking sector were defined. FinTech develops independently from the banking sector; however, the banking sector is a major implementation field for FinTech solutions. Therefore, in the model, we took into account the variables determining new technologies *inside* the banking sector, *outside* the banking sector and the variables relating to

Table 9.1 Description of the explanatory variables used in the model

Category	*Variables*	*Symbol*
Banking sector	Tier 1 ratio (common equity to risk-weighted assets)	Tier1
	Size of banking sector as the logarithm of total banking sector assets for each country	Assets
	Return on assets	ROA
	Return on equity	ROE
Concentration ratios derived from ECB statistics adopted as indicators of market structure	Banking sector concentration, defined as the share of the five largest credit institutions in total assets[2]	CR5
	Herfindahl-Hirschman Index for assets (sum of squares of individual banks' market share)	HHI
Cyclical factors	GDP growth and GDP *per capita*	GDP
Variables describing digital technologies *inside* the banking sector	Value of card payments with cards issued by payment service providers (in billion EUR). The payment value of all payments made with a payment card issued by payment service providers in the reporting country (in billion EUR). Includes all payments made with a payment card issued by a payment service provider regardless of the cardholder's residency or where the payment was made. Each country is required to report the number of cards issued by payment service providers, including cards issued for both domestic and foreign markets.	Card
	ATMs in the reporting country. ATMs that allow authorized users to withdraw cash. Authorization is usually performed through a payment card. Other forms of authorization are permitted depending on the functionality of the ATM and the account. The variable also includes devices with a wire transfer function.	ATM
	Value of wire transfers and direct debits initiated electronically (in million EUR). This variable covers the payer's payments to the beneficiary. It is a wire transfer order to credit a beneficiary's account at this or any other bank. Funds are transferred from the payer's paying agent to the beneficiary's paying agent. The variable includes wire transfers and direct debits in electronic form only.	eCredit
	Individuals (ages 16–74) who used online banking in the previous 3 months before completing the survey as a percentage of the population. Online banking covers electronic transactions such as wire transfers, direct debit, balance checking and/or account history.	INTER
Variables describing digital technologies *outside* the banking sector	Proportion of people (ages 16–74) using mobile devices to access the Internet, including phones, smartphones, portable computers, tablets and other devices used away from work and home in the previous 12 months. Share of total population in a given age group.	Mobile_U
	Share of people (ages 16–74) ordering products and services online. Purchase or order of a product or service for personal use within previous 12 months. Share in total population in a given age group.	Mobile_O

(*Continued*)

Category	Variables	Symbol
Variables describing FinTech in general	The value of the KFTX Stock Index was created to track the capitalization of innovative companies in the financial sector.	KFTX
	FinTech equity financing in relation to GDP for country *c* in year *t*; data from the study: Cornelli, Doerr, Franco, & Frost (2021), pp. 31–43.	*FinTech*1
	Number of transactions in the FinTech sector in relation to GDP for country *c* in year *t*; data from the study: Cornelli, Doerr, Franco, & Frost (2021), pp. 31–43.	FinTech2

Source: Own analysis.

the FinTech sector (Pawłowska, 2022). Second, the analysed phenomenon was empirically measured based on a quantitative study using econometric techniques on a constructed panel of data. The panel data included annual data at the national level of 28 EU economies. Data in the panel covered the macroeconomic situation (e.g., GDP growth) in individual EU economies, the level of concentration in individual banking sectors, the situation in the banking sector and bank performance, e-banking and the FinTech sector.

Data for the panel came from the European Central Bank and Eurostat. Additionally, we take into account new FinTech variables from the study: Cornelli, Doerr, Franco, & Frost (2021). We also took into account as FinTech variable the Nasdaq Financial Technology Index (KFTX) (see Table 9.1).

It should be noted that FinTech solutions have emerged in the last 5–6 years, so analysing them in earlier periods is difficult. Another limitation, in addition to missing data, was the need to standardize the data for the study. The definitions of the variables used in the construction of the data panel describing the development of the FinTech sector and new technology in the banking sector are presented in Table 9.1.

It should be noted that KFTX does not refer to individual business classifications. A company is included in the index if it provides digital solutions for the financial market. The incomes of companies included in the index are usually based on the fee-based model. The index was first listed on July 18, 2018, at which time it amounted to 1,000 points. There are prior values for the index; however, they result from the so-called back-testing (conducted by the stock exchange) of the share prices of the companies making up the index. Very useful information for the panel model was the value of FinTech credit in the European markets. However, due to significant data gaps and a short time series, the variable could not be used in the estimations of the panel data and was ultimately not used in the empirical model. Certainly, the values for this variable will be supplemented over time. The value of FinTech credit will become a key variable for analysing the financial innovation sector.

Finally, panel data covered the years from 2010 to 2020 and included data from EU economies. Some variables have been available since 2013. Due to missing data, this was an unbalanced panel. Descriptive statistics of the collected data are presented in Table 9.1 of the Appendix.

9.5 Econometric models and results

To verify the research hypothesis, the econometric models were estimated based on the panel data. In this chapter, we present the contraction and results of these models based on three equations. The first model based on equation (9.1) concerns the impact of the digital techniques outside and inside banking sector on the performance of the EU banks. The second model based on equation (9.2) concerns the impact of the digital techniques on the performance of the EU banks, but also concerns the impact of the COVID pandemic on the performance of banks. Furthermore, the third model based on equation (9.3) concerns the determinants of the development of the FinTech sector. The three models mentioned were estimated using panel data analysis techniques.

9.5.1 Model 1

In the first model, the dependent variable is banks' profitability, while the independent variables are GDP, vectors of banking performance variables, concentration of the banking market and explanatory variables concerning new technologies and digitalization. Profitability was measured by ROA and ROE indices published by the European Central Bank for particular banking sectors. The model uses two types of variables to describe the new technology (inside and outside the banking sector) and variables describe the FinTech sector. Equation (9.1) represents the output specification of the constructed econometric model:

$$Y_{c,t} = \mu_t + \gamma_c + \alpha_1 GDP_{c,t} + \beta_k \sum_{k=0}^{n} X_{c,t} + \alpha_2 MS_{c,t} + \alpha_3 BaTech_{c,t} + \alpha_4 NTech_{c,t} + \varepsilon_{c,t} \qquad (9.1)$$

where the explained variable $Y_{c,t}$ is the profitability of banks in country c in year t. Profitability is expressed in the model as return on assets (*ROA*) and return on equity (*ROE*) in country c in year t.

As explanatory variables, the following variables were used in country c in year t: $GDP_{c,t}$ is the business cycle variable, $X_{c,t}$ is a vector of control variables that reflect bank performance in banking sectors; $MS_{c,t}$ is a vector-specifying concentration in banking sectors, $BaTech_{c,t}$ is a vector of variables that capture digital technology inside banking sector; $NTech_{c,t}$ is a vector of variables that capture digital technology outside banking sector.

The individual explanatory variables in the model are described below:

- as variable describing $GDP_{c,t}$ was adopted GDP *per capita* in country *c* in year *t*;
- the vector of control variable $X_{c,t}$ describes the situation in the banking sector: *Tier1 ratio* and *Assets* in country *c* in year *t*;
- the concentration ratios $MS_{c,t}$ as indicators of market structure: the share of the five largest credit institutions in total assets ($CR5_{c,t}$) and as the HHI for assets (the sum of the squares of the market share of individual banks),[3] for country *c* in year *t*.
- the variables derived from payment statistics from the ECB were adopted as variables describing the new technology ***inside*** **the banking sector** $Ba_{Techc,t}$ in country *c* in year *t*: *INTER*, *ATM*, *eCredit* and *Card*.[4]
- as variables describing the new technology ***outside*** **the banking sector** $N\_Tech_{c,t}$ sector, we considered: *Mobile_U* and *Mobile_O* for country *c* in year *t*. Also, we used the KFTX index *(KFTX)* in year *t*.

Finally, on the basis of Equation 1, five estimates were made, the results of which are presented in Table A2. In the fifth estimation, the HHI index was used as a concentration indicator, in the first four CR5 was used.

9.5.2 Model 2

In the second model in case to evaluate the impact of the COVID pandemic on the performance of banks, the new variables were constructed concerning the pandemic and the FinTech sector. Whole model is described by Equation 9.2.

In case to test the impact of a pandemic on the banking sector was defined additionally a binary variable defining the COVID-19 pandemic (COV):

- COV = 1 for 2020 year, COV = 0 otherwise.

Furthermore, we take into account the following new FinTech variables from the study Cornelli, Doerr, Franco, Frost, (2021):

- *FinTech1* is define us a FinTech equity financing in relation to GDP for country *c* in year *t*;
- *FinTech2* is defined as a number of transactions in the FinTech sector in relation to GDP for country *c* in year *t*;

Equation (9.2) represents the second specification of the econometric model:

$$Y_{c,t} = \mu_t + \alpha_1 GDP_{c,t} + \beta_1 COV_{c,t} + \alpha_2 MS_{c,t} + \alpha_3 BaTech_{c,t} + \alpha_4 NTech_{c,t} + \alpha_5 Fintech_{c,t} + \varepsilon_{c,t} \tag{9.2}$$

where the explained variable $Y_{c,t}$ is the profitability of banks in country *c* in year *t*. Profitability is expressed in the model as return on assets (*ROA*) and return on equity (*ROE*).

$GDP_{c,t}$ is the GDP growth in country c in year t, $MS_{c,t}$ is a vector specifying concentration in banking sectors in country c in year t like in Equation (9.1). As $Ba_{Techc,t}$ we take *INTER* in country c in year t; As $NTech_{c,t}$ we take *Mobile_U* in country c in year t, like in Equation (9.1).

As variables describing FinTech sector development variables was taken the following variables: *FinTech1* and *FinTech2*, in country c in year t, like in Equation (9.1).

9.5.3 Model 3

In the third model we take into account the impact of the COVID pandemic on the FinTech development.

Equation (9.3) represents the third specification of the econometric model:

$$Y_{c,t} = \mu_t + \alpha_{11} GDP_{c,t} + \beta_1 COV_{c,t} + \alpha_2 MS_{c,t} + \alpha_3 BaTech_{c,t} + \alpha_4 NTech_{c,t} + \varepsilon_{c,t} \quad (9.3)$$

where the explained variable $Y_{c,t}$ is defined as the FinTech sector development. As variables describing FinTech sector development variables was taken the following variables: *FinTech1* and *FinTech2*, in country c in year t, like in Model 2.

Also, the explanatory variables are defined as in Equations (9.1) and (9.2).

Finally, on the basis of Equations (9.1), (9.2) and (9.3), nine estimates were made, the results of which are presented in the Tables 9.3 and 9.4. Table 9.2 in the Appendix shows the descriptive statistics of the variables selected for three models.

9.5.4 Description of model results

Table 9.2 in the Statistical Appendix presents the results of the panel regressions based on Equation (9.1). The coefficients of the model (1) were estimated by linear regression on panel data using the STATA package.[5]

In Table 9.3, the positive and significant coefficient α_3 was found for ATMs located in the reported country (Columns 1 and 2), percentage of people using online banking (Columns 1–3) and the KFTX index (Columns 1, 2 and 5). This means that new FinTech in the banking sector had a positive and significant impact on the profitability of banks in the EU. In Table 9.3, a negative and significant coefficient α_3 was found for the variable for electronically initiated direct debits, *eCredit* (Column 3). Variables defining mobile technologies (*MOBILE_U* and *MOBILE_O*) also affected the level of profitability in the banking sector. In Table 7.3, a negative and significant coefficient α_4 was found for the variables indicating the share of people using mobile devices to access the Internet (*MOBILE_U* and *MOBILE_O*) and for the variable indicating the share of people ordering products and services online (Columns 2 and 4). However, the coefficient of the variable *INTER* turned out to be positive, which means that Internet use for Internet banking affected banks' profitability (Column 5). This implies that new FinTech had a negative and significant impact on profitability in the EU. In addition, a negative and significant α_2 coefficient was found for two concentration indexes. This means that concentration measured by the sum of the assets of the five largest banks (CR5) and the Herfindahl-Hirschman Index had a negative and significant impact on banks' performance in the EU. This is not consistent with the field research indicating that in a market with higher concentrations, banks are more likely to show collusive behaviour, and their oligopoly rents will increase their performance (profitability). On the one hand, new technologies inside the banking sector had a positive impact on bank performance. On the other hand, new technologies outside the banking sector had a negative impact on bank performance.

Table 9.4 in the Statistical Appendix presents the results of the panel regressions based on equations (9.2) and (9.3). In estimations 1 and 2 based on equation (9.2), the dependent variable was assumed *ROA*. In estimation 3 and 4 based on equation (9.3) in case to test the impact of a pandemic on the FinTech sector, the dependent variable was defined as the FinTech sector development.

The results of the quantitative study presented in Table 9.4 showed that the COVID-19 pandemic negatively affected the performance of traditional banks. In addition, the use of technological solutions in banks also positively affected their profitability as indicated by the positive and significant coefficient on the variable *INTER* (Column 1). On the development of the FinTech sector, COVID-19 pandemic, affected positively as indicated by the estimation results (Column 4). The growth of the FinTech sector is positively affected by the growth of the variable INTER and Mobile indices in the stock market (Column 4). However, the COVID-19 pandemic can be said to have caused accelerated development of digital technologies and the FinTech sector. In estimations 1 and 2, a positive effect of the variable KFTX was shown, which may mean that the situation on the stock market has a positive effect on profitability.

To sum up, the results of the models allowed us to verify the hypothesis that new technologies have an impact on bank performance. Also, the findings confirm the impact of the COVID pandemic on the FinTech and traditional banking sector. However, the results showed that the pandemic had a positive impact on the development of the FinTech sector (see Table 9.4, estimation 4). But new technologies outside the banking sector may weaken the results of traditional banks, as clients may be more likely to use their solutions (see Table 9.3, estimations 2 and 4). On the one hand, the pandemic contributed to an economic downturn and decline in banks' results, but on the other hand, it caused the development of sales channels using new FinTech technologies.

Due to the pandemic worsening situations for both individual and business customers, banks' financial performance was expected to deteriorate. Economic lockdowns are bound to result in higher special-purpose reserves due to a decline in bank asset quality. At the same time, the decline in customer business activity reduces banks' margin of revenue. In such a tough situation, FinTech solutions are proving to be a source of cost reductions for banking operations through the efficiency gains offered. Improving data statistics in this area remains an important issue that will improve monitoring of this phenomenon and analysis of the competitive advantage of FinTech providers compared to traditional banking services. For our analysis, FinTech credit would be an important variable (see Claessens et al., 2018). The next research step will be to calculate the model again based on the data of the subsequent years of the pandemic and other FinTech variables. However, banks appear to be able to survive a crisis of distrust, while this may be difficult for FinTech leaders due to the nature of their business.

9.6 Conclusions

New digital technology has created a vast field of new unregulated players in financial markets. Nevertheless, traditional banks still remain the most important player in the financial sector but in the case of operating in the market for a long time they must constantly adapt to the changing reality in order to not fall out of the leadership role. The pandemic forced the banking sector to implement innovations and catch up with emerging, advanced IT solutions. However, a lack of supervision over FinTech players gave them a competitive edge over the banking sector. Many factors, both internal and external, influenced the performance of the banking sector. It has become a challenge for mature, traditional institutions to function in a rapidly changing environment. The development of technology is both an opportunity and a threat. It offers cost reductions and entrance into niche micro-markets. Banks must compete not only with other traditional banks but also with players for whom there are no geographical or technological boundaries. For traditional and regulated banking companies, such competition is extremely difficult. Does this mean that banks will lose their position to FinTech companies? In our view, banks' public trust puts them in a stronger position than all other payment providers.

In this study, we try to isolate the channels through which the FinTech sector interacts with the banking market. However, the biggest limitation of our study was the selection of appropriate variables for the model and data. Although most of the data were from the ECB, there are many gaps in the constructed data panel across variable categories. The FinTech sector has the strongest impact on individual customers of the banks and community groups involved in financing specific ventures. Unfortunately, such activity eludes traditional market monitoring; hence, shortages and data gaps occur. Private, unregulated and unsupervised companies are not subject to the same disclosure requirements as banks. In a way this is from where the competitive advantage and flexibility of the FinTech sector comes. The FinTech companies develop very fast. Nevertheless, banks still remain the most important players in the financial sector. The balance of power in the banking sector seemed stable until the pandemic. The need for self-isolation and new technological solutions allowed for the entry of new players who could flexibly adapt to an unprecedented situation. However, it seems that traditional banks still prove to be leaders in implementing new technological solutions.

Notes

1 The KBW Nasdaq Financial Technology Index tracks the performance of companies that leverage technology to deliver financial products and services. Index-eligible components are selected by the KBW Index Committee. The Committee selects

financial technology companies with products that are distributed nearly exclusively electronically, with limited to no "bricks and mortar" and with a revenue mix that is predominantly fee-based, as determined by Keefe, Bruyette & Woods (2016). The Index includes US-listed companies. The Index is not limited by industry classification because financial technology companies are not easily categorized into a single industry group. Listings of index are open access data.
2 The first model was estimated based on cross-sectional data using the MFE estimator, the second and third models were estimated based on cross-sectional data using simple FE estimator.
3 MFE is multiple levels of fixed effects estimator (including heterogeneous slopes).
4 Fixed-effects estimator (FE).
5 Due to the problem of causality in estimations 3 and 4, the variable KFTX was not used.

References

Besanko, D., Thakor, A. V. (1987). Collateral and Rationing: Sorting Equilibria in Monopolistic and Competitive Credit Markets. *International Economic Review*, 28 (3), 671–689.

Besanko, D., Thakor, A. V. (1993). Relationship Banking, Deposit Insurance and Bank Portfolio Choice. In: *Capital Markets and Financial Intermediation*, ed. by X. Vives and C. Mayer, Cambridge University Press, Cambridge, 292–318.

Blakstad, S., Allen, R. (2018). FinTech Revolution. Springer, Cham, 121–132.

Boyd, J., De Nicoló G. (2005). The Theory of Bank Risk Taking and Competition Revisited. *Journal Finance*, 60 (3), 1329–1343.

Cornelli, G., Doerr, S., Franco, L., Frost, J. (2021). Funding for FinTech s: Patterns and Drivers. *BIS Quarterly Review*, 31–43, September.

Claessens, S., Frost, J., Turner, G., Zhu, F. (2018). FinTech Credit Markets around the World: Size, Drivers and Policy Issues. *BIS Quarterly Review*, 23, September, 29–49.

European Central Bank. (2018). "How Does the ECB Supervise Banks that Use FinTech?" 27 March 2020, available online https://www.bankingsupervision.europa.eu/about/ssmexplained/html/FinTech. pl.html (20 March 2020).

European Commission (2020a). Komunikat Komisji do Parlamentu Europejskiego, Rady Europejskiego Komitetu Ekonomiczno-Społecznego i Komitetu Regionów w sprawie strategii UE w zakresie finansów cyfrowych, COM, 24 września 2020; https://ec.europa.eu/search/?QueryText=FinTech&op=Search&swlang=en&form_build_id=form-8Bwn3FeT0YoCoFDGQfKKNmPd9baHEgIDRwwxPnvxGI8&form_id=nexteuropa_europa_search_search_form.

European Commission (2020b). Komunikat Komisji do Parlamentu Europejskiego, Rady Europejskiej, Rady, Europejskiego Komitetu Ekonomiczno-Społecznego i Komitetu Regionów pt. "Europejska strategia w zakresie danych", COM 66 final, 19.02.2020 r.

Financial Stability Board (2019). FinTech and Market Structure in Financial Services: Market Developments and Potential Financial Stability Implications, available online https://www.fsb.org/wp-content/uploads/P140219.pdf (11 November 2021).

Frost, J. (2020). *The Economic Forces Driving FinTech Adoption across Countries,*. University of Toronto Press, 70–89.

Goetz, M. R. (2018). Competition and Bank Stability. *Journal of Financial Intermediation*, 35, 57–69.

McKinsey & Company. (2020). *Global Banking Practice: The 2020 McKinsey Global Payments Report*, available online https://www.mckinsey.com/industries/financial-services/our-insights/the-2021-mckinsey-global-payments-report.

Navaretti, G., Calzolari, G., Pazzolo, A. (2017). FinTech and Banking: Friends or Foes? *European Economy: Banks, Regulation, and the Real Sector*, 2. https://www.google.com/url?sa=t&rct=j&q=&esrc=s&source=web&cd=1&cad=rja&uact=8&ved=2ahUKEwi25_KW1_HmAhXLxaYKHZujDUQQFjAAegQIARAC&url=http%3A%2F%2Feuropean-economy.eu%2Fwp-content%2Fuploads%2F2018%2F01%2FEE_2.2017-2.pdf&usg=AOvVaw0-JoPn8cR3rwnd7X-Xcz0Y

Nicoletti, B. (2017). The Future: Financial Services as Platforms. *The Future of FinTech*. Palgrave Macmillan, Cham.

Pawłowska, M. (2022). Digital Techniques in the Financial Sector, Impact on Market Structure and Risk, Oficyna Wydawnicza SGH, Warszawa.

Pawłowska, M., Staniszewska, A. (2021). Impact of FinTech on the Level of Competition in the EU Banking Sector. *Financial and Economic Systems: Transformations and New Challenges*, ed. by Z. Ftiti, H. Ameur, and W. Louhichi, World Scientific Publishing, London, 537–560.

Scardovi, C. (2019). Singularity Bank: AI and Runaway Transformation in Financial Services. EGEA Sp.A., Milano.

Sironi, P. (2022). *Banks and Fintech on Platform Economies: Contextual and Conscious Banking*. Wiley, London.

Visa. (2020). The Visa Back to Business Study, Global Small Business and Consumer Insights: Powering Recovery Through Digital and Contactless Payments amidst COVID-19, available online https://www.google.com/url?sa=t&rct=j&q=&esrc=s&source=web&cd=&ved=2ahUKEwjtwo6Um7ntAhWtCRAIHXbjCSUQFjAAegQIAxAC&url=https%3A%2F%2Fusa.visa.com%2Fdam%2FVCOM%2Fglobal%2Frun-your-business%2Fdocuments%2Fvisa-back-to-business-study.pdf&usg=AOvVaw1_haPKO9_7H9zubjdz8u2V (11 November 2021).

Internet Sources

European Central Bank. (2019). "Data from: Payment Statistics, Full Report" (Dataset). European Central Bank, available online https://sdw.ecb.europa.eu/reports.do?node=1000004051 (20 March 2020).

Eurostat open source data base. (2021). Available online https://ec.europa.eu/eurostat/web/main/data/database;

Eurostat open source data base. (2020). E-commerce for Individuals, available online https://ec.europa.eu/eurostat/statistics-explained/images/c/ca/E-commerce_statistics_for_individuals_-_graphs_and_tables_06-2021.xlsx-1.xlsx, (11 November 2022).

KBW Nasdaq Financial Technology Index, open source listings available online https://indexes.nasdaqomx.com/index/History/KFTX, on 20th Jan 2023.

Keffe, Bruyette & Woods (2016). Introducing the KBW Nasdaq Financial Technology Index, North America Equity Research, Fintech, Industry update, July 18.

Appendix

Table 9.2 Summary statistics of the main variables in the model

Variable names	*Mean*	*Std. Dev.*	*MIN*	*MAX*
Assets	12.8266	1.85279	10.0031	16.315
CR5	62.0285	18.1816	26.18	97.28
HHI	0.13645	0.156726	0.0245	1.3
ROA	0.6116	0.782862	−2.55	3.04
ROE	7.1482	8.3403	−29.28	24.07
Tier1	17.3965	4.17968	10.89	35.21
KFTX	1128.053	231.638	849	1434
ATM	41915.2	237.083	196	86767
eCredit	89139.57	275248.3	196.4	1546847
Card	699.847	1721.94	2.4	12470.4
INTER	51.229	23.345	24.66	98.1367
Mobile_U	60.7971	15.7902	24	88
Mobile_O	50.229	19.5151	10	84
*FinTech1**	48.44	10.6071	2	90
*FinTech2**	60.7971	15.7902	24	88
GDPpc	35023.55	22098.2	6812.406	118823.6
GDP	2.975	2.78129	−1.4	25.1

Source: Own calculations on the basis of ECB, Eurostat data (open source). This table provides summary statistics (mean and standard deviation [Std. Dev.] for all variables in the model. Data are observed yearly from 2013 to 2020). *Data concerning FinTech are observed yearly from 2010 to 2020, data are missing for Romania and Croatia (see: Cornelli, Doerr, Franco, Frost, 2021).

Table 9.3 Empirical results for the model for the period 2013–2020 (MFE)

	(1)	*(2)*	*(3)*	*(4)*	*(5)*
	ROA	*ROA*	*ROA*	*ROA*	*ROA*
Assets	0.0083	0.0333	0.0923***	0.0025*	0.3320***
	(0.0329)	(0.0338)	(0.0291)	–	(0.0654)
KFTX	0.0003*	0.0003**	–	–	0.0005*
	(0.0001)	(0.0001)	–		(0.0003)
ATM	0.0007***	0.0006***	–	0.0007***	0.0012***
	(0.0002)	(0.0002)	–	(0.0001)	(0.0004)
CR5	−0.0031	−0.0056**	−0.0030	−0.004**	–
	(0.0022)	(0.0023)	(0.0022)	(0.002)	–
HHI	–	–	–	–	−3.8172***
	–	–	–	–	(1.2499)
Tier1	−0.0163*	−0.0127	−0.0187**	−0.011	0.0384**
	(0.0091)	(0.0085)	(0.009)	(0.0069)	(0.0184)
INTER	−0.0010	0.0078	–	−0.001	0.0173***
	(0.0019)	(0.0036)	–	(0.0002)	(0.0037)
Cart	−0.0001	–	–	–	–
	(0.0000)	–	–	–	–

(Continued)

Table 9.3 (Continued)

	(1)	*(2)*	*(3)*	*(4)*	*(5)*
	ROA	*ROA*	*ROA*	*ROA*	*ROA*
GDP	−0.0053	−0.0020	−0.0007	−0.0006	0.0177
	(0.0101)	(0.0097)	(0.0110)	(0.0098)	(0.0273)
MOBILE_O	–	−0.0127***	–	−0.0045*	–
	–	(0.0043)	–	(0.0026)	–
MOBILE_U	–	–	0.0021	−0.0029***	–
	–	–	(0.0026)	(0.0001)	–
eCredit	–	–	−0.0001*		–
	–	–	(0.0000)		–
Constant	0.7894	0.4860	1.9264***	0.8876***	2.9804***
	(0.5339)	(0.5059)	(0.4958)	(0.1893)	(0.9457)
Observations	192	192	187	199	197

Source: Own calculations. Standard errors in parentheses, ***$p < 0.01$, **$p < 0.05$, *$p < 0.1$.

Table 9.4 Empirical results for the model for the period 2010–2020 (FE)

	(1)	*(2)*	*(3)*	*(4)*
Variables	*ROA*	*ROA*	*FinTech1*	*FinTech2*
CR5	−0.009	−0.010	0.002**	−0.000
	(0.008)	(0.010)	(0.001)	(0.000)
FinTech1	−0.0793	–	–	–
	(0.1370)	–	–	–
FinTech2	–	4.182	–	–
	–	(3.550)	–	–
KFTX	0.001***	0.001**	–	–
	(0.000)	(0.000)	–	–
Mobile_U	0.011	0.013	0.001	0.000**
	(0.007)	(0.009)	(0.001)	(0.000)
INTER	0.018**	0.021**	−0.001*	0.001***
	(0.008)	(0.010)	(0.001)	(0.000)
GDP	−0.359	−0.544	0.125***	0.020**
	(0.280)	(0.357)	(0.028)	(0.008)
COV	−1.083**	−1.056*	0.078	0.041***
	(0.512)	(0.539)	(0.058)	(0.009)
Constant	1.550	3.140	−1.473***	−0.251***
	(3.180)	(3.989)	(0.329)	(0.086)
Observations	227	227	227	227
Number of id	26	26	26	26

Source: Own calculations. Standard errors in parentheses, ***$p < 0.01$, **$p < 0.05$, *$p < 0.1$.

10 Competition between banks and FinTechs in the context of the COVID-19 pandemic

Stanisław Kasiewicz, Lech Kurkliński and Jacek Woźniak

10.1 Introduction

In the literature there are different opinions about who will be the winner of the ongoing rivalry between banks and FinTechs, including BigTechs. One group of experts believes that traditional banks, such as dinosaurs, are doomed to extinction. Another group of specialists says that banks are not very flexible, but these entities will be able to survive in the market (Walker, Morris, 2021, pp. 1–4). This problem shows the importance of various aspects of modern competition. It is moving to the digital sphere systematically, even accelerated by the COVID-19 pandemic. Therefore, the strengths and weaknesses of the main market players require analysis and the identification of success factors of financial institutions in the current and future market. The wave of new technologies, the concept of Open Banking, as well as new regulations, especially the PSD 2 directive in the EU, have opened the banking services market to new non-banking competitors. They are called FinTechs – not licensed firms focused on the use of modern technologies to provide financial services. Practically, we are observing the creation of a new industry consisting of such companies. It impacts disruptions in the market because of the different battlefields of competition under digital circumstances. That is why these questions arise: how are banks and FinTechs progressing regarding new business strategies and models? What are the advantages of digital competition? Who will be the winner in the financial services market? Should the regulator change its attitude to the principles of digital competition? In this chapter, the authors try to answer these questions, or at least provoke a discussion on this subject.

10.2 The impact of the pandemic on banking sector development

The COVID-19 pandemic is having a huge impact on the economy and entire societies on a global scale, including the banking sector, which has not yet completely recovered from the previous crisis. Despite the passing of more than a decade since the collapse of the global financial system in 2007–2009, the consequences can be observed to this day. But the long-term activities of regulators are focused on increasing capital adequacy ratio and other prudential requirements, and an improvement in risk management has brought results. This does not mean that

DOI: 10.4324/9781003310754-10

today's banking systems are completely safe and there will be no serious threats in the near future. They are primarily associated with many unfavourable macroeconomic and political challenges facing the world as a result of the COVID-19 pandemic and global instability. Technological change also plays a special role, with its destructive consequences for the banking sector.

The impact of the COVID-19 pandemic on banks and other financial service providers can be classified as direct and indirect. The most important effects are as follows (Resti, 2021, pp. 8–9; OECD, 2021):

1 Human behaviour caused by fear of health and various other types of restrictions.
2 Changing payment preferences, the proliferation of digital transactions and the reduction of cash turnover.
3 Increased competition from new non-bank market players.
4 Accelerating banks' digital transformations.
5 Increasing threats from cybercriminals.
6 Change in the organisations caused by the wide use of teleworking.
7 Reduction of bricks-and-mortar bank branches.
8 Macroeconomic turbulences: GDP drops, deterioration of the situation of selected groups of borrowers, changes in the real estate market, both residential and commercial, supply chain problems, and intensification of inflation.
9 The need to modify supervisory processes over the financial market.

The COVID-19 pandemic has prompted people to change their ways of meeting needs and the priorities they adopt. The majority of human activities are directly or indirectly related to financial services, e.g., payments or mortgage credit. The COVID-19 pandemic has been modifying the way such processes are carried out for over two years. Sanitary restrictions have primarily resulted in an increase in the prevalence of e-commerce on a global scale, as well as the use of electronic payments. Online sales have spread in relation to goods and services already purchased in a remote form, but also many others so far sold exclusively in stationary mode.

The results of global research show an increase in the share of customers preferring e-commerce (51–100% of all expenses) to over 45%. This is almost a 100% increase compared to the period before the COVID-19 pandemic. The use of cards (credit and debit) has increased, including contactless solutions such as Apple Pay, Google Pay, and online banking, i.e., non-cash transactions. However, major changes have occurred in the field of mobile payments (e.g., e-wallets and QR codes) (World Payments Report, 2020, p. 27). These trends have become entrenched after the end of the lockdowns, and payment service providers expect a return to only 30% of pre-pandemic levels of cash turnover (Resti, 2021, p. 8).

A similar situation occurred in Poland, albeit to a lesser extent. For example, the growth of active users of mobile applications increased by 17.6% (ZBP, 2021). Globally, over a two-year period, there has been overall growth of more than 50% in the use of digital payment channels. There is also an increasing popularity of electronic channels in every age group of consumers, with the largest increase, i.e., over 60%, recorded in the group of "young" customers (World Payments

Report, 2020, p. 8). This is naturally accompanied by an accelerated reduction of stationary bank branches, which in Poland during the pandemic (from March 2020 to March 2021) amounted to 9.9% (KNF, 2022). Similar tendencies are observed all over the world, especially in the USA and Europe (Neely, 2021).

On the basis of the presented results from global research and specific national data (regarding Poland), it can be concluded that the implementation of payment processes (but also more broadly relations with customers of financial institutions) fundamentally changes its form. This is an indicator of the popularity of digitalisation in financial services in the post-pandemic era. Therefore, banks face the challenge of "fitting" into this trend (Vasiljeva, Lukanova, 2016). Specifically, an increase in the use of digital platforms is observed, primarily by non-banking entities. To a large extent, this applies to technology giants – BigTechs. But they show that anti-competitive behaviours and unfavourable tendencies concentrate in the market. Under these circumstances, some banks are also trying to create digital platforms and ecosystems. This is due to benefits coming from the services offered by third parties, including non-financial products. The pandemic has increased interest in new business models, ranging from "Banking as a Platform" to "Banking as a Marketplace".

The lockdowns imposed during the first wave of COVID-19 led to a surge in interest in teleworking. In particular, the financial sector, including traditional institutions, has adopted a new operating pattern. Large European banks are now moving towards a "new normal" in which 40–60% of the working hours take place remotely (Resti, 2021, p. 8). With teleworking, new challenges have emerged. On the one hand, they concern some limitations of functionality, problems with the efficiency of operations and communication, as well as ICT threats. On the other hand, there were significant cost savings, the possibility of using a new process approach, and new HR policy.

The proliferation of teleworking, remote transactions, and the use of innovations in the form of cloud solutions, digital platforms, etc., have even multiplied the problem of cybercrime. The attacks on the IT structures of the financial sector increased by 238% in the first weeks of the COVID-19 pandemic (Resti, 2021, p. 15). This is one of the most important challenges facing financial institutions (banking and non-banking), supervision but also the clients themselves. The growing use of teleworking and online shopping is putting pressure on the real estate market. On the one hand, the demand for commercial space decreased, but on the other hand, housing conditions (location, size of apartments, own garden) became more important. Low-interest rates encouraged mortgage financing. But the eruption of inflation and rising interest rates have started serious problems for customers. It is particularly visible in the countries of Central and Eastern Europe.

The crisis related to the COVID-19 pandemic has triggered a decline in GDP, but the recession has affected selected social groups and economic activities in different ways. Some industries have been facing financial problems in a particularly drastic way, such as tourism, communication, gastronomy, etc. (for banks it means an increase in credit risk). Because of this problem, unprecedented support under public programmes has been observed, either directly in the form of grants or guarantees for bank loans. Sovereign debts have risen sharply. This has led to a massive issuance of money. Together with other factors (such as problems with supply chains, fluctuations in energy prices, political tensions), they have created inflationary pressures and an increase in interest rates (good for bank margins, but bad for the depreciation of fixed-rate instruments). After the collapse of the GDP in the first half of 2020, and then optimistic rebounds in economic growth, there are mixed forecasts for the next years (IMF, 2022).

The COVID-19 pandemic also has implications for banking supervision. First of all, all aspects of the digitisation of financial institutions and the swelling risks came to the fore. In addition, the fairness of competition between various entities in the conditions of the digitisation of financial services (e.g., the problem of regulatory arbitrage between banks and FinTechs, or the market power of BigTechs) drew more attention. There are also consumer protection issues (e.g., privacy) arising from the use of innovations such as artificial intelligence, processing of huge databases from various sources, etc.

In general, the COVID-19 pandemic has accelerated the trends observed so far, which in particular are important for competition between banks and new entities – FinTechs.

10.3 Principles of digital competition

Building new foundations of digital civilization, as well as revolutionary technological changes in the financial sector, it is necessary to intensify research on the features and rules of digital competition. Some publications have been written about it (Teece, 2012; Tirole 2020, p. 2; Petit, 2020), but there are still no clear answers to a few key questions:

1 Can we define the principles of digital competition?
2 Why has the discussion on the rules of competition become an important issue in the theory and practice of the digital financial services market?
3 Will the present or recommended regulations of the digital market allow for the limitation of market power and the unfair practices of technology giants?

The respected rules of competition determine basic problems such as the behaviour of service providers in the fight/competition for the favour of customers, the system of regulating the market, and competitive and antitrust policy. Without an in-depth analysis of these principles, it is difficult to prepare appropriate strategy and business models for financial institutions. The emerging formal and informal rules of competition related to the digital sphere will determine the future of banks and their rivals.

The competition in the digital market seems to be different from the traditional one. At least this observation is confirmed by the ineffectiveness of present methods of protecting fair competition and the formation of uncontrolled monopolistic phenomena. Reasons are related to specific principles, mechanisms, and accepted values determining the proceeding of rivals on the digital market. In the case of the financial services market, competition is heavily determined not only by competing firms (e.g., banks, FinTechs, BigTechs) but also by other important stakeholders like regulators, supervisors, central banks, and infrastructure firms. These institutions have a significant impact on the rules of operation, attitudes, behaviours, and decisions of market players. It is commonly emphasised that modern competition is becoming more complex and dynamic, the boundaries of the banking industry are blurring.

Contemporary digital competition has been diagnosed in some publications (USC, 2020; Stigler Center, 2019; Furman, 2019; Crémer, de Montjoye, Schweitzer, 2019). What are the distinguishing features of digital competition in the financial services market? First of all, information and everything related to it have become the most important. New technologies have allowed for multiple access and huge possibilities (e.g., using artificial intelligence) to process data from own and external sources. This has its consequences, inter alia, in the sphere of marketing, risk management, quality of services, etc. On the one hand, the asymmetry in access to information between clients and professional market participants has decreased (e.g., by allowing easy comparison of offers). On the other hand, the main overlords of ecosystems – digital platforms have gained a huge information advantage over their ordinary participants. This remark applies not only to consumers but also to companies that have to accept rules imposed by ecosystems. If we add the power of ecosystem administrators to control access to platforms by acting as a gatekeeper or entry point, this situation gives a considerable competitive advantage (obtaining the simultaneous position of a controller and a market player) (de Lis, Ortun, 2018). It is skilfully used by BigTechs – global technology giants (e.g., in terms of pricing and promotion policies, and the operation of internet search engines) (Tirole, 2020). Fortunately, so far, this phenomenon is observed in the financial services market only to some extent. Undeniably, the multilateral nature of digital platforms creates a lack of transparency in the flow of information, which makes it easier to manipulate and arbitrarily allocate places to generate income (Petit, 2020, pp. 10–16). Traditional financial institutions are basically deprived of such opportunities.

In the financial sector, there has been a jump in efficiency (e.g., through automation, transference of a large part of the activity to the cloud, and increased flexibility to use it). However, technology has led to the unbundling of the banking value chain. Under these conditions, it became possible to compete in parts of this value chain. There is no need to build large, complex, capital-intensive organisations (like traditional banks), so the entry barrier has lowered, which is crucial for competition. Especially in the banking sector, where there is a second barrier – a need to obtain a licence. The possibility to operate with smaller, unlicensed companies (FinTechs) significantly changes the rules of the game. New business models are emerging, benefiting from these new conditions. In the last few decades, the market has been characterised by statics, now it has moved to being considerably more dynamic (de Lis, Ortun, 2018). Prudential regulations also played an important role (especially after the global financial crisis), which significantly constrained banks, but not companies dealing cut off from the aforementioned banking chain values.

Rapid technological advances and disruptions are prompting business transformations, accompanied by a high degree of uncertainty. All these factors give a signal to look for a new approach to competition. If observed trends in this area persist and remedial measures are not taken, this situation may lead to significant structural changes, not necessarily beneficial for customers and economic development. Also, this problem should be addressed through ethical values, maintaining honesty and transparency of economic activity.

That is why the European Union attaches great importance to the formulation and respecting of the rules of competition in the unified market for financial services. These principles include three objectives: the development of technologies that serve citizens, a fair and competitive digital economy, and an open, democratic, and sustainable society. Those particularly important for the development of FinTechs (Amstad, 2019): the principle of transparency, open standards between market participants, and technological neutrality (EC, 2018).

The open standard focuses on what procedures, processes, and analyses should be done by the regulated entity to keep entry open for newcomers. It allows access to the full specification (e.g., technological) which is not limited by the law, financial, or trade secrets of the company that developed the standard.

Technological neutrality means that regulators monitor the technology by focusing on the analysis of the functionality of the financial service, not on an entity. For example, a technology-neutral regulation sets out detailed anti-money laundering requirements, whether customer service is done at a bank branch or through an online solution.

Transparency enables effective and clear information for all stakeholders about all aspects specified in an open standard. Access to a standard should be ensured on fair, reasonable, and non-discriminatory terms.

There have been discussions of different imperatives that should be included in a company's decision-making process if they intend to meet the demands of digital competition. We can find recommendations to (Kimura, Reeves, Whitaker, 2019):

- increase in the pace of organisational learning,
- use ecosystems,
- take into account activities in the physical and digital world in a combined way,
- use imagination and constant creation of new ideas, and
- achieve resilience under uncertain conditions.

New technologies have become an accelerator in the disruption of the traditional competition system. Technological progress has always been an important factor in change, but it was not expected to explode and contribute to building a new quality of the financial service market. The ingenuity in taking active actions of innovators to reach the expectations and needs of customers is astonishing. Technologies have generated new competitors in the banking services market and have become an impulse to shape different characteristics and effective rules of digital competition. They inspired traditional financial institutions to change their strategies and business models, to search for new tools to compete. They have left regulators and supervisors shocked by the need to seek solutions to a number of pressing challenges: when to regulate digital markets and how.

The most dangerous for traditional banks seem to be the activities of BigTechs. On the one hand, they create progress, but on the other hand, they cause negative effects. This is due to the formula of their operation, which cannot be covered by the current legal framework regarding competition and antitrust regulation. Petit (2020, p. 4) argues that BigTechs can be classified as entities having combined monopoly and oligopoly characteristics (using the term "moligopoly"). Technology and innovation are fundamental for digital competition. That is why the primacy of BigTechs is beyond dispute and there is no indication that the situation will change quickly in the future. The positive and negative effects of the strongest players (e.g., in the sphere of innovation, acquisitions, and customer rights) imply different attitudes (Deller, 2021, p. 26). There are two extreme camps on conducting regulatory policy to eliminate the undesirable behaviour of BigTechs (Bostoen, 2018). Polarly opposed opinions cause an impasse. This is compounded by the problem of quantification and assessment of the impact of BigTechs' actions. It also turned out that imposing penalties (e.g., by the EU) on technology giants is not an effective tool. It is clear that to a large extent the process of organising digital competition will depend on the effectiveness of global regulators, but the interests of world powers are divergent. While EU legislative initiatives on the digital single market are worth supporting, they do not seem to be able to fundamentally change the prevailing rules for competition in digital markets.

10.4 Analysis of the competitive advantages of banks and FinTechs

The competition between banks and FinTechs takes place on many levels today. It concerns not only regulatory aspects but also technological, cost, marketing, etc. Therefore, in order not to lose market share, banks should identify the key factors of competitiveness in relation to FinTechs' activity. According to the IMF in 2019 the global market share of FinTechs was 6% (Polandrani, 2019) but particularly in US personal loans: 2013 – 5%, 2018 – 38% (Nelly, 2021). The list of the required bank actions should include (*FinTech Futures*, 2018; Cavaglieri, 2021; Piechowiak, 2021):

- offering more advanced digital services and a pro-innovative attitude,
- full support of top managers for digital strategies, integrated with HR policy towards development and acquisition of talents, representing required skills and cultural predispositions,
- paying more attention to *customer experience*, as well as undertaking extensive activities to recognise the specificity of Customers 4.0,
- increasing the flexibility and attractiveness of market offers and at the same time representing an openness to internal structural changes,
- treating tradition, reliability, and safety as the foundation of a company, which cannot be lost,
- maintaining and increasing a group of loyal, satisfied customers, e.g., thanks to the high quality of services offered (including traditional banking services),

- the ability to take quick advantage of the opportunities created by new regulations (making use of experience in compliance),
- cooperation with FinTechs, as well as taking market and operational risks, related, e.g., to opening up to new customers and digital transformation.

On the other hand, the factors for increasing the competitiveness of FinTechs towards banks are (Pollari, 2016; Vasiljeva, Lukanova, 2016; Carstens, 2019; de la Mano, Padilla, 2018):

- expanding brand recognition,
- high level of innovation – often associated with the creation of the market for new financial services, as well as the use of the demand-pull model of innovation,
- strong position and cooperativeness in the technological environment – FinTechs are often IT companies themselves,
- focus on value delivered to customers and trust-building,
- operations based on innovative business models adapted to the digital environment,
- focus on creative employees (e.g., technologists, IT specialists, business analysts, etc.), as well as building intellectual capital,
- increasing (in the case of BigTechs already global) effect of operation and at the same time lower regulatory restrictions than for the banking sector,
- extensive IT budget, as well as improvement of the operational and market risk management system.

Practically, banks and FinTechs "fight" for the same customers, mainly for the generation of Customers 4.0, but for the banking sector, it is not a priority. Nevertheless, for winning this rivalry, referring to the *World Payments Report 2020* (p. 18), banks should focus on: innovations delivered to customers (79% of indications), digital transformation of internal processes (75%), compliance with regulations (73%), increasing the efficiency of processes (68%), risk optimalisation (65%), as well as crisis management, in the aspect of building market resilience (62%). The areas listed above are difficult to develop for a large number of banks – especially under the conditions of the COVID-19 pandemic. This is due to the fact that they are mostly oriented towards the "pursuit" of FinTechs, which – by their nature – have often become "technology pioneers". On the other hand, banks are trying to maintain the expected level of profits, that is why they are wary of risky investments. The deteriorating financial situation of society (e.g., groups of borrowers) and macroeconomic turbulence do not help to achieve the ambitious goals of the digital transformation. Taking care of financial efficiency blocks short-term innovativeness and willingness to take risks by banks, from which FinTechs benefit. During the COVID-19 pandemic banks would rather "stick" to the existing market segments, without aggressively entering into relations with completely new customer groups. In addition, the demand for higher-quality digital services is increasing, but many banks are not fully prepared for this challenge (Bosch, 2021).

The above presented opinions on a global scale were confronted with the results of a survey conducted by the authors of this chapter (Kasiewicz, Kurkliński, Woźniak, 2021), which was carried out during the period May–July 2021 with the support of the Polish Bank Association. The respondents were specialists and managers dealing with financial technologies in banks, representatives of FinTechs and software companies, as well as experts and academics (87 selected persons). The evaluations provided by bankers and experts can help to identify key areas for banks to compete and shape their advantage over FinTechs in the reality of the Polish financial services sector (Figure 10.1.A-D). The areas were assessed on a 5-point scale. Level "1" meant low importance and level "5" very high importance. Focusing on the current level of maturity of the digital transformation of banks, the key areas of building a competitive advantage (both groups of respondents) are the development of digital payments and adaptation to regulatory changes (Figure 10.1.A). On the other hand, the basic area for banks to achieve a competitive advantage over FinTechs and BigTechs in the next five years will be risk management. In particular, this area should be properly managed by banks and adapted to the realities of the post-pandemic environment, taking into account the potential of FinTechs to have greater freedom for more aggressive market penetration (Figure 10.1.B). From the perspective of the banks' competitors, it is worth noting that FinTechs (without BigTechs) gaining competitive advantage will primarily concern the areas: technology, data and analytics, the customer in the centre of interest, prices, as well as cost-efficiency. In turn, the main advantage of BigTechs gaining competitive advantage will be: technology, network architecture, data and analytics, the customer in the centre of interest, availability of equity/financing, prices, as well as cost efficiency (Figure 10.1.C-D).

These results (based on the above-mentioned survey) conclude that banks wanting to compete with FinTechs constructively (currently and over the next five years) should focus on: the development of IT infrastructure (both: own sources and outsourcing), creating a pro-innovative culture in their own hierarchical structures, as well as identifying the needs of new customer groups (especially Customers 4.0), acquiring and analysing data and attracting talent who are able to carry out the "full" (i.e., also cultural, not only technological) digitisation of banks. Nevertheless, they should pay attention to the appropriate pricing strategy, as well as risk management, which determines the dynamics of innovative processes and the penetration of new, attractive markets to a large extent. The banks' risk aversion and creation of the image of a "safe but not very progressive entity" will cause a widening technological gap in front of FinTechs. Banks must bear in mind that FinTechs (and partly BigTechs) at the same time are developing in the areas of: IT technology, satisfying customer needs (even creating these needs – and not like banks that "chase" the digital needs of customers), and creating optimal pricing and marketing strategies. All this indicates that banks must take into account the directions of FinTechs and BigTechs' activities and priorities, mainly related to the identification of market niches and digitisation of services.

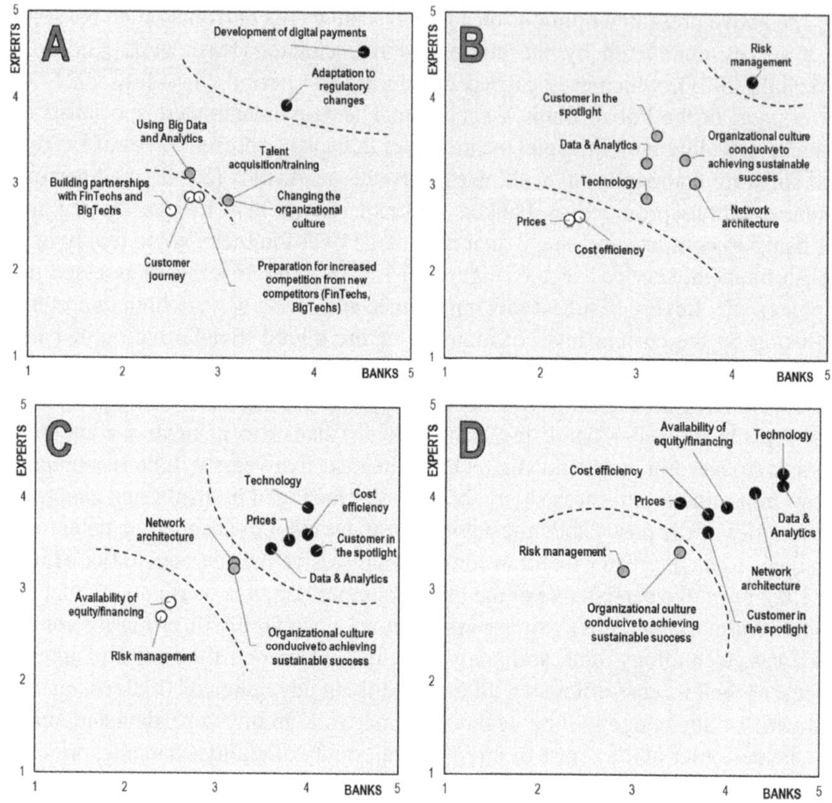

Figure 10.1 Competition between banks and FinTechs – in the opinion of banks and experts

(A: the current level of advancement of the digital transformation of banks; B: areas where banks can gain a competitive advantage over FinTechs and BigTechs in the perspective of five years; C: areas where FinTechs [without BigTechs] can gain a competitive advantage over banks in the perspective of five years; D: areas where BigTechs can gain a competitive advantage over banks in the perspective of five years).

Source: Own elaboration.

10.5 Prospects for the development of competition between banks and FinTechs

Experience during the COVID-19 pandemic shows that competition between banks and FinTechs is accelerating. However, research on the Polish market from 2021 showed it is not currently perceived as a serious challenge (Kasiewicz, Kurkliński, Woźniak, 2021). A similar opinion was also expressed in the report from the European Systemic Risk Board (ESRB)'s Advisory Scientific Committee (Beck et al., 2022). However, when analysing the prospects for the development of this competition, it is necessary to take into account the tendencies in this field (Dealroom, 2019, pp. 14–30):

1 The prospect of the introduction of digital currencies by central banks, with all its structural consequences.

2 The new regulations, especially the PSD 2, open access to information previously reserved only for banks (development of the open banking concept).
3 The prudential regime maintains the phenomenon of regulatory arbitrage, which hampers banks and gives FinTechs more freedom.
4 Robo-advice, artificial intelligence, machine learning, and augmented and virtual reality technologies make overall management more efficient, easier, and create products tailored to the individual needs of customers.
5 The spread of innovation in the lending sphere weakens the attractiveness of traditional loans.
6 Cost challenges faced by large organisations such as banks, in the face of the flexibility and lean structure of FinTechs.
7 Collecting data from various sources (Big Data, Internet of Things) and offering personalised services based on them.
8 Digital platforms are displacing single services/products, and online intermediation increases efficiency and scalability.
9 The proliferation of digital two-way markets dominated by FinTechs and especially BigTechs.
10 Faster processing of transactions (e.g., international transfers).
11 Advances in the use of credit scoring algorithms and advanced predictive analytics, allowing for better risk estimation.
12 The use of innovations (new technologies) both in creating threats (especially cyber threats) and combating them.

Analysing the above factors, the key role of technology is clearly visible. In this context, the weak competitive struggles of incumbent operators with FinTechs undermine the position of banks. But it does not prejudge the final result of this battlefield.

In general, competition and its exacerbation bring benefits for socio-economic development and, above all, for customers. This is also the case with financial services. The observed technological revolution and competition between banks and FinTechs cause an increase in efficiency and quality of services. New technologies reduce the existing asymmetry of information and force even greater customer focus. It can make relatively easy comparisons, choices, and flexible reactions to emerging offers (accept new products, change the current service provider). This leads to a weakening of customer loyalty and an increased risk of losing the customer base. For traditional banks, for which this is one of the basic assets, it is the main problem. This trend will be strengthening, and therefore it will be forcing an activity to keep track of the competitors and constantly maintaining the attractiveness of the offer. In the next stage, new business models that are already flexibly adapted to the changing market situation are becoming more important. This approach is associated not only with technological changes (e.g., abandoning rigid mainframe-based IT systems in favour of cloud solutions) but also with cultural changes related to service providers, customers, as well as regulators and supervisors. The speed of social absorption of innovation will determine the pace of transformation in the financial market.

There is a decline in the number of bricks-and-mortar branches. This trend has accelerated even more during the COVID-19 pandemic, and it seems to be continuing. This forces the restructuring of incumbent banks. They must also make changes in the functioning of their headquarters, which results in pressure to increase efficiency and the use of new technologies and change the philosophy of operation (customer relations, management, attitude to risk, etc.). The necessity to reduce margins and maintain satisfactory financial results is increasing. Therefore, one of the observed effects is the phenomenon of concentration on the market, because the scope and cost intensity of adjustments, but also economies of scale, definitely create preferences for larger players (Resti, 2021).

Despite the reserve presented by a large number of traditional banks, an expansion of acquisitions and partnerships with FinTechs should be expected. This direction allows for innovations introduced by more agile entities to be embraced, and at the same time for the preservation of the institutional existence of banks. Competition from BigTechs remains a greater challenge, as shown, e.g., by experience from China. Their competitive advantage is very strong, which includes, huge databases of customers, having global digital platforms, where they decide on the rules of participation for third parties. If the financial services market developed in this direction, incumbent banks would be relegated to "warehouses" of money or suppliers of products on platforms controlled by non-banking entities, and banks' offers would be commoditised. Some banks have already recognised this threat. They are creating their own platforms, offering products from other financial service providers as well. "Banking as a Platform" or "Banking as a Marketplace" business models are gaining popularity. Some banks have started to partner with BigTechs. Incumbent operators can continue to use their strengths, which include customer trust, in a sense of security regarding not only the savings (e.g., covered by institutional deposit protection systems) but also data and privacy. Still, banks have a chance to make the right digital transformation in terms of technological solutions, attractive products, customer contacts, cultural aspects, and maintain their market position.

To a large extent, in what way BigTechs will occupy the financial services will be determined by regulations. Regulators may not allow them to control this market because of potential, excessive systemic risk. It could be done by imposing stronger prudential standards. But currently, existing solutions open the gate to at least partial circumvention of the applicable, strict regulations, including obtaining a full license for banking activities (e.g., using the "Banking as a Services" business model). Nevertheless, despite increased supervision, it remains an important banking privilege to accumulate deposits protected by public cash guarantee schemes. This allows for relatively cheap financing and practically maintains the compulsion to have an account with a licensed bank. However, there is a very serious threat associated with the possible introduction of digital currencies by central banks, as indicated by one of the scenarios for the development of the financial services market presented at the end of this subchapter.

Digital disruptions pose a huge challenge for regulators. They need to adapt to new circumstances, facilitating competition and allowing innovation to permeate into the market, while at the same time keeping financial stability. It is not easy to coordinate prudential rules with competition policy, e.g., managing barriers to entry without destabilisation of the system (low regulation for entrants can foster competition). But this may destabilise incumbents by reducing their profitability, increasing risk-taking incentives and shifting the systemic risk to non-bank entities. The U.S. announcement shows that new market players (including FinTechs) and digital branches of existing banks are taking over a significant part of mortgage credits and, of course, payments (Neely, 2021). Lower requirements for small, non-systemic institutions may foster competition and market development, or this objective can be achieved by applying the same rules (same risk, same regulation), but verified by the proportionality principle. But where is the border between systemic and non-systemic institutions? The proportionality approach, however, encounters great difficulties in practical implementation and usually remains only as a declaration. In addition, consumer protection issues are important like data control, transparency of processing, and security of transactions. There is also a risk of price discrimination, especially with regard to global digital platforms. Therefore, the adopted regulatory policy may become an important determinant of the development of competition between banks and new players, i.e., FinTechs, and even more BigTechs.

10.6 Conclusions

The considerations carried out in this chapter show the comprehensive impact of the COVID-19 pandemic on the financial services market. The most important observations include the fact that development trends, which have accelerated as a result of the spread of the coronavirus, indicate the need to have strategies and business models that are adapted to the conditions of competition in the digital environment.

The degree of digital transformation varies between banks. This advancement is relatively better in relation to the strategy. The groundbreaking new business models are used much less. Overall, the implementation of digitalisation is fragmentary. The focus is on technological factors and other important aspects (e.g., risk management, organisational culture, leadership) are changing to a much lesser extent. Thus, there is still great potential for actions that banks can take to keep up with competition from new market players. However, a large number of banks do not appreciate this threat yet.

Answering the question of what competitive advantage digitisation gives, attention should be paid not only to technological innovations but also to their connection with all spheres of the functioning of financial institutions and the departure from the usual perception of the banking services market. This attitude must include the ability to compete at almost every stage of the banking value chain, reducing market entry barriers, increasing the ease of switching service providers, unlimited time and geographical accessibility, changes in information asymmetry, etc. As a result of digitisation, customers have gained very significant benefits, but the question of whether serious monopolistic long-term threats have emerged at the same time. This applies primarily to the activities of technology giants. They are using the features of digital competition, such as intensified economies of scale, network effects, market control possibilities (e.g., within ecosystems), and problems with transparency in the digital sphere (e.g., price policies).

Who will be the winner in the financial services market? So far, in most markets, banks can manage to maintain their dominant position, although in some markets they are starting to lose it significantly, e.g., in payments or offering certain types of loans. Market development scenarios may be different, covering a wide spectrum of possibilities:

1 Incumbent banks will maintain their dominant position in the financial market.
2 The role of traditional banks (even after a digital transformation) will systematically decline. Big technological companies will be able to offer financial services more widely through partially regulated subsidiaries. They can capture the majority of the market.
3 The third scenario is related to the emission of digital currencies by central banks. This potential phenomenon could be crucial for changes to the model of today's financial intermediation. The retail customers will move away from incumbent banks, and the depositary role will be taken by central banks. This will create a more comfortable field for other financial service providers (FinTechs and BigTechs), offering specialised products tailored to individual needs. The banks will have to compete with new competitors but are practically deprived of their main advantage - the role of a safe depository institution of customers' money.

All of these scenarios are possible. The battle between banks and tech companies is not yet over.

The final question is related to the regulators. Should they change their attitude towards the principles of digital competition? There is undeniable evidence that the current regulatory system for digital competition has fundamental weaknesses. Despite attempts to control this field, there are still many unregulated problems. This is one of the most important challenges facing regulators around the world.

References

Amstad, M. (2019). Regulating FinTech: Objectives, principles, and practice. *Asian Development Bank Institute Working Paper Series 1016*, 1–13.

Beck, T., Cecchetti, S., Grothe, M., Kemp, M., Pelizzon, L., and Serrano, A.S. (2022). Will video kill the radio star? Digitalisation and the future of banking. *Reports of the ESRB Advisory Scientific Committee*, 12, January.

Bosch, R. (2021). *Digital banking: is your bank a leader or laggard?*. https://www.bearingpoint.com/pl-pl/our-success/thought-leadership/digital-banking-is-your-bank-a-leader-or-laggard/ (22.06.2021).

Bostoen, F. (2018). Neutrality, fairness or freedom? Principles for platform regulation. *Internet Policy Review*, 7(1), 1–19.

Capgemini Research Institute (2020). *World payments report 2020: Will covid-19 spark the end of cash payments?* https://www.capgemini.com/news/press-releases/capgeminis-world-payments-report-2020-will-covid-19-spark-the-end-of-cash-payments.

Carstens, A. (2019). Big tech in finance and new challenges for public policy. *SUERF Policy Note*, 54, 2–10.
Cavaglieri, Ch. (2021). *Challenger and mobile banks. Find out how the new wave of digital banks, such as Monzo, Starling and Revolut, are aiming to shake up the banking sector*. https://www.which.co.uk/money/banking/bank-accounts/challenger-and-mobile-banks-aj0mj7w688r5 (20.05.2021).
Crémer, J., de Montjoye, Y.-A., and Schweitzer, H. (2019). *Competition policy for digital era. Final Report*. Brussels: European Commission.
de la Mano, M., and Padilla, J. (2018). Big Tech banking. *Journal of Competition Law & Economics*, 14(4), 494–526.
Dealroom. (2019). *The State of European Fintech, About Finch Capital*, October. https://dealroom.co/blog/the-state-of-european-fintech-report-2019-edition (20.12.2021).
de Lis, S. F., and Ortun, P. U. (2018), *Digital transformation and competition in the financial sector*, BBVA Research, https://www.bbvaresearch.com/wp-content/uploads/2019/01/Digital-transformation-and-competition-in-the-financial-sector.pdf (5.05.2022).
Deller, D., Doan, T., and Mariuzzo, F. (2021). *Competition and Innovation in Digital Markets*. BEIS Research Paper No. 40, Centre for Competition Policy, UEA, www.gov.uk/beis, 1–56.
European Commission (EC). (2018). *FinTech Action plan: For a more competitive and innovative European financial sector*. European Commission. https://ec.europa.eu/info/publications/180308-action-plan-fintech_en (15.01.2022).
European Commission (EC). (2020). *Shaping Europe's Digital Future*. European Commission. https://ec.europa.eu/info/strategy/priorities-2019-2024/europe-fit-digital-age/shaping-europe-digital-future_en (15.01.2022)
FinTech Futures. (2018). *The five attributes of a successful digital banking experience*. https://www.fintechfutures.com/2018/11/the-five-attributes-of-a-successful-digital-banking-experience/ (24.05.2021).
Furman, J. (2019). *Unlocking digital competition*. Report of the Digital Competition. ExpertPanel. https://assets.publishing.service.gov.uk/government/uploads/system/uploads/attachment_data/file/785547/unlocking_digital_competition_furman_review_web.pdf (19.02.2022).
IMF. (2022). *World economic outlook update, rising caseloads, a disrupted recovery, and higher inflation*. https://www.imf.org/en/Publications/WEO/Issues/2022/01/25/world-economic-outlook-update-january-2022 (10.02.2022).
Kasiewicz, S., Kurkliński, L., and Woźniak, J. (2021). *Strategie i modele biznesowe banków wobec konkurencji ze strony FinTech-ów*, Warsaw: Warsaw Institute of Banking (not published).
Kimura, R., Reeves, M., and Whitaker, K. (2019). *The New Logic of Competition. Winning the '20s*. Boston Consulting Group.
Komisja Nadzoru Finansowego (KNF). (2022). *Dane miesięczne sektora bankowego – grudzień 2021*. Komisja Nadzoru Finansowego. https://www.knf.gov.pl/?articleId=56224&p_id=18 (10.02.2022).
Neely, M.-C. (2021), *The Fintech Revolution in Banking*. https://www.stlouisfed.org/publications/regional-economist/fourth-quarter-2021/fintech-revolution-banking (15.02.2022).
OECD. (2021). *The COVID-19 crisis and banking system resilience: Simulation of losses on non-performing loans and policy implications*. OECD Paris, https://www.oecd.org/daf/fin/financial-markets/COVID-19-crisis-and-banking-system-resilience.pdf.
Petit, N. (2020). *BigTech and the Digital Economy*. Oxford: Oxford University Press.

Piechowiak, Ł. (2021). *Challenger banki w natarciu. Czy Polska ma szansę na swojego jednorożca?*. https://fintek.pl/challenger-banki-w-natarciu-czy-polska-ma-szanse-na-swojego-jednorozca/ (17.04.2021).

Polandrani, P. (2019). *FinTech Trends: M&A and Mobile Payments Driving Recent Growth.* https://www.globalxetfs.com/fintech-trends-ma-and-mobile-payments-driving-recent-growth/ (7.05.2022).

Pollari, I. (2016). The rise of Fintech opportunities and challenges. *JASSA: The Journal of the Securities Institute of Australia*, 3, 16–20.

Resti, A. (2021). *Did the pandemic lead to structural changes in the banking sector?*. Economic Governance Support Unit (EGOV) Directorate-General for Internal Policies.

Skinner, C. (2020). *Doing Digital. Lessons from Leaders*. Marshall Cavendish International, Singapore.

Stigler Center. (2019). *Committee for the Study of Digital Platforms. Market Structure and Antitrust Subcommittee*. Draft, 15 May 2019.

Teece, D. J. (2012). Next-generation competition: New concepts for understanding how innovation shapes competition and policy in the digital economy. *Journal of Law, Economics & Policy*, 9, 97.

Tirole, J. (2020). *Competition and the Industrial Challenge for the Digital Age*. www.tse-fr.eu › TSE › documents › doc › tirole (25.03.2021).

United States Congress (USC). (2020). *Investigation of Competition Digital Markets Majority staff report and recommendations*. United States Congress, House of Representatives. https://judiciary.house.gov/uploadedfiles/competition_in_digital_markets.pdf?utm_campaign=4493-519 (28.01.2022).

Vasiljeva, T., and Lukanova, K. (2016). Commercial banks and Fintech companies in the digital transformation: Challenges for the future. *Journal of Business Management*, 11, 26–32.

Walker, T., and Morris, L. (2021). *The Handbook of Banking Technology*. Wiley, New York.

ZBP. (2021). *Raport NetBank 1Q/2021*. https://www.zbp.pl/raporty-i-publikacje/raporty-cykliczne/raport-netbank (10.02.2022).

Abstracts

Chapter 1

The introduction provides the motivation underlying this book and briefly describes its subject: the impact of the pandemic on bank stability, performance and credit policies, as well as the extent of banks' and financial markets' strategic adjustments to the challenges brought about by the COVID-19 pandemic. The structure of the chapters is then briefly summarized. It starts with the impact of the pandemic on macroeconomic policies (Chapters 2–4) which is followed by the impact on the enterprise sector (Chapters 5 and 6) and on banking industry performance (Chapters 7 and 8). The last two chapters discuss the pressures coming from the FinTech sector (Chapters 9 and 10).

Chapter 2

The chapter examines whether and to what extent government interventions influence changes in sovereign risk. Using sovereign ratings as the main measure of the sovereign risk of 35 OECD countries, we investigate (i) how government interventions – bailout, liquidity support, blanket guarantees, and nationalization – implemented during the global financial crisis (GFC) (2008–2016) affected changes in sovereign risk and (ii) the relation between COVID-19-related measures and changes in sovereign risk (December 2019 versus December 2020). Our results reveal that bailouts were the main intervention measure affecting the changes in sovereign risk during the GFC. As for the COVID-19 intervention measures, despite the measures being sizeable, the sovereign risk does not seem to be permanently affected, as most countries did not experience a significant change in their ratings.

Chapter 3

Starting from the introduction of the Euro as a common currency, significant changes in the architecture of bank supervision in Europe have occurred. In particular, exogenous events such as the global crisis, the sovereign debt crisis in some European countries and recently the shock given by the pandemic have produced noticeable changes in the architecture of bank supervision in Europe. As a result, the authorities in charge of the responsibility for monetary and financial stability have changed in many countries and a trend toward more cross-border cooperation between supervisors has emerged. The evolution in the bank supervisory architecture gradually have empowered the European Central Bank (ECB) of greater and greater powers, in particular regarding the largest banks in the Eurozone. All this considered, this chapter aims to analyze the causes and the consequences of these changes focusing on the critical issues concerning the new role played by the ECB which has to find a new balance between independence and accountability maintaining the effectiveness of its action as bank supervisor.

Chapter 4

This chapter tackles the issue of macroprudential policy in the European Union during the COVID-19 pandemic, with the main focus on events from 2020. Local changes in the restrictiveness of macroprudential requirements (capital buffers) are compared using various measures of restrictiveness (capital requirement, surplus capital, bank lending capacity). Additionally, the main reasons for changes in the restrictiveness of macroprudential policy have been identified, using the qualitative and quantitative analysis. The study sheds light on the positive impact of the loosening of macroprudential policy on the expansion of bank assets. Therefore, it pointed at potential macroeconomic benefits of the macroprudential policy conducted during the pandemic proving its countercyclical nature.

Chapter 5

Tail events, due to their nature, occur very rarely and are therefore often regarded as an element of surprise. However, business continuity management (BCM) as a part of enterprise risk management (ERM) should protect businesses from disruption in case of such events. In this chapter, we investigate whether businesses of different sizes were ready to withstand the consequences of the outbreak of the global SARS-CoV-2 pandemic in 2020. To this aim, we analyse the results of a global survey conducted during a major lockdown period (April–May 2020) by applying multiple correspondence analysis (MCA) and clustering. Our findings indicate that the financial sector was the best prepared for tail events, which may be attributed to regulations enforced for most financial institutions. Although around a half of businesses did not have a business continuity plan (BCP), having one helped adjust to the new conditions efficiently.

Chapter 6

Using a proprietary quarterly database of lending decisions (N = 3,687) from 31 March 2019 to 31 December 2020 for small- and medium-sized enterprises (SMEs), this chapter investigates how the financial measures introduced by Law Decree No. 18 of 17 March 2020 in terms of moratorium of interest could have effectively slacked liquidity shortfalls during the COVID-19 outbreak. Findings suggest that a public measure of assessment works better in the case of low risk and large firms as well as in the presence of personal guarantee and a strong relationship lending story.

Chapter 7

The last evidence emphasizes that the economic effect of the COVID-19 pandemic resulted in a change in credit standards and a reduction in loan demand. However, this phenomenon is not confirmed in all markets. The aim of the chapter is to verify the research question: how the COVID-19 pandemic affects bank lending activity in European countries. The analysis has been extended by the importance of bank-specific and macroeconomic factors. The survey is carried out on 652 commercial banks in European countries, using data from the period 2018 Q3–2021 Q1. The study contributes to the ongoing discussion of customized modifications to business models that appears to be the most promising strategy to sustainably increase lending during and after the COVID-19 pandemic.

Chapter 8

The COVID-19 pandemic has disrupted bank recovery after the global financial crisis, creating strong disruptions in macroeconomic trends and resulting in largely expanding budget deficits in 2020 and in reversing the tendency to control public debt through the region. The aim of this chapter is to analyze the impact of the pandemic on bank performance in the CEE region, represented by bank stability, bank profitability and credit accessibility. The empirical findings allow to formulate conclusions that some countries, such as Croatia, were disproportionally affected in terms of GDP growth and bank profitability, while some banking sectors (such as the Czech Republic and Estonia) have exposed strong resilience to the external shock, but for some the shock strengthened the already detrimental trends (Poland and Hungary).

Chapter 9

The aim of this chapter is to investigate the impact of innovative financial technology (FinTech) on EU banking performance. The IT revolution brought new factors that influenced the traditional banking market. Banks were forced to compete not only with other players from the banking sector but also with unregulated FinTech companies. Furthermore, we take into account the impact of the COVID pandemic, which forced the banking sector to accelerate of implement innovations and catch up with emerging advanced IT solutions, in case to compete with new FinTech companies. Based on the quantitative analysis on panel data, this chapter confirms that new technology has had an impact on bank performance. Also, the findings confirm the impact of COVID pandemic on traditional banking sector and FinTech sector.

Chapter 10

There is a problem: Who will be the winner of the ongoing rivalry between banks and FinTechs, including BigTechs? The digital environment is gaining more attention from a business competition point of view. Even this issue has been accelerated by the COVID-19 pandemic. Therefore, the strengths and weaknesses of the main market players require analysis and the identification of success factors of financial institutions in the current and future market. It impacts disruptions in the market because of the different battlefields of competition under digital circumstances. That is why these questions arise: how are banks and FinTechs progressing regarding new business strategies and models? What are the advantages of digital competition? Who will be the winner in the financial services market? Should the regulator change its attitude to the principles of digital competition? In this chapter the authors try to answer these questions, or at least provoke a discussion on this subject.

Index

Note: **Bold** page numbers refer to tables; *italic* page numbers refer to figures and page numbers followed by "n" denote endnotes.